Watching Fishes

Life and

Watching Fishes

Behavior on Coral Reefs

ROBERTA WILSON

JAMES Q. WILSON

HARPER & ROW, PUBLISHERS, New York
Cambridge, Philadelphia, San Francisco, London
1817 Mexico City, São Paulo, Singapore, Sydney

For
Flower, Punk, Big Star, Big Tuna,
The Colonel, Torso, Precious Burden, Big Sam,
Sweet Kathy, Nell, Little Tuna, and James:
perennial diving companions and
friends of fishes

FIRST EDITION

Designer: Patricia Dunbar

Library of Congress Cataloging in Publication Data

Wilson, Roberta
  Watching fishes.

  Bibliography: p.
  Includes index.
  1. Fishes   2. Coral reef fauna.   I. Wilson, James Q.
II. Title.
QL617.W55   1985   597.092   84-48205
ISBN 0-06-015371

85 86 87 88 89 10 9 8 7 6 5 4 3 2 1

Contents

Acknowledgments

We wish to thank several scholars who read and commented on various portions of this work. Professor Eugenie Clark, of the University of Maryland, Les Kaufman, Curator of Education of the New England Aquarium, Professor Karel Liem, of Harvard University, Alex Kerstitch, of the University of Arizona, and C. Lavett Smith, Curator of the American Museum of Natural History, have saved us from many errors (no doubt many remain) and made valuable suggestions. To all of them we are much indebted.

Most of the research was done in the pleasant surroundings of the libraries of the Museum of Comparative Zoology of Harvard University and the Marine Biological Laboratories of the Woods Hole Oceanographic Institution—libraries whose staffs are uniformly welcoming and helpful, for which we are very grateful.

It has been a special pleasure to work with Buz Wyeth at Harper & Row and to have had the editorial assistance of Terry Karten. Pat Dunbar, who designed the book, deserves particular thanks.

CENTRAL AND EASTERN PACIFIC OCEAN

TROPIC OF CANCER

Hawaii

Marshall Islands

EQUATOR

Gilbert Islands

Rangiroa

French
Polynesia

Fiji

TROPIC OF CAPRICORN

NEW ZEALAND

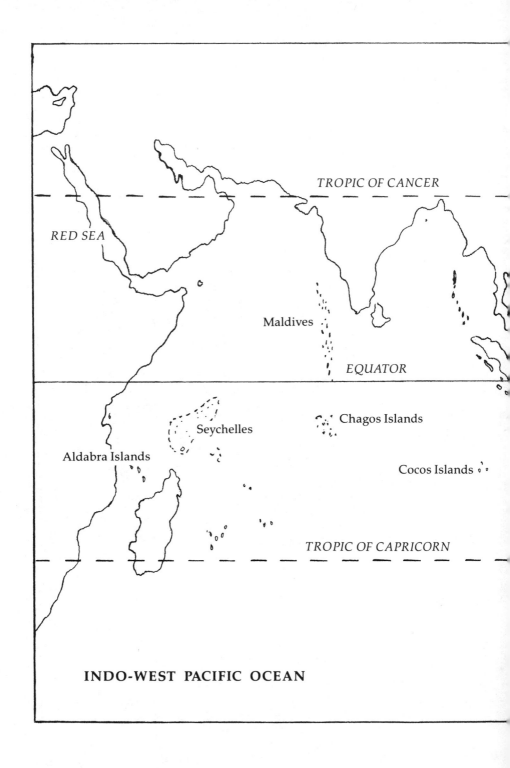

TROPIC OF CANCER

RED SEA

Maldives

EQUATOR

Seychelles

Chagos Islands

Aldabra Islands

Cocos Islands

TROPIC OF CAPRICORN

INDO-WEST PACIFIC OCEAN

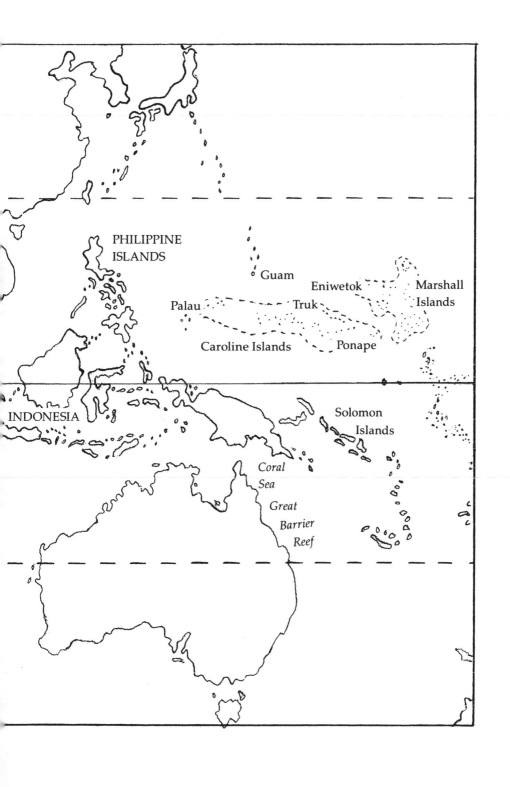

Preface

The coral reef is no longer the rarely seen realm of mystery and exotic life that it was when we began exploring it twenty years ago. Millions of people have put on masks and snorkels to get at least a glimpse of that world, tens of millions have seen underwater motion pictures taken by Jacques Cousteau, the photographers of the *National Geographic,* and others, and hundreds of thousands have used scuba equipment to experience the extraordinary sensation of moving effortlessly and weightlessly among the fishes and plants of the reef. Thus there is little need for yet another book to draw attention to the existence of this world or to rhapsodize about its wonders.

What is needed is a book that explains how that world works. The same self-contained underwater breathing apparatus—scuba—that has opened up the coral reef to human exploration has also revolutionized the scientific study of it. Two decades ago much, if not most, of what was known about the behavior of tropical fishes and marine invertebrates had come from the dissection of captured specimens or from the observation of them in laboratory tanks and aquariums. Hardly any studies of reef animals had been made in their natural habitat. Hence, although scientists acquired a firm grasp of the physiology of these animals and identified and classified hundreds of species, what they knew about how fishes, snails, crabs, and shrimps actually lived on the reef was often based on the assumption that these creatures behaved in the ocean in much the same way they behaved in a laboratory setting. There were good reasons from the very first to be skeptical of that assumption; after all, one of the most important forms of behavior, reproduction, often cannot be observed in tanks because most species will not reproduce while in captivity.

And if they will not breed in a tank, why should one suppose they act naturally in other respects?

Today, scientists have available countless studies done on the reefs of tropical marine animals and plants in their natural settings. As a result, much of what was once thought to be true is now known to be either wrong or at least incomplete. Fishes that were once believed to be territorial turn out not to be that at all; fishes that seemed in tanks to lead solitary lives are now known to be part of elaborate social communities; a world that was once thought to be characterized by ceaseless predation is now known to involve a substantial amount of mutually beneficial behavior; and sharks, which traditionally seemed to be nothing more than mindless, unpredictable eating machines, now appear to behave in rather predictable ways, to be capable of learning, and in the case of some species, to live in groups.

Although such studies are available to scientists, they have not been available to the general public. They appear in obscure, specialized journals, are written in the technical language of biologists and zoologists, and rarely supply an overview of an entire field of inquiry. But their contents, once understood, are fascinating. It is our purpose in writing this book to provide for the lay reader or the beginning student of marine biology an easily understood summary of what scientists have discovered about life on the coral reef.

This is not a fish identification book. An ample supply of such books already exists, many conveniently printed on waterproof plastic pages so that they can be taken along on a boat or even carried with a diver underwater. We have included many photographs, but although they may be helpful in identifying some creatures, their purpose is to illustrate the life and behavior of tropical fishes and invertebrates.

The organization of the book reflects our desire to explain to the reader what he or she is seeing and why reef animals behave as they do. Accordingly, each chapter takes up one or more of the major activities of fishes and invertebrates so that the reader will understand how they swim or otherwise get about, how fishes use their ability to see and smell, what role color plays in organizing reef life, how reef animals reproduce, which fishes create social communities and for what purposes, what fishes form schools and why, which species are territorial, and how species cooperate by cleaning, protecting, or feeding one another. We have included a separate chapter on sharks largely because of the popular interest in, and popular misconceptions about, those remarkable creatures. We have ended the book with an account of twenty-four hours on a typical reef, a guide to what a snorkeler or diver is likely to see at dawn, during the day, at dusk, and at night.

No previous knowledge of science is needed to read this book; people who have never even taken one snorkeling trip out over a reef can learn a great deal from the book, but those who have already done some exploring on their own will learn even more because they will have already seen—and, we hope, wondered about—the brightly colored fishes that dart about in what seems to be an almost random pattern but which in fact is governed by a clear, if only imperfectly understood, logic.

To grasp that logic, it is important to understand that behavior, any behavior, is governed by both inherited predispositions and learning. What we see when watching a damselfish defending its little patch of algae is the combined result of thousands of years of evolutionary adaptation by that species and of trial and error during this particular fish's lifetime. How much of the behavior of that damselfish represents an innate predisposition (that is, its genetic inheritance) and how much represents things it has learned for itself is not yet very clear but is becoming clearer all the time.

One thing that certain fishes learn is what routes to take from where they spend the day to where they feed at night. In a pioneering demonstration of social learning among fishes, Gene S. Helfman and Eric T. Schultz of the University of Georgia transplanted some French grunts *(Haemulon flavolineatum)* from their customary location to a new coral head. Within two days, they had learned from the resident French grunts which were the best routes to swim to find feeding areas. By contrast, a control group of French grunts, transplanted to a reef lacking any established grunts from which the newcomers could learn, wandered about more or less at random and were unable to find their way back to where they started out.

The customary modes of human speech are not well suited to making important distinctions between learned and innate behavior. When divers ask one another why one fish is blue, another is striped, and a third changes color, they often speculate that these fishes appear that way "in order to" hide themselves, or attract mates, or sneak up on prey. Our language tends to use words that emphasize, whether intentionally or not, the goal-seeking behavior that we impute to other humans. People act because they have motives or are more or less clever about arranging their affairs. When someone wears a certain color and style of clothing, it is "in order to" be inconspicuous in a crowd or to attract favorable attention; if someone speaks softly in some cases and loudly in others, it is because he or she wishes to persuade or denounce.

All this may be a useful and even correct way of describing human affairs, but it is a misleading way to explain differences in color and behavior among fishes. The fishes found on the reef today are the current and still changing product of eons of evolutionary adaptation. If some are blue and others are striped, if some are aggressive and others seem shy, it is not because they have consciously evolved "in order to" conceal themselves or learned how to conceal themselves and then passed on that acquired ability to their offspring. They are the survivors of a very long process of natural selection that has made them—for the moment—well fitted to survive a bit longer in that particular environment.

Natural selection, a part of evolution, involves the interaction of two things: variations in the environmental conditions and variations in the genetic makeup of a species. Variations in the environment make it more advantageous for a species to have one trait—say, a blue color—than to have another. Variations in genetic makeup that occur naturally owing to sexual reproduction and the appearance of mutants give to some members of a species that trait (say, a deeper blue color) to a greater degree than others. Those individuals with the useful trait will survive longer and hence be more likely to find a mate. The genes that produce the deep blue color are thus more likely to be passed on to offspring than the genes that produce a lighter blue color. Even if having a deep blue color confers for any given fish only a very slight advantage in its environment, the greater reproductive success of fishes with that trait will come, over thousands of years of mating on a given reef, virtually to extinguish fishes lacking the trait. But environmental conditions may change, and having a blue color may as a result no longer confer any particular advantage; it may even become a liability. Mutations, or genetic accidents, will also occur. For example, a fish with blue and white stripes might result randomly from the mating of all-blue male and female fishes. If this new color pattern is advantageous, the fish having it will enjoy greater reproductive success and, over more hundreds of thousands of years, the species will change color. But if no such mutants appear, the entire species of blue-colored fishes may slowly die out.

Because natural selection operating over eons leads to the adaptation of species living on a reef to a particular reef, people sometimes suppose that every single observable feature of a fish must be there "for a reason"—that is, all of its features must supply some evolutionary (or reproductive) advantage. But that is not necessarily the case.

It is possible for some features of a fish to be irrelevant to its reproductive success. Plate 23 shows a clown or whiteblotched triggerfish *(Balistoides niger)*, photographed on a reef in the Philippines where it sports a most improbable pattern of bright colors and large white polka dots. Now, it is possible that these colors are useful to it in that environment, but it is also possible that they are of no use at all; for a species with that color pattern to survive, it is only necessary that the pattern confer no disadvantage, however slight. Whether this fish does or does not benefit from that pattern we cannot say; in the short run, no one can say.

The basic unit for the analysis of fishes, or of any animals, is the species. Throughout this book we shall describe how members of various species behave; because the same species may have, depending on where it is observed, differing popular names (and sometimes no name at all), we shall always give the scientific name for the species under discussion. By supplying all these Latin terms, which some find distracting, we are trying to make it easier, not harder, for the reader to understand how tropical fishes behave. In general, the most important forms of fish behavior are distinctive to a species, although an individual member of that species may have learned, by trial and error, to engage in that behavior in slightly different ways. Thus, knowing exactly who is and who is not a part of a given species is important.

Roughly speaking, a species is a population of individuals that are capable, under ordinary and natural circumstances, of breeding with one another. In a zoo, a scientist might be able to get a lion and a tiger to mate, producing as an offspring a "liger" or a "tiglon." But in their natural habitat, lions and tigers do not mate. They are not members of the same species. By the same token, a scientist may be unable to get two clownfish to mate in a laboratory tank, whereas on the reef they mate regularly. They are members of the same species. Members of different species, in short, are reproductively isolated from one another.

The science of classifying species, called taxonomy, is accepted internationally and enables scholars around the world to study life and ponder evolutionary development with a minimum of confusion. The modern system dates back to the mid-eighteenth century, when the Swedish biologist Carolus Linnaeus devised a two-part scheme for naming plants and animals, giving each reproductively integrated group an italicized "specific" name for its species and one for its genus. The names are usually Latin or Latinized in form. The genus, which may consist of several related species, is given first and capitalized, and the species name appears last and is never capitalized. Sometimes the name of the taxonomist who first classified a species is added at the end in unitalicized letters. Thus the clown or whiteblotched triggerfish (Plate 23) is named *Balistoides niger* (Bonnaterre). In some identification books it is listed as *Balistoides niger* (Bonnaterre) = *B. conspicillum* (Bloch and Schneider) to clarify that it was classified independently in two different regions but is now known to be the same fish. Because Bonnaterre classified this triggerfish first (1788), his name takes precedence. To our minds, Bloch and Schneider's species label (it means "conspicuous") is more apt than Bonnaterre's "niger," or "black," but rules are rules and Bloch and Schneider were thirteen years too late.

Every genus is grouped into a family, which for animals is a name ending in "-idae." The genus name may or may not be derived from the family name. In the case of the triggerfish, it is; the triggerfish belongs to the family Balistidae. ("Balist" comes from the Latin word for catapult and is the root of the English word ballistics, meaning the study of the propulsion of projectiles; hence trigger, the sharp, hinged dorsal spine that the triggerfish can erect in a moment and lock into place.) Families are in turn grouped into orders (Pisces for fishes), orders into subphyla (fishes are vertebrates, or members of the subphylum Vertebrata), and subphyla into phyla (Chordata for fishes). Finally, our triggerfish joins the vast and diverse kingdom of the animals (Animalia), sharing with us *Homo sapiens* the last three designations.

This classification system may seem confusing at first, but as we said before, without it, the same fish may have a different name in every region it inhabits. For example, *Carcharodon carcharias,* the great white shark, has at least six different common names, some contradictory: in Australia it is called the white pointer and in South Africa the blue pointer. If you want to look up a fish, it is much better to know its Latin name, and you need only be concerned with its genus and species. Having said all that, we must admit that the proliferation of coral reef studies made possible by the advent of scuba equipment has resulted in a proliferation of new classifications and reclassifications of coral reef inhabitants. Every month, journals seem to include an article with a title such as, say, "A New Species of Balistid Fish: *Balistoides tranquilus* (Annabelle)." That taxonomy is constantly growing and changing means that we snorkel and dive in exciting times.

Finally, a word about the sometimes confusing usage of "fish" and "fishes." "Fish" is both singular and plural; when plural it refers to more than one fish *within* the same species. The plural "fishes" is used when two or more species are involved; hence the title of our book.

CHAPTER ONE

Coral Reefs

A coral reef in the sea is like an oasis in the desert. The warm, tropical seas are poor in nutrients and devoid of shelter, but the reef teems with life, supported by the food found there and protected by a rock-hard, elaborate architecture that resists wave action and provides niches in which many fishes find safety from predators. The result is the world's oldest ecosystem and what may be the most complex animal and plant community on earth, rivaled only by the tropical rain forest.

On land, an oasis exists where water can be found at or near the earth's surface, nourishing plant and animal life that could not survive in the barren desert. But there is no counterpart to the providential underground stream that can explain the existence of a coral reef and its nurturing environment. What accounts for the abundance of food on a reef in the midst of an ocean deficient in food? How can something—food and shelter—be manufactured out of what appears to be nothing?

Part of the answer is the coral polyp, a simple, multicellular animal that produces a stony skeleton and forms colonies with adjoining polyps; together, the linked skeletons of these creatures can result in a colony weighing many tons and occupying dozens of cubic feet of space. Neighboring colonies form reefs that may extend for hundreds of miles.

But the polyp cannot by itself create and supply with food the inhabitants of the tropical reefs with which divers and snorkelers are familiar. Left alone, a coral polyp grows slowly, far too slowly to build —and after a disaster to rebuild—a large reef. Moreover, a polyp is an animal; it consumes food but does not create it, except insofar as the polyp itself is eaten by a few predators. Finally, polyps, being animals, do not require light and thus need not live near the surface of the ocean, where the sun's rays can reach them. Reefs built by polyps alone would not only be much smaller and sparser than those that exist, they might well exist at great depths where no diver would ever see them. (Some corals have been found at depths of up to 18,000 feet.)

The key to the ability of the polyps to be productive, shallow-water reef builders and food suppliers is some tiny, yellow-brown plants, the zooxanthellae, which live inside the polyps. The zooxanthellae (the word means, roughly, "animal-loving plants") are algae that have entered into a mutually beneficial, or symbiotic, relationship with the polyps. The zooxanthellae take up carbon and phosphates dissolved in the sea water and, by photosynthesis, convert them into oxygen and various organic compounds, such as sugars and amino acids, which the polyp then converts into proteins, fats, and carbohydrates. Moreover, the zooxanthellae consume the polyp's waste products, such as carbon dioxide and ammonia, and produce from them fresh supplies of oxygen and food.

Because the zooxanthellae are plants, they require sunlight to engage in photosynthesis. As a result, reef-building corals flourish only in shallow tropical and semitropical waters, within 100 yards of depth. In fact, the most luxuriant reefs are very close to the surface; the best diving is typically to be found at depths not much greater than seventy-five feet. The algae are important to corals in another way. To grow, corals must manufacture their skeletal material from calcium particles extracted from the water around them. A polyp can do this without zooxanthellae, but only very slowly. The algae facilitate the conversion of calcium and carbon dioxide into calcium carbonate in a form akin to limestone, the principal ingredient of the coral reef. Because calcification, like growth, is promoted by the zooxanthellae, a coral skeleton will grow about fourteen times faster in sunlight than it will in darkness.

This efficient association of polyps and zooxanthellae is the most important but by no means the only community relationship on the reef. Other calcium-secreting organisms, such as many coralline sponges that grow on deep forereefs (the most seaward parts) away from sediment, contribute heavily to the rigid limestone reef mass as it grows, but it is the corals that define its structure and, in combination with the zooxanthellae, supply a significant part of the food that makes it possible for the reef to support so much life in the midst of an oceanic "desert."

The results of this partnership are "oases" so vast and so varied as to invite comparison with the earth's greatest sights. The Palancar Reef off Mexico's Yucatan coast is a submarine Bryce Canyon, a spectacle of towering pinnacles interrupted by cavernous recesses, archways, finger canyons, and tunnels. The Gulf of Elat (sometimes called Aqaba) in the Red Sea is a vast, steep ravine, its upper shallows lined with fringing reefs. Belize, the only true barrier reef of the Atlantic, has the varied architecture of a sunken badlands, with buttes and shallow valleys and a low chaparral country interrupted by a collapsed limestone cave, or "blue hole," the submarine equivalent of Carlsbad Caverns. Ponape, an atoll in the Pacific Caroline Islands, is like a terraced garden around the base of an ancient, collapsing mountain. Smaller, conical coral formations rising out of shallow sandy plains form patch reefs in all seas, such as those between the Queensland coast and Australia's offshore barrier reef—individual, self-contained hilltown communities. The forereef of Andros Island in the Bahamas drops off from the intense growth at its alpine crest down a sheer slope to the black deep of the Tongue of the Ocean, like a great Rocky Mountain wall.

The parallel between earth and water should not be overdrawn, however, for unlike the terrestrial landscape, reef topography has been built by living organisms. Its edifices represent millions of years during which the skeletons of living coral animals and the remains of other reef creatures were cemented together in a continuing process of calcification. The luxuriant life that a reef fosters is a testimony to the ability of its inhabitants to adapt to massive changes in the structure of the earth and the conditions, even the shape, of the oceans.

REEF HISTORY

The seemingly delicate ecosystem of the reef has not only survived innumerable threats to its existence, it has sometimes prospered from them. Violent storms may topple large sections. Catastrophic weather pattern changes will raise or lower the ambient water temperature, killing vast tracts of coral (although a few corals can survive extreme temperature ranges, most do not flourish below 23 degrees Celsius and seem to do best between 25 and 29 degrees). Floods wash sediments down the mouths of rivers and out into the ocean, where they cover coral surfaces or change the salinity level on the continental shelf. Tidal aberrations expose shallow corals to the killing air. In the past two decades the crown-of-thorns sea star *(Acanthaster planci)* has ravaged acres of coral in the Pacific. Destruction and pollution caused by man threaten corals everywhere.

Concerns about these threats sometimes make us forget how old, and thus how enduring, the reefs are. Their history stretches back two billion years and is recorded in fossils that dot the earth's continents. The earliest reefs, built in Precambrian times, were produced from limestone deposits made by algae. Thereafter, throughout their existence, reefs have resulted from some kind of animal-plant associations that produced limestone secretions. Although zooxanthellae may have played a role in earlier reefs, the productive association between zooxanthellae and the scleractinian, or stony, corals that persists in modern reefs developed in the middle of the Triassic period in the Mesozoic era, over 200 million years ago. This "recent" alliance enabled corals to deposit skeletal calcium carbonate about ten times faster than their ancestral predecessors.

Several times before the appearance of this partnership, in the preceding Paleozoic ages, gradual but devastating climatic changes caused significant setbacks or mass extinctions. Four such major collapses have been identified by scientists; they have been described by Norman D. Newell. Following each disaster, the reef community revived, and each time with a more diverse assemblage of species. For example, in early Cambrian times stony spongelike reefs flourished, affording shelter to ancient reef populations. And during the Cretaceous period at the end of the Mesozoic era there occurred a golden age of enormous molluscs, the rudist clams, ancestral relatives of the giant clams of today's Indo-Pacific, the tridacnids. This "Clam Camelot," as Les Kaufman calls it, formed dramatic reef structures (although nowhere near as large as modern reefs) that suffered extinction in the last major reef collapse about 65 million years ago. From fossil records we have learned that modern reefs probably harbor the greatest number and variety of plant and animal species ever to coexist at one time. Catastrophe, it seems, led to the subsequent multiplication, not the diminution, of life forms over time, at least in the ocean.

In the past two decades our understanding of the geological conditions that favored the formation of today's reefs has been enhanced by the science of plate tectonics, the theory that explains how certain geological disruptions—shifts in the underlying crusts or "plates" of the earth's surface—result in continental drift and fragmentation. These shifts affect reefs, because when land masses are rearranged, they cause major changes in global weather patterns. The consequent environmental changes that occur in the temperature, salinity, depth, and nutrient-bearing currents of the sea alter the growth and the pattern of reefs.

Toward the end of the Paleozoic era, plate shifts in the earth's surface joined the major land masses of the earth into a single continent that scientists have named Pangaea. Primitive reef-building species during this time were broadly distributed in the tropical oceans surrounding the remainder of the earth's surface. It is theorized that, over time, more plate movements caused both changes in world climate and the draining of shallow sea areas around Pangaea's land mass, leading to another catastrophe for the reef community. As a result, the seas were devoid of reefs during the first 10 million years of the Mesozoic era. Then further spreading of the sea floors with consequent upheavals under the earth's crust slowly split apart the plate bearing the Pangaean supercontinent. By the end of the Mesozoic era favorable environmental conditions fostered the development of a reef community in what is today the Mediterranean, where fossil records indicate the emergence of six new coral species, the ancestors of the present-day corals.

The Mediterranean reef declined during Cenozoic times as a result of changes wrought by the continents' drifting into the geographical arrangement familiar to us today. This time, however, there has not been a mass extinction of reef life. Many Old World species rode along with their continental shelves as they shifted to new locations, migrant colonizers of unfamiliar areas. Those pioneers fortunate enough to shift into the right environmental conditions adapted and diversified, creating the results that we now enjoy when we snorkel or dive.

TODAY'S REEF GEOGRAPHY

Reefs are at present primarily concentrated in two major areas: the tropical western Atlantic, including the Caribbean, and a much larger tropical Indo-Pacific region stretching from Africa's east coast and the Red Sea to the central Pacific and Australia. In addition, isolated reef communities flourish near Hawaii, near the Pacific coast west of Panama, and in the Sea of Cortez (the Gulf of California).

Scarcely any reefs are found on the western edges of the continents because of the pattern of the oceans' currents. The great clockwise flow of the Gulf Stream brings warm tropical water up from the equator to the east coast of Florida and the southern edge of the Atlantic states and then swings out toward Bermuda. In the southern hemisphere, the counterclockwise flow of equatorial water brings tropical temperatures down to the eastern shores of Australia, where the Great Barrier Reef is found. By contrast, the western coast of North America is washed by the cold Japanese current and the western coast of South America by the cold Humboldt current coming up from Antarctica. There are some exceptions where pockets of warm water, such as the one trapped in the Sea of Cortez or the one off the west coast of Panama, make possible the growth of reefs on the western edges of a continent.

Within the Indo-Pacific region, a series of reefs in the west-central Pacific constitute the most richly speciated area in the world's oceans (see map in front of book). Centered around the Philippine and Indonesian islands, this region spreads to the Great Barrier Reef. It combines stable food supplies, minimal fluctuations in the weather, and a large area of shallow seas interrupted by numerous chains of islands and the small continent of Australia. In some places, the currents flow in patterns that favor cross-speciation. From an evolutionary standpoint, there are more young families of coral in this fertile region than in other places, indicating that these waters serve as evolutionary centers. Counts of the average ages of corals have led some scientists to conclude that evolution may be going on twice as fast in the Indo-Pacific as in the Atlantic. As a result, this part of the world is the scuba diver's paradise, providing the greatest assemblage and diversity of reef life to be found anywhere.

In the Austral-Asian archipelago, large areas of shallow water uninterrupted by deep-sea valleys help to stabilize fluctuations in the climate, and the proximity of land helps to support marine life. Ninety percent of the world's marine fauna cluster about continental shelves, in the shallows around islands, or on seamounts just below the surface. Shallow-growing corals need a hard substrate on which to anchor. The many groups of islands in the Austral-Asian region furnish more substrate than is found in other tropical seas. Australia, a small continental land mass, is more hospitable to reefs than large continents are because it affects the surrounding climate less drastically while still providing continental-shelf shallows.

Still, diversity is pronounced on many reefs in addition to the rich area just described. Moreover, the combination of species varies from region to region, so that each community is unique in its composition. Each is affected by its immediate environment and by its proximity and access through currents to other reefs. The result, as James W. Valentine and Eldridge M. Moores have emphasized in their analysis of the effect of plate tectonics on life in the sea, is that today's reefs, dispersed as they are, have a provincial character. Once established, adult breeding fishes and invertebrates tend to stay put. In later chapters, we shall glimpse a few examples of provincial variations of behavior that occur within the same family of animals, or even within the same species, as these animals adapt to local habitats. A few fishes, such as the familiar sergeant majors of the genus *Abudefduf,* are circumtropical, found on virtually every reef, whereas other species appear to be endemic only to certain ones. This is analogous to the terrestrial distribution of animals found on separated continents that were once united.

Regional Barriers

The breaking up of Pangaea into smaller units provided more continental shelf area to harbor life but also created barriers to cross-speciation. These barriers include the vastness of the eastern Pacific Ocean and the Atlantic Ocean and the continental linkup of North and South America by the Isthmus of Panama.

The east Pacific barrier, first noted by Charles Darwin in *The Origin of Species,* is between the western Pacific Austral-Asian region and the eastern Pacific shallows along the tropical west coast of the New World. These reef areas are separated not only by great distance but also by a deep sea floor that affects currents and temperatures. Only a few species have managed to make a trans-Pacific migration. Many of those that have done so are known to have long floating larval lives; it is thought that they survived the long crossing in the early stages of life. Six others are species of sharks—strong swimming, pelagic (that is, open-ocean) roamers that are presumably able to undertake great journeys as adults.

Curiously, all these pioneers seem to have journeyed from west to east despite the predominantly east-to-west direction of most trans-Pacific currents. These migrants apparently rode the comparatively narrow west-to-east equatorial countercurrent. As far as can be determined, no migrants have gone in the opposite direction, westward from islands on the New World continental shelves to distant Pacific islands. John C. Briggs, a marine scientist who has studied the species that have crossed the Pacific barrier, theorizes that most of them are good competitors, dominant forms that evolved in the hospitable warm seas of the Indo-Pacific, able to invade peripheral areas and compete in their insular, undisturbed habitats where reef fishes were comparatively scarce. But another student of marine population distribution, G. J. Vermeij, argues that it is not always the strongest species that migrate and stresses the varying effects of specific habitats on species dispersal. Vermeij points out that adapting to unique environments such as reefs results in specialized ways of making a living that in themselves inhibit geographic range. The Hawaiian Islands, lying isolated in between the eastern and western Pacific, have developed an ecology of their own, with few links to the westerly reefs.

Another barrier created as the New World separated from the Old consisted of the distance across the Atlantic, the depth of its valleys, and the Isthmus of Panama, which rose and connected North and South America in Miocene times, preventing further intermixing of tropical species from the two oceans. Briggs estimates that there are less than a dozen shore fishes common to the tropical waters on both sides of the isthmus. Separated by such barriers, the ancient migrants from the now destroyed Mediterranean reef have gone about their evolutionary adaptation processes in relative isolation from one another, contributing to the overall diversity.

Atlantic-Pacific Contrasts

After the closing of the Isthmus of Panama, the number of different Atlantic corals declined as a result, it is thought, of a general cooling of the world's climate that brought more severe temperature fluctuations to the Atlantic than to the tropical Pacific, where the vast, island-dotted shallows provided a more stable expanse for growth and diversification. In the Atlantic, only about sixty coral species flourish, in contrast to the more than 700 that have been identified in the Indo-Pacific. The degree of diversity among fishes and invertebrates differs correspondingly. Species counts are incomplete, but those that have been made indicate dramatic contrasts. Over 500 Atlantic fish species have been classified, but the Philippines, New Guinea, and the Great Barrier Reef harbor over 1,500 species each. Three thousand species are estimated for the combined Austral-Asian archipelago, a number that constantly increases as new species are identified.

Conventionally, coral reefs are divided into three types: fringing, barrier, and atoll. These three basic labels, first used by Charles Darwin, are valuable but somewhat arbitrary categories to which several other descriptive terms have since been added, such as bank reefs, patch reefs, and table reefs. No two reefs are, of course, exactly alike, for each is shaped by a unique environment. In theory, a single reef might, over geologic time, progress through all three stages.

Atlantic reefs are generally smaller and have shallower lagoons than their Pacific cousins. Some reefs seem to be combinations of types. The Atlantic's only true barrier reef is a long coral ridge that runs parallel to the coast of Belize in Central America, separated from it by a lagoon too deep to support coral. Typically, Caribbean reefs are fringing ones that ring island shorelines fairly close in, rooted on rocky substrate and often connected to the island itself. A few resemble mini barrier reefs. Farther out from shore in deep water, submerged bank reefs of various shapes occur, with no distinctly delineated lagoons or with shallower lagoon channels than those of barrier reefs. The Yucatan shelf reefs east of Mexico and those off the Florida Keys are of this type, although some scholars would term the latter "fringing-barrier." Atolls—rings of coral reefs and islands that surround a lagoon where a volcanic mountain has subsided—are absent in the Atlantic. They are primarily a western Pacific phenomenon, although Lighthouse Reef, Glover's Reef, and Turneffe Reef off the coast of Belize are circular in shape and are sometimes called atolls. Patch reefs can be found dotting submarine landscapes everywhere. They are simply isolated coral-head communities surrounded by sandy or grassy bottoms, perhaps rising to sea level or nearly so. They come in all sizes, depending on their growth stages, and many have densely speciated communities.

In the Pacific, Australia's Great Barrier Reef is perhaps best known. Unrivaled anywhere in size, it consists of approximately 2,-500 individual reefs that range from the inshore shallows to the deep continental shelf drop-off. Fringing reefs decorate the shores of east Africa, the Red Sea, and the Seychelles. But Indo-Pacific reefs are predominantly atolls. They spread from the Laccadive and Maldive islands eastward through the South China Sea to the vastness of the central and south Pacific, where the great atolls of Kwajalein, Truk, Eniwetok, and Bikini support endless variations of the reef communities.

The common star coral, *Montastrea annularis,* is one of the Atlantic's principal reef builders. It generally grows in massive boulder-shaped heads but may in crowded environments take a branching shape. A young *M. annularis* one-half meter square will already be the basis of an infant patch reef, harboring a few small fishes and invertebrates. Growing at an average rate of ten millimeters in diameter a year, a single colony may attain a diameter of five meters and be perhaps three meters high. Such a coral head will be, it is estimated, 400 to 500 years old. A 1973 census of a medium-size patch reef two-and-a-half meters in diameter located off the Bimini Islands yielded 563 fishes of thirty-nine species. (The census was done by poisoning the water with rotenone and counting the kill.) The widespread elkhorn *(Acropora palmata)* and staghorn *(A. cervicornis)* corals, found most often in the shallowest habitats, are important builders of Atlantic reef crests (see Plates 1 and 5).

Star corals are also found in the Pacific, but they are not the predominant reef builders. Because there are so many Pacific species, it is difficult to generalize about reef-building corals there. Among the commoner ones are the hump corals of the family Poritidae, especially *Porites lutea,* which forms large, rounded, brown-colored colonies in shallow waters; the branching *Acropora* flower corals, which include various species of staghorn and table corals (see Plate 2); and the cauliflower or bush *Pocillopora* corals (family Pocilloporidae), which are intricately branched housing projects for large colonies of fishes and crustaceans (see Chapter 11).

The extreme shallows of many Pacific and some Atlantic reefs, such as those in the Windward Islands, are often characterized by an encrusting zone of coralline algae. These algae, which like corals secrete calcium skeletons, produce a hard substrate important for the establishment of many sessile animals (that is, animals attached to some surface), including corals.

In addition to the reef-building hard or stony corals, there are soft corals, produced by polyps that do not secrete hard skeletons; they are members of the subclass Octocorallia (or Alcyonaria) of the class Anthozoa. Octocorallia, as their name implies, always have eight feathery feeding tentacles grouped around each polyp, as opposed to six or multiples of six in hard corals.

Atlantic soft-coral populations also differ from those of the Pacific. The Atlantic has an abundance of gorgonian soft corals, such as sea fans, sea whips, and sea rods (see Plate 10), all plantlike in appearance and displaying only a narrow range of colors, mostly purplish gray. Gorgonians derive their name from a horny but flexible substance called gorgonin, which, together with needle-shaped calcareous spicules, supports their structure. Like flowers and shrubs, they indicate current direction and intensity as their soft bodies yield to its velocity. Gorgonians do grow in the Pacific but are comparatively sparse and inconspicuous there.

Unique to the Indo-Pacific are soft corals (order *Alcyonacea*) that bestow on the reef the appearance of a summer garden in full bloom. They exist in a riot of colors. Some, such as the sarcophytons (see Plate 4), can be massive or encrusting and contribute to the lush appearance of the surrounding reef. The translucent, treelike, branching varieties are often found in sheltered areas. They abound, for example, on the superstructures of the sunken ships at the bottom of Truk lagoon. To feed, their elastic bodies, reinforced with calcareous spicules, can expand from small globules when pumped up with water (see Plate 9). Each such coral colony has its own microcommunity of tiny fishes and invertebrates living in its branches.

Typical Reef Zones

Just as different terrestrial habitats have plants and animals adapted to their special environmental qualities, so do differing reef zones tend to have predictable coral colonies. Each reef is somewhat distinctive, depending on how its location affects salinity, temperature, currents, sedimentary deposits, and underwater terrain. A typical profile of a fringing reef is depicted in the drawing on page 18. Beginning at the shore is a bed dotted with sea grass and small corals in a lagoon area that stretches to the reef crest. This area is subject to tidal changes but to relatively little current. The crest may break the water's surface or lie just underneath. Its outer, seaward, current-washed slope is called the reef front, or the forereef, terms that can be confusing to the novice approaching from the shore. It is populated with the most diverse coral and fish populations until it drops off to depths too great for photosynthesis. As a rule of thumb, the greatest diversity in animal life occurs about one-quarter of the way down the reef structure. Thus, the best diving can be done in relatively shallow water.

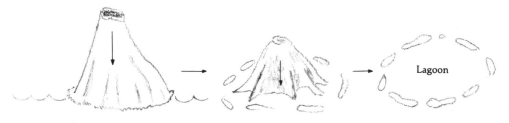

Incipient reef growth   Developing lagoon

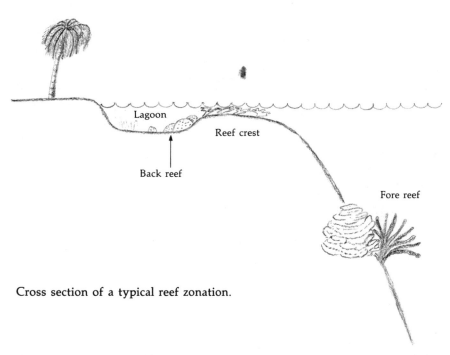

Cross section of a typical reef zonation.

A barrier reef profile is rather like that of a fringing reef writ large. The lagoon area will be wider and deeper, with little or no coral growing in its depths. An atoll's lagoon may have patch reefs within it, but the bulk of growth will be outside the crest on the downward slopes of its seaward edges.

POLYP LIFE

Reef-building corals, the scleractinians,* are colonies formed of small polyps that are little more than stomachs, cemented together by their calcium secretions to form living, carnivorous rocks. But what powerful, enduring stomachs! Each stomach wall has six, or some multiple of six, tentacle extensions around its single opening that enable it to trap, from the surrounding water, zooplankton: small animal life that rides the currents or propels itself along, some of microscopic size and some large enough for a diver to see. Each polyp tentacle is armed with a weapon deadly to its tiny prey, a poison-bearing, barbed, hairlike stinging cell called a nematocyst. When not feeding, corals retract their tentacles and show only their hard surfaces. When extended, however, the delicate, floral patterns of the tentacles give the stony corals a deceptively soft, fuzzy look, camouflaging for the human eye what is actually a bristling, explosive-charged armory (see Plate 7). A helpless zooplankton carried into contact with a tentacle triggers the nematocyst's poisonous discharge; digestion begins even before the tentacle sweeps the zooplankton into the polyp's stomach.

As if writhing tentacles disguised as flowers were not enough of a nightmare for planktonic animals, the coral polyps of many species continually produce an exterior coating of sticky mucus that traps zooplankton. Long strands of mucus up to three or four inches long, called mesenterial filaments, extrude from the polyp stomachs or from the edges of their mouths, entangling prey. The strings, which bear their own nematocysts, periodically are drawn back into the stomach cavity for digestion, aided by the constant pulsations of little hairs, called cilia, around the polyp mouth. These filaments work in tandem with the tentacles when they are feeding, but sometimes they trap prey even when the tentacles are retracted. And that's not all. Waving, hairlike cilia create currents that wash through the polyp's stomach. These cilia serve many functions. They draw mucus-trapped food inward; they cleanse the coral interiors with an up and outward spiral current; they aid in reproduction, acting as a transport service; and they have been observed, in at least a few Atlantic species, to reverse direction and carry particulate matter inside for digestion when the

---

*The reef-building corals belong to the phylum Coelenterata (or Cnidaria). Coelenterates take their name from the Greek word *coel,* which means hollow; the word "coelem" has come to mean the body cavity of any animal. In the case of coelenterates, they are little more than body cavities.

tentacles and mucus threads are resting.

Although each polyp is an individual animal that can survive by itself, its usual mode of life is communal. Colonies of polyps are interconnected. Above the stony cup (calyx) that forms the base for each polyp, a horizontal sheet of tissue connects the adjoining sides of body walls. Through this connective tissue the colony is capable of cooperative food sharing. Digested nutrients can be passed throughout the community, from polyp to polyp, transported by amoebocyte cells.

Most stony corals feed nocturnally, but some kinds habitually feed during the day and all are capable of some daytime feeding. In a study of thirty-five species of Atlantic corals, J. B. Lewis and W. S. Price found that the feeding habits of corals are of three kinds. Those that feed around the clock rely primarily on their tentacles for capturing prey. A limited number of nocturnally feeding corals depend on mucus nets for trapping zooplankton. The largest number of species, including the familiar star, staghorn, and brain coral species, use a combination of feeding techniques. Although they are mostly nocturnal, some of them trap food with mucus strands during daylight hours, even though their tentacles are usually retracted then. On occasion, however, the polyps will be active, with tentacles extended in the day.

In laboratory experiments Lewis and Price noted that corals respond both to tactile stimuli on their tentacles and to smells. When brine shrimp were released into the water, nearby polyps "woke up"; their cone-shaped mouths opened wide and expanded upward well above the stony calyx and their tentacles unfolded and lashed about vigorously. Night divers can see these feeding practices. Patient observation will reveal how each tentacle acts independently, how the mouth sinks inward to receive the bounty from the tentacle tips, and, if the prey is large enough to be visible, as it often is, how quickly it is shattered on contact, before the meal is swallowed.

Growth and Reproduction

Corals grow by budding polyps that are arranged in patterns according to their species. In some species new polyps arise around the base of old ones, a process termed extratentacular. In others, buds form from the oral discs—the area around the mouths—of old polyps, which gradually lengthen out and divide to make two individuals; this is intratentacular budding. Brain corals are intratentacular budders that never completely separate their discs, their rows of polyps all arising from a single, shared disc that becomes a convoluted trench; hence its brainlike resemblance.

Polyps also reproduce sexually. Eggs and sperm develop in the stomach walls of the polyps. Waterborne sperm, released through the polyp mouth, are drawn inside other polyps in currents created by the beating cilia. Eggs are fertilized internally, develop briefly, and leave the parent polyp in a free-swimming larval stage (the larvae are called planulae), becoming themselves a part of the zooplankton. The timing of the larval release varies widely depending on the species and the region, but it occurs with marked seasonality and sometimes in lunar cycles. Although cast adrift in the sea, each larva carries with it two special legacies: a portion of its parents' zooxanthellae (an inheritance enabling it to meet its symbiotic needs) and a built-in preference for the proper substrate. Those larvae that survive settle, after a few days or weeks, onto some appropriate hard surface and found their own colonial empires.

Polyps can also reproduce by regeneration from broken pieces. On fragments of sufficient size, soft tissues begin to grow at the line of breakage a few weeks after detachment, secreting a new base of calcium carbonate, a survival skill we shall consider later in this chapter in a section about reef destruction and recovery.

Coral Enemies

The stinging nematocysts of coral tentacles serve not only hunting purposes but defensive ones as well, protecting the sessile (that is, attached) polyps from the fish and invertebrate predators that feed on them. Even so, corals are vulnerable to many enemies that either have devised ways to avoid the nematocysts or are immune to them (see Chapter 11). Several fishes eat living corals, notably the few species of parrotfishes that crunch on live coral, the triggerfishes that bite off chunks to get at invertebrates inside, filefishes, and many butterflyfishes. Curiously, Indo-Pacific corals are more subject to fish predation than Atlantic corals. One theory is that the richer coral cover on Indo-Pacific reefs has reduced the amount of plant food available and thereby caused more fishes to adapt to coral or partially coral diets. A host of invertebrate predators also specialize in coral, such as fireworms, small box crabs, snails, and nudibranchs (snails without shells). Where wounds are not severe, corals have remarkable powers of polyp regeneration, although they must combat invading sponges, worms, and other sessile animals looking for a base.

As coral grows, it builds outward or upward on its secreted skeletal base in a layerlike pattern. Both the older, non-polyp-bearing portions and damaged areas of living sections are vulnerable to boring animals: sponges, molluscs (snails), and many kinds of polychaete marine worms (see drawing below). Some corals become so weakened by these infestations that they collapse. When they do, they may become foundations for new reef builders and other attached animals.

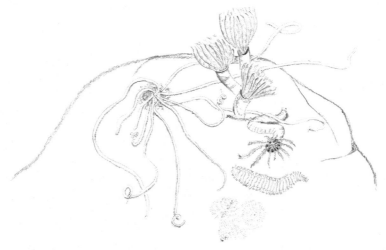

A variety of polychaete worms. Clockwise from top: Featherduster colony (sabellids); fan worm (serpulid) in calcareous tube attached to dead coral patch; bristleworm (or fireworm); Christmas-tree worm (serpulid of genus *Spirobranchia*), a boring polychaete; terebellid with long tentacles extending through its gill mass from burrow: a photosensitive worm seen nocturnally. All shown here are sedentary except the bristleworm.

The habits of some territorial damselfishes are destructive to the corals they claim as property. The Caribbean threespot damselfish *(Stegastes planifrons = Eupomacentrus planifrons),* whose algae-farming practices are described in Chapter 8, cultivates algal mats on live staghorn *(Acropora cervicornis)* and common star coral *(Montastrea annularis),* defending them from herbivorous intruders. The threespots establish their farms by biting living coral tissues. The lesions that result are overgrown by filamentous algae within two or three days. Kaufman, who studied this phenomenon on a Jamaican reef, reported that one-tenth of a square meter could be converted into an algal garden within one month by a constantly nipping threespot. The wounded coral is thereby exposed to further destruction by boring organisms and by other herbivores, such as schooling striped parrotfish *(Scarus iserti = S. croicensis)* that, attracted by an algal meal, overwhelm the defending threespot's defenses and erode the coral surface with their scraping teeth. Similar coral mortality has been observed on the Great Barrier Reef branching corals, *Acropora palifera,* in which the damselfish farmers, *Dischistodus perspicillatus,* establish territories.

Sediment that settles over coral is another danger. Under natural reef conditions, without unusual deposits of sediment, corals are able to keep themselves clean. Polyps inflate hydrostatically, produce mucus, and transport particles away with the energy produced by the tiny beating cilia around the polyp mouths. A recent study of the Atlantic large cupped boulder coral *(Montastrea cavernosa)* showed that under normal reef conditions sediment was removed as rapidly as it was deposited. Corals that live in shallow, sandy habitats, such as the small Atlantic starlet coral *(Siderastrea siderea),* are especially adapted to survive silt conditions. But too much sediment and the coral dies.

The effects of storms, pollution, and other catastrophic enemies of coral are considered below in the section about reef destruction and recovery.

Coral Competition

Coral growth is subject not only to predation from swimming fishes and crawling or drilling invertebrates but also to competition from other coral species. As they must all anchor on hard surfaces, and as they all grow in size once anchored, space for growth and sunlight for their zooxanthellae becomes scarce; just as trees in crowded forests compete for space, so do corals. Different species grow at different rates; thus, it is thought that some fast-growing species will (literally) overshadow nearby slow-growing ones and kill them, or portions of them, although this has not been well demonstrated.

We do know that some corals can combat crowding from a neighbor. When competitors grow close enough together (within about two centimeters), some species will extend their mucus strands through their polyp walls to digest the tissue of intruding rivals, thereby destroying the intruders.

Several scientists have noted dominance hierarchies among coral species on widely separated reefs. An extensive study of Atlantic coral interactions made by Judith Lang for her Ph.D. thesis at Yale University revealed a clear-cut ranking among coral species. Watching the behavior of corals transplanted among reefs as distant from one another as Jamaica, Panama, Curaçao, and Bonaire, Lang found a consistent pattern of aggression. No species ever attacked its own kind. Curiously, a given coral under attack from another does not seem to fight back against its persecutor, but will attack another species lower in the pecking order. In fact, in crowded conditions a coral may be eating the tissues of a neighbor on one side and at the same time be under attack on its other side. In a laboratory experiment, a mushroom coral *(Scolymia lacera)* deprived of light gradually weakened until its polyps detached from its skeleton; nevertheless, the polyps continued to feed on a nearby subordinate species.

Since the more aggressive coral families seem to be small, compact, and slow growing, Lang suggests that attack by mesenterial filaments is a means of protection against rapidly growing corals. She found that in habitats shared by mushroom corals and a coral they consistently attack, *Scolymia cubensis,* the latter species is far more abundant. Although it may not be "dominant" in contact situations, it seems to be superior in numbers. The Caribbean large-cupped boulder coral *(Montastrea cavernosa)* has specialized, extra-long sweeper tentacles, named for their distinctive waving actions. The sweepers have outsized nematocysts and are extended primarily at night, when they trap zooplankton food (see Plate 8). C. A. Richardson, P. Dustan, and Lang have found evidence that the sweeper tentacles are also used for defense in coral space competition, in fighting off the mesenterial filament attacks of the more aggressive boulder coral, *M. annularis*.

Pecking orders seem to vary according to region, so that every reef has a unique combination of coral competitors. A species that dominates one reef may be a second-class citizen on another. C. R. C. Sheppard, who compared two oceans, noted that families of corals that are highly aggressive on Atlantic reefs tend to be less dominant in an Indian Ocean setting. There is recent evidence that soft corals, the alcyonaceans, can compete effectively with the stony scleractinians. In an experiment on the Great Barrier Reef, researchers relocated colonies of three species of soft corals next to stands of two hard corals and compared the results with undisturbed control areas. Where the two types of corals were in direct contact, the researchers noted significantly high levels of hard-coral mortality. About half of the Great Barrier Reef soft corals contain toxic substances that not only aid them in defense against predators but apparently also are useful in aggressive competition. Research in coral interactions is young, much of it undertaken only in the past five years. Further studies will undoubtedly reveal much more about the behavior of the reef builders.

All corals adapt their shapes to some degree in the scramble for light. Some species, such as the table corals, can make do with a small foothold on the substrate, growing outward from small pedestal bases into intricate branching forms that maximize their surface areas, thereby competing with massive species (see Plate 2). Other corals have adapted to shaded habitats, growing under overhangs and even in caves. Such species—at least 150 have been recorded on the Great Barrier Reef alone—tend to be small in size, often encrusting or two-dimensional in growth form. They may have fewer polyps than sun-dwelling corals, but these house a larger number of zooxanthellae, perhaps to maximize the light-gathering area. If a coral grows in a place entirely without sunlight, however, it will have no zooxanthellae. The shade coral most familiar to Indo-Pacific divers is the widely distributed, brilliantly colored *Tubastraea coccinea* (see Plate 6). Corals not evolutionarily adapted to shade are devastated if deprived of their accustomed sunlight. They soon expel their zooxanthellae and die.

THE FOOD WEB

The richness of marine life in all seas is dependent on tiny microscopic plants, the phytoplankton (floating plants). These are algae, plants so simple that they lack roots, stems, and leaves and sometimes consist of but a single cell. They bear within their minute bodies, however, a most important ingredient: chlorophyll, the key to photosynthesis. They convert the energy of the sun into energy for other living things, turning the ocean's chemicals into organic compounds (such as car-bohydrates) and releasing oxygen as they do so. The plants are pro-ducers in the food web, providing nourishment for ocean herbivores, and thus, ultimately, for the carnivores. These phytoplankton, the counterparts of terrestrial plants, float in the upper layer of the oceans only as deep as light can penetrate. Unlike corals, they flourish most abundantly in cold waters. There, they are the underpinnings of the food web, providing sustenance both to zooplankton (floating ani-mals) and to small fishes.

The food web builds and spreads from the consumption of phyto-plankton, with bigger fishes eating smaller ones and being in turn eaten, their waste products sinking to the sea floor where bacteria and other decomposers of dead organic matter recycle them into organic nutrients. Upwellings of deep currents and the vertical migrations of marine animals recycle the rich organic compost from the sea floor to upper water levels. Additional organic material enriches the seas from continental runoffs and the decomposition of larger, inshore plants. Cold currents—such as the Humboldt, which flows northward from the Antarctic along the coast of Chile to Ecuador, turning west to cross the tropical Pacific—carry the rich phytoplanktonic nutrients along with them. Loaded with food, the Humboldt supports huge pelagic schools of fishes, such as anchovies, that provide important commercial fishing opportunities off the South American coast. Around the Galapagos archipelago, on the equator 600 miles off Ecuador, planktonic nutrients swept along by the cold currents darken the ocean so much that divers may feel as if they are immersed in pea soup. Yet it is this very darkness—or the plankton that cause it—that makes possible the large schools of fishes that are found in the Galapagos and the sea lions that feed on the fishes.

If cold, upwelling currents are the source of much of the nutrients that enter the ocean's food web, how do the nutrient-poor tropical seas support huge, complex coral reef communities? In part they do so by scavenging from the ocean the relatively small amount of phytoplanktonic life that manages to find its way into warmer waters. Plankton counts of water samples taken from in front and in back of a reef reveal dramatic differences: very few nutrients survive the screening processes of reef life. Even most plankton originating in the reef itself, such as particles of algae or larvae, are consumed before they get very far. The seaward side of a reef, the forereef, is always the most elaborately populated, its residents clamoring for first choice. Here is where the most coral arms reach out for plankton, where filter-feeding sponges abound, and where schools of planktivorous fishes hover, mouths agape. Some organic food is washed into the sea from land nearby—if there is land nearby. Many nocturnal fishes sleep in hiding places by day on the reef and migrate well away from it at night to forage in sandy areas or to feed on night plankton. They thus transport back organic matter from outside the reef, which they deposit in the form of wastes, a contribution that has been measured for at least one reef species. Still, these sources are not nearly enough to support the richness of a reef.

Most of the needed food seems to be generated within the reef itself. The formation of these nutrients is initiated by the photosynthesis carried on by zooxanthellae inside corals, anemones, and a few other organisms that harbor them and by the many varieties of algae that encrust dead surfaces, grow in the underlying skeletal pores of live coral, and thrive in the sand. This solution to the puzzle of reef nutrition was first documented by the brothers Harold and Eugene Odum, ecologists sent by the United States Atomic Energy Commission to study the Eniwetok atoll reef in connection with nuclear test explosions conducted there in the early 1950s. They were able to calculate Eniwetok's biomass: the dry weight of all its living matter. Depending on the reef zone, the algal biomass was two to four times as great as that of the herbivores and approximately forty times that of the carnivores, enough to explain the miracle of the oasis in the desert. The Odums stressed the role of the corals in forming a bridge between the plant and the animal worlds, hosting some algae inside the polyps and providing external surfaces on which more could grow.

Since the Odums' research, several marine scientists have demonstrated that reef productivity is also enhanced by those territorial fishes that farm algal gardens. The algal mats not only supply the herbivorous fish farmers with food but also attract small invertebrates, whose numbers have been shown to be greater in these mats than in comparable algal masses outside such territories. Furthermore, the growth of blue-green algae, which promote nitrogen fixation and thus organic productivity, is greater inside these territories. In one experiment, Susan H. Brawley and Walter H. Adey removed damselfishes of three different farming species from their territories and found that a rapid reduction in brown and filamentous algal biomass resulted. Studies of territorial damselfishes in the Indo-Pacific support these findings. Although the role of herbivorous fishes (and invertebrates) in reef ecology is not fully understood, recent investigations have increased our understanding of the sources of reef nutrients.

REEF DESTRUCTION AND RECOVERY

Between the turn of the century and 1962, 200 hurricanes and over 200 less catastrophic tropical storms battered the Caribbean, or about six-and-a-half storms a year. Although no storm hits every reef, each cuts a violent path, its heavy wave action toppling corals and injuring fishes. Obviously, shallower habitats are affected the most. Deep slopes, particularly below about sixty feet, are more stable environments. Since careful records are just beginning to be kept of reef populations before and after storms, and then only in a few places, we do not yet know how to predict with accuracy the time it takes for reefs to recover. Some fast-growing corals can recover within one or two years; others take decades. We do know that some storms are devastating, such as Hurricanes Hattie and Gerta, which pounded the barrier reef off Belize in 1961 and 1978. D. R. Stoddart, who surveyed the effects of Hattie, estimated eight years afterward that the worst-affected reefs might take twenty to twenty-five years to recover. After inspection three years later he reconsidered and speculated it might take sixty to one hundred years. Observers of damage in other regions have reported much faster recoveries. Differing recovery rates probably reflect not only the severity of the storm but the growth rates and resilience of the particular coral species involved. Some scientists have suggested that reefs lying in storm belts adjust to their weather patterns—their corals have adapted to stress—and suffer less damage than those that are hit less frequently. But coral storm damage has not been studied long enough for anyone to be certain.

Reefs, however, have always had to deal with storms, and obviously, over geologic time, they have found ways to reconstitute themselves following a disturbance. There is even considerable support among ecologists for the notion that storms of moderate intensity play a beneficial role in redistributing species, maintaining diversified populations, creating space for new colonization, and weeding or thinning out dominant corals. Many reef-building corals regenerate from broken pieces. Extreme shallow-water families, such as the brittle staghorn and elkhorn species *(Acropora cervicornis* and *A. palmata),* are particularly vulnerable to storms, yet they seem especially adapted to their turbulent, wave-tossed reef positions. Lightweight fragments can be carried considerable distances by heavy wave action before reestablishing themselves and sending out new growth, and they can do this even if they settle on a soft substrate. Breakage is an important way for corals to distribute themselves and to avoid overcrowding.

In the aftermath of Hurricane Gerta a group of scientists who studied the Belize reef suggested that long-term reef calcification and growth rates may be positively affected by moderate storms. They noted that close to half of the broken branches of elkhorn coral regenerated and overall 39 percent of the detached coral colonies survived. This created a larger number of coral colonies, although of smaller size than before the storm. Survival was highest among the larger-size pieces. The researchers hypothesized that for the fast-growing elkhorn coral, which reaches a "survival" size in about ten years—the average time between hurricanes at Belize—fragmentation may be the main means of reproduction and dispersal in that region. Other observers have suggested similar benefits for staghorn coral in other areas.

Severe storms may not be followed by such successful recovery, however. Following Hurricane Allen in 1980, a team of researchers tagged fragments of staghorn in three reef zones off Jamaica. Although initially many broken pieces survived, five months afterward the mortality rate was substantial. There had been nearly a hundred-fold long-term decrease in survival from the original poststorm number of colonies. Apparently the tissues of the staghorn were too sorely stressed to sustain recovery.

Perhaps more serious destructive effects than direct storm violence are long-term changes in water temperatures and salinity levels. Such changes were apparently wrought by shifts, during the winter of 1982–1983, in the movement of the El Niño current that flows off the western coast of Panama. The side effects of that season's cyclical reversal of Pacific wind and water currents are still being evaluated and are thought to be more pronounced than in any other year of this century. Water temperatures in some Pacific reef areas were raised to as high as 31 degrees Celsius, well above the tolerance level of corals, leading to a rapid decline of several reefs during the spring of 1983.

Damage by the Crown-of-Thorns Sea Star

Beginning in the mid-1960s something akin to an underwater plague struck huge sections of the Great Barrier and other Indo-Pacific reefs. An unexplained population explosion of coral-eating crown-of-thorns sea stars, each able to devour about two square feet of coral in a day, marched through coral forests, alarming marine scientists everywhere (see Plate 11). Year after year the devastation widened. Unlike storms, which disturb the shallower zones, the crown-of-thorns can reach deep areas and destruction is thorough at many depths. All kinds of eradication schemes were suggested and some, futilely, attempted. But the crown-of-thorns infestation disappeared by itself when sea star populations returned to "normal," and by the mid-1970s complete or nearly complete reef recoveries were reported throughout the tropical zone.

Scientists are not certain why the outbreak began or why it ended, but many now think it was not the unmitigated disaster that was first feared. Some compare the recent rampage by armies of the crown-of-thorns to forest fires that periodically clear out overcrowded tree communities and make way for new competition and colonization.

The sea stars are tentatively viewed as a natural phenomenon that, like recurring moderate storms, help to diversify a reef.

Man-made Pollution

In addition to storms, reefs in some areas are occasionally damaged by unusually low tides that expose corals to the air and dry them out. In the Gulf of Elat in the Red Sea, an unexpected low tide in 1970 killed between 80 and 90 percent of the reef-building corals in the reef flat area. Because an extensive census of its population had been conducted in the previous year, the recovery could be measured accurately. Coral communities were regularly monitored in two similar areas, one near the port of Elat, where two major oil terminals pollute the waters, and the other, a control reef, five kilometers away. Part of the recovery was from regeneration and part from the settlement of larval planulae that established new colonies. Three years afterward, the rate of coral regeneration from fragments was comparable at both reefs, but coral recolonization from the free-swimming planulae was twenty-three times greater at the control reef in healthy waters than at the reef near the port. The reproductive systems of the corals and the health of their planulae were affected by the pollution. The observing ecologists estimated that within another two or three years the control reef would be fully recovered (it should be remembered that shallow-water corals are generally fast-growing varieties), but reached the conclusion that when man-made pollution complicates natural catastrophes, reefs are unable to return to their former configurations.

There is little, if anything, we can do about natural disturbances to coral reefs. Left alone, they seem to do fairly well by themselves. Viewed from an evolutionary perspective, corals have had millions of years to adapt to such phenomena. But encroachments by man that change the quality of the marine environment can be, and have been, calamitous. Too often they come too rapidly and too severely for reefs to recuperate. It is one thing for a colony of staghorn coral to break apart in the shallows and quite another for a large, mature dome of star coral several hundred years old to lose its reproductive ability from pollution or to be smothered in silt from harbor dredging.

ARTIFICIAL REEFS

Space-hungry settlers of the American West who jumped the starting gun in the 1889 rush for free land in the Oklahoma Territory were called Sooners. Space-hungry marine dwellers also have plenty of sooners in their midst. Artificial reefs have been constructed in many places in the Atlantic and Pacific oceans during the past two decades to serve as living laboratories for a variety of marine study projects. Invariably, colonization by fishes, invertebrates, and algae is swift. Divers constructing a study reef from concrete blocks and Portland cement in the Sea of Cortez in the mid-1970s found that aggressive spotted sand basses *(Paralabrax maculatofasciatus)* claimed shelter spaces while the structure was still being assembled. Within ten days after its completion, algae growth blanketed the reef, and within a month, fishes representing fifteen different species had established themselves. Eventually fifty-seven species were present. Such speed in occupying shelter and capitalizing on the availability of firm substrate has been observed in similar experiments in many places, including the accidents of sunken ships, reaffirming the importance of reef architecture in marine communities (see Plates 3 and 4).

Corals seem to be the last animals to colonize artificial reefs, appearing about one year after reef construction. They seem to prefer authentic, biologically produced limestone, and so they must wait until coralline algae and other calcium-secreting organisms have encrusted man-made structures. Other invertebrates and fishes are not so fussy and welcome any new housing project, whether it be a tower supporting an offshore drilling rig, a sunken ship, or even old rubber tires.

New denizens arrive in fairly predictable patterns. Among fishes, the first to come are newly hatched larvae settling from the plankton and juveniles and subadults that have difficulty in competing for housing elsewhere against established adults. Other earlybirds are opportunistic fishes with relatively large home ranges that need places to hide or rest: carnivores such as the many species of groupers and snappers, and foragers such as parrotfishes, surgeonfishes and grunts, which are used to a lifestyle of moving between one patch reef and another. Territorial fishes that defend their homesites, notably the damselfishes, are among the last to take up residence. Although coral matures slowly in contrast to the rest of the immigrants, eventually artificial reefs resemble natural ones in the extraordinary diversity of their flora and fauna. More than nineteen years of observations of Randall Reef (named for John E. Randall, its initiator), constructed with 800 concrete blocks in 1960 off St. John in the Virgin Islands, point to the predictability and stability of reef communities. There are always regional variations, and initial colonization has a random quality to it, but once established an orderly equilibrium predominates.

APPROACHES TO REEF STUDIES

Studies of aspects of coral reefs fairly tumble over one another these days. Twenty years ago many marine biologists published reports in journals often mainly given over to terrestrial matters. For example, students of fishes (ichthyologists) shared, and still share, with students of snakes (herpetologists) a scholarly publication established in 1913, *Copeia.* Behavioral studies first found room in the pioneering journal founded by Konrad Lorenz and Wolfgang Wickler, *Zeitschrift für Tierpsychologie* (Journal of Animal Psychology). A few marine journals existed, but nothing like today's proliferation, in which a flood of studies appear and theories are debated by an international community of scientists.

One of the liveliest international discussions among reef ecologists is that concerned with explaining the basis of species diversity in reef life. In the past decade, researchers have generally held one of two opposed views. One, familiarly called the chaos theory, was advanced principally by the Australian ecologist Peter F. Sale and is supported by Rand Dybdahl, Frank H. Talbot, Barry C. Russell, and others. It emphasizes the chance nature of reef colonization (Sale initially called it a "lottery" system), holding that the nature of species turnover, as determined by periodic census counts of defined areas, is a random process that results in great variability. Just so many niches are available, and when one is vacated, it is the luck of the draw, rather than the competitive abilities of the fishes, that determines the next occupant.

The opposing viewpoint, the order theory, stresses the predictability of reef populations and their behavior. It holds that in the long run, through several generations of fishes, the reef community, despite some species turnover, is orderly and stable, with a constant composition of species. Because reef fishes have adapted to very specialized habitats, they are able to live in close proximity with quite diverse neighbors without crowding one another out or spending undue energy in competition. The chief spokesmen of the order theory are C. Lavett Smith (curator of the American Museum of Natural History), G. S. Helfman, James C. Tyler, John Ebersole, and others.

These opposing theories have been useful in stimulating research to further our understanding of the ways in which densely crowded, diverse populations live together successfully. In the past five years almost every scholarly article concerned with the broad ecology of reef populations has addressed itself in some degree to these opposing viewpoints. To some extent the differences between them are exaggerated. Some of the most recent studies emphasize that differing intervals between reef censuses and the different sizes and varying geologies of reefs studied in this pioneering era of reef research account in part for different findings. As more studies are done in more underwater locations, compromise views have emerged.

Reefs are not benign, unchanging environments. Divers typically explore them in fair weather and may often be deceived by their calm appearance. But the reefs experience and survive great natural catastrophes and also intense predation; they recover from the disasters and accommodate to the predation in quite predictable patterns. Patch reefs that have been subjected to rotenone poisonings and studied during the aftermath have been shown to be recolonized immediately, their new communities resembling their past ones, just as artificial reefs develop similarly to natural ones. A study made after an accidental poisoning of a nature reserve reef from chemical contamination in the Gulf of Elat following a fire in the port showed that the fish populations recovered fully within a year, immigrating in much the same pattern as reported earlier for artificial reefs. From this perspective, the enduring resilience of reefs is an inescapable conclusion and immensely impressive. But within that stable environment, the behavior that occurs—techniques of swimming, modes of reproduction, the use of the senses, the extent of social life, the acquisition and defense of territories, the development of symbiosis and mimicry— is so incredibly diverse as to make one wonder how anything even approaching stability can occur. Describing and explaining behavior on the tropical reef is not like giving an account of life in a small town, but akin to describing and explaining life in London, Tokyo, or New York City. It is to this task that we now turn.

CHAPTER TWO

Swimming

*H*umans quickly learn that moving through water is harder work than moving across land. It takes five to ten times as much energy for a human to swim a given distance on the surface of water as it does for him to cover the same distance running. Man naturally envies the fishes for their apparently effortless movement underwater, especially those with the classic fish shapes designed for speed and endurance, the fusiform fishes.

Fusiform means "spindle-shaped" and comes from the Latin word for spindle, *fusus.* According to the branch of physics called fluid dynamics, an ideal streamlined body will be tapered at each end, with its deepest part at a point about one-third of the way back from the nose (see the jack on page 40). This form minimizes the amount of turbulence created by the body as it moves through water; the less turbulence, other things being equal, the less effort required to achieve a given speed. The fusiform shape is exemplified by fast-swimming predator fishes, such as jacks, tunas, mackerels, and barracudas. It is no accident that torpedos also have a fusiform design, and thus before people learn the word "fusiform," and whence torpedos derive their shape, they often say that barracudas and similar predators have torpedo-shaped bodies. So obvious are the advantages of such a shape that we sometimes assume that fishes lacking it are at a disadvantage.

In fact, for many reef fishes, swimming speed is not very important. The reef provides an environment that enables a variety of fish forms to survive and prosper. If no reefs existed, the fusiforms would long since have destroyed all but a few bottom-dwelling species and some others with unusual defenses because there would be no place for poor swimmers to hide. But a reef, with its myriad holes and food sources, constitutes a habitat that permits all manner of adaptations. Perhaps in no other aspect of fish life has the variety in the natural environment allowed natural selection to produce such a variety of fish behavior.

For a few fishes, swimming ability is hardly important at all. Sedentary bottom dwellers such as the frogfishes (Antennariidae) and the scorpion or stonefishes (Scorpaenidae) have forfeited agile motion for the ability to capture prey by camouflage and deception, as will be described in Chapter 3. If provoked, these sluggish fishes are barely able to rise up more than a few inches and to flutter awkwardly for a few feet to a new anchorage. And of course squids and octopuses do not swim at all; they move about by jet propulsion, ejecting a stream of water through a special nozzle on their bodies.

For other fishes, the ability to swim is more important, but for many of these, hovering and turning are of greater importance than speed or power. Butterflyfishes, for example, thrive on a diet of coral polyps and the tentacles of featherduster and Christmas-tree worms. These food sources cannot swim, but they can retreat into their protective hard shells. Thus, what is valuable to a butterflyfish, and what has enabled it to survive over the centuries, is the capacity to hover motionless while picking at the coral and to dart swiftly, though over only short distances, up to a featherduster worm before it retracts.

Butterflyfishes, angelfishes, damselfishes, and surgeonfishes have slender, compressed bodies that they propel, in varying styles, with the rowing motion of their pectoral fins, much like the swimming methods of some of the thicker-bodied wrasses and parrotfishes.

These oarlike fins are of little value for sustained bursts of speed but are invaluable for braking, pivoting, and reversing direction. As with all fishes, shape and lifestyle are closely related.

MOVING IN WATER

No matter how various their swimming styles, all fishes must cope with certain common features of their underwater environment. Water is 800 times as dense as air, much more viscous (resistant to flowing), and incompressible. The effort to move through water creates drag on the fish's body as it attempts to push the water aside and produces turbulence along its sides and in its wake. The streamlined —that is, fusiform—fishes have shapes that minimize this drag and turbulence. For a while, some observers thought that the slimy mucus with which fishes are coated also helped to reduce drag, but we now know this is not the case. When scientists measured the drag on fish-shaped objects suspended in a moving stream of water, they found that coating the objects with slippery stuff had no effect on the resistance they encountered.

The maximum speed a fish can attain underwater is determined by the relation of its muscle power to its form. It is possible to calculate the theoretical speed limit of any given underwater creature. This led to the paradox (Gray's paradox, to be exact) that is the marine equivalent of the well-known story about the scientist who proved that a bumblebee cannot fly. In 1936, Sir James Gray calculated that, given its shape, a porpoise would have to have muscles capable of generating seven times as much power as any known mammalian muscle to account for the porpoise's top speed of 20 knots (about 23 miles per hour). In short, it is theoretically impossible for the porpoise to swim as fast as it does. Strenuous efforts have been made since 1936 to resolve this paradox. Scholars have revised upward their estimate of muscle power and downward their estimate of drag. But the paradox persists. In 1978, C. C. Lindsey summarized the state of affairs by observing that "the gap between the swimming fish and the scientists is closing, but the fish is still well ahead."

If water creates problems, it also provides benefits. Chief among these is that the buoyancy of water renders the effects of gravity nearly inconsequential. The supportive water makes it possible for the fish to move in three dimensions and unnecessary for it to devote much energy—in some cases, any energy—to staying off the bottom. But for a fish to be truly weightless, it must be neutrally buoyant—

that is, the weight of the water it displaces must exactly equal its own weight. Evolution did not equip fishes with this precise body weight, but it did equip most of them with a gas bladder.

A gas bladder is a built-in buoyancy compensator. It is a gas-filled bag, situated near the center of the fish, that can expand or contract in order to keep the fish weightless in water. There are two types of these bladders, open and closed. Fishes with open bladders must take in air at the surface of the ocean and force it through a duct into the bladder. They are not dependent on the air for breathing (as are, for example, sea snakes) but for buoyancy. As these open-bladder fishes descend, the pressure of the surrounding water compresses the bladder and so the fishes lose buoyancy, making it easier for them to descend. As they rise, the bladder expands and they gain buoyancy, making it easier to move upward. When the bladder expands, excess air must be bled off through the throat if the bladder is not to rupture. (In some advanced open-bladder fishes, the excess air is reabsorbed by body tissues.) Because open-bladder fishes must periodically recharge their air supply, they tend to live at shallower depths; because air lost during an ascent can only be replaced at the surface, they tend to remain at the same depths for long periods.

Closed-bladder fishes are a more recent evolutionary development. They can inflate their bladders with air extracted from the water by their gills and carried to the bladders through a complex array of capillaries. To deflate, they reabsorb excess air back into the bloodstream. Since they need never go to the surface for air, many need never leave the safety of the reef and hence are not so dependent on the ability to defend themselves in open water or to evade predators with sustained high-speed swimming. The advent of closed swim bladders meant that fins no longer had to be designed for relatively long open-water chases and escapes. Most coral reef fishes have closed bladders, a fact that permits evolution to select fins that are appropriate for many things other than speed, such as hovering, turning, and backing.

There are a few fishes, however, without swim bladders at all. The bottom dwellers, such as blennies, lizardfishes, clingfishes, and many gobies and scorpionfishes, can survive by remaining negatively buoyant and capturing their food through concealment. The clingfishes and some gobies have even developed suction discs for holding fast to rocks or coral; for them, a swim bladder would be quite disadvantageous. Lizardfishes have evolved long, strong pelvic fins that are not well adapted for swimming but are ideal for balancing themselves on the sand while awaiting their prey.

Sharks and rays have no swim bladders but are nonetheless excellent swimmers. When we understand how they manage this, we can better appreciate the advantages of bladders to the reef fishes. To swim and stay afloat at the same time, the sharks and rays must gain lift as well as propulsion from their bodies and fins, though some are assisted by buoyant livers. What they lack in natural buoyancy they make up for with aerodynamic principles.

The eagle rays (*Myliobatidae*) and mantas (*Mobulidae*) have developed pectoral fins that are so broad as literally to be wings. As the drawing on page 34 makes clear, these rays actually fly through the water, much as a hawk flies through the air. Once they attain sufficient momentum, they can glide in the water; when their momentum slackens, they will sink unless they start flapping again. Lindsey has suggested that all rays began as sedentary bottom dwellers, feeding on molluscs and crustaceans. In time, natural variation within the species enabled some to lift off the bottom and to discover that they could survive above it, feeding on plankton and other floating prey. The familiar stingray still lives on the bottom, capable of generating only enough lift to rise a few feet and coast from one spot to another when disturbed. The eagle rays and mantas have besides their pectorals only tiny pelvic fins, which may be used to kick back when the ray leaves the ocean floor and starts its flight. The long, whiplike tail plays no role in propulsion.

Sharks, on the other hand, propel themselves with a powerful side-to-side sweep of their bodies. But if that was all they did, they would sink, literally swimming themselves into the bottom, much as an airplane without wings would fly itself into the ground. To stay afloat, sharks gain lift from their well-developed pectoral fins, which, situated near the shark's center of gravity, slope down and backward like the small wings on a high-speed jet fighter. The lower flap of a shark's asymmetrical tail also produces some lift. If only the tail fin generated lift, the shark would be driven nose down into the bottom; counterbalanced with the lift provided by the pectorals, however, the tail fin supplies the balance the shark needs in the absence of a swim bladder.

Modern fishes—that is, those more recent in evolutionary development than the primitive sharks, rays, and certain bony fishes—are called teleosts; this group includes most coral reef fishes. Because they have swim bladders, they can develop through natural selection more complex and flexible fins. Some can afford to sacrifice power for control. Their fins are built around light, bony rays, each ray set into its own balled socket and controlled by its own set of muscles that can incline, elevate, or depress each section of the fin.

Because their tail, or caudal, fins need not supply lift, they can be symmetrical. Being symmetrical, they are more efficient at providing propulsion. (The lift the shark gets from its tail fin depends on its attacking the water unevenly, producing more pressure on the lower surfaces than on the upper ones.) Similarly, because the pectoral fins need not supply lift, they can become specialized for other purposes. They can be held close to the body to reduce drag and increase speed or they can be extended in order to increase drag and so serve as a brake. One pectoral fin can be extended and the other held close in order to make the fish pivot. For slow swimming—for example, grazing on a crop of algae—the tail fin, which consumes much energy, can be held motionless and power supplied by the pectorals, which, with a rowing motion, can propel the fish slowly with little energy use. The fins on the fish's back, the dorsal fins, can be folded down for streamlining or held erect for defense or display. Because all its fins are needed for lift and power, the shark must sacrifice some maneuverability. In the eyes of a diver, even a large shark can change direction with frightening rapidity, but in the eyes of a reef fish, it must seem a speedy but clumsy oaf.

TYPES OF SWIMMING

Fishes swim in different ways. Beginning with the work of C. M. Breder in the 1920s, careful efforts have been made to describe, classify, and measure these various means of locomotion. Although the nomenclature and the mathematics used to describe fish locomotion have become quite complex, the basic classificatory system is still largely as Breder first outlined it. Here, we shall discuss only the major types of swimming motion. It is important for the reader to remember that not only are we omitting some subtypes, we are also describing types that, although they are named after certain species of fishes, in fact are common to many other species as well.

The first and in many ways the simplest type of swimming is "eel-form" (technically, "anguilliform," after the common eel, *Anguilla*) (see drawing on page 40). As the name suggests, this swimming motion involves undulations of the whole length of the fish's body, the amplitude of the undulation increasing toward the tail. These undulating motions generate a backward thrust of the body against the water, thereby driving it forward. (Of course, many fishes other than eels undulate their bodies to some degree, but because of their fins and their differing body structures, the effect is not the same.) Eel-form swimming is effective but not particularly efficient because the undulations increase drag. It is employed, therefore, mostly by bottom dwellers that need not move quickly or efficiently. Not only eels but also blennies swim this way, as do flounders (which undulate vertically, top to bottom, rather than horizontally) and certain slow-moving sharks (such as the nurse and wobbegong sharks). Interestingly, many young fishes swim in this fashion before acquiring their adult form of motion. Eel-form swimming is the marine equivalent of the way snakes move on land; because the undulations of the eel press on water throughout its length and all around its body, the eel can move faster in the water than the snake can on land.

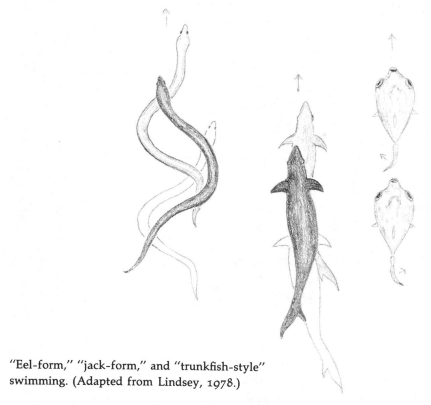

"Eel-form," "jack-form," and "trunkfish-style" swimming. (Adapted from Lindsey, 1978.)

The roaming reef predators display "jack-form" swimming (technically, "carangiform," after the Carangidae family, which includes jacks, scads, and pompanos). Although there is some variation in body shape among the fishes using jack-form swimming, in general they have certain features in common: a head like the nose of an aircraft, often sloping down on the top (like the nose of the supersonic Concorde), and a tapered posterior that ends in a forked tail (technically, a lunate caudal fin). That portion of the body (called the caudal peduncle) that connects with the forked tail is narrowed.

A jack, like other carangiform swimmers, is adapted for acceleration. It thrusts its rather stiff body from side to side, creating propulsion without much waving of the body, encountering less resistance than eel-form undulations produce. The forked pattern of the tail reduces drag; the narrowed portion of the body connected to the tail minimizes recoil and thus helps to keep the body still. Jack-form fishes are splendid, efficient swimmers, as they must be to catch their prey. Because of the great energy required by their powerful caudal thrusts, they have a higher proportion of blood-rich red meat and a more highly developed gill system than do slower swimmers.

The least efficient sustained swimmers are those that move trunkfish style (they are "ostraciform" swimmers, after the family Ostraciidae, which includes trunkfishes and cowfishes). Like the jacks, they use their tails for propulsion, but in so inept and clumsy a manner as to make it clear that speed is not their objective. Pufferfishes (Tetraodontidae) and porcupine fishes (Diodontidae) swim in a variation of the trunkfish style. Lacking speed, they must depend on body armor or the secretion of toxic substances for protection. And since they are armored, they cannot easily move their tails as do the jacks. Muscles on either side of their bodies alternately contract, producing a sculling effect. Always in motion, whether moving forward or hovering, they derive most of their propulsive power from their small pectoral, dorsal, and anal fins.

Triggerfishes, filefishes, butterflyfishes, and trumpetfishes all employ variations of a swimming style called "balistiform" (after the family Balistidae, which includes the triggerfishes and filefishes). They move by undulating their dorsal (that is, back) and anal fins. This undulation, like that of eels, produces a backward thrust against the water. Unlike the eels, however, only certain fins, and not the whole body, undulate. Such fishes can move faster than eels or trunkfish but not as fast as jacks. Their great advantage is the rather precise control of their movements that is achieved by undulating fins. In fact, by reversing the pattern of undulation, the fish can back up.

There are other swimming forms, some with characteristics that overlap those already discussed, and there are many fishes that combine these forms or use a different one under special circumstances. For example, regardless of how most fishes habitually get around, in an emergency they will use their tail fins.

For most fishes, like most guards in basketball, what counts is not how fast they can move at top speed but how quickly they can accelerate. But for fishes, unlike basketball players, the ability to keep energy in reserve for sudden, short bursts can make the difference between life and death. As N. B. Marshall remarks, "Quick acceleration rather than sustained swiftness is likely to be the vital aptitude of most fishes."

The most significant variation among the swimming equipment of reef fishes is found in the placement and use of the pectoral (that is, chest) fins. Set low and angled, as on sharks, they provide lift. Set high and forward, as on snappers and jacks, they can act as brakes. Set very low and rigid, as on lizardfishes, they serve as props but can, with a quick flex, jerk the fish up to catch an unsuspecting prey. And on most fishes, the pectorals control pitching (the up-and-down motion of the body) and yawing (the side-to-side motion).

Pelvic fins also serve various purposes. When the fish brakes, its pelvic fins can be angled to counteract the unbalancing effects of a sudden reduction in lift and increase in drag. When the pectorals are displayed in order to attract a mate, the pelvic (or the ventral) fins can take over the maneuvering function.

To swim, fins are not enough; they must be activated by muscles. Swimming muscles account for the bulk of a fish's body mass. Among fishes, bigger almost always means stronger (although, as we shall see in a Chapter 8, not necessarily braver). These muscles are arranged in sections called myomeres, which in turn are made up of intricate layers folded into W-shaped patterns. Marshall calls them conical Chinese puzzles. Each side of the fish's body has an identical set of myomeres, divided along the horizontal axis into an upper and a lower system. Alternating contractions of the myomeres on one side cause corresponding stretching of those on the other and result in waves of motion passing along the body.

Covering these muscles is skin tissue, which is laid out in a spiraling pattern around the fish's body, some in left-handed directions and some in right-handed ones, with the angles of the spirals determined by how deep-bodied the fish is. The result is a kind of latticelike arrangement that conforms to the principles of a geodesic curve, each spiral taking the shortest distance to wrap about the fish's body.

All fishes have skin, but not all have scales. The very fastest fishes, such as tunas, tend to have scales so smooth as to feel almost like skin. Manta rays, mackerels, many eels, and some gobies and blennies have no scales at all. Most reef fishes, however, have scales, which presumably protect their bodies from the abrasive surface of the coral heads among which they must move.

CHAPTER THREE

Eating

Divers can see many forms of fish behavior—schooling, swimming, even territoriality—but rarely do they see, or think they see, a fish eating. It is unusual ever to watch a fish swallow another fish, yet we know from examining the stomach contents of fishes that many species are piscivores. And although we know that many species eat things other than fishes, and thus we would not expect to see them engaged in hungry pursuit, we seldom observe them swallowing anything at all. We can easily watch birds eat, but not fishes. Like the dog that did not bark in the Sherlock Holmes story, the fact that fish do not appear to eat ought to be an important clue to the existence of unusual patterns of behavior.

Part of the reason we rarely see piscivorous (fish-eating) fishes eat is that most divers are not in the water when piscivores are feeding. By and large, fish eating occurs in the half-light hours of dawn and dusk; in technical language, it is "crepuscular." Most divers are underwater during the day, when predation is rare, or at night, when on the reef potential prey fishes are secure in their coral holes and many piscivores are hunting off the reef. And those carnivores that do eat at night, the nocturnal predators, are usually after smaller stuff, such as microscopic animals or small crabs. Many of these carnivores range well off the reef, hunting over sandy bottom areas. But another reason that eating is hard to observe is that much of it occurs faster than the eye can follow.

Most fishes are teleosts, bony fishes. The most notorious predators, sharks, are not teleosts (they will be discussed later). A teleost represents the highest stage of evolution among the fishes; it is, in a sense, the most modern of fishes. And of the teleosts, coral reef fishes display the greatest evolutionary development. Among the ways in which a teleost's bodily structure is especially advanced is its mouth. The bony fishes have developed an incredible variety of oral machinery, all specialized to solve various eating problems created by the defensive tactics or armor of their prey. One characteristic of many teleosts is a "protrusible" jaw—that is, one that can be extended (see drawing on page 45). This enables them to rely on suction as well as pursuit in order to feed. By extending their jaws, these fishes enlarge the size of their mouths. When they open their mouths, the water pressure inside is less than the pressure outside. This difference in pressure causes water, and whatever is carried in the water, to rush into their jaws. They literally vacuum up their meals. Their mouths then close and excess water exits through the gills. All this happens so quickly that even a person watching a fish at close range in an aquarium will not see the food move; one moment it is in front of the fish, the next instant it is inside.

The specialized eating machinery is not limited to protrusible jaws. In the throats of these fishes is a second set of jaws, called "pharyngeal" (pronounced "far-*in*-gee-al") jaws, which grind up whatever prey the fish has sucked in. This means that such fish can shop quickly and do the kitchen work later. Snails, for example, need not be laboriously extracted from their hard shells before they can be eaten. Algae need not be separated from the chunks of coral in which they are often embedded. The snails are picked up or algae-covered pieces of coral are bitten off; these are then passed on to the pharyngeal jaws, which crush the hard material and extract the digestible food. Many of these fishes have special glands that secrete a mucus to line their

Protrusible jaw of slingjaw wrasse *(Epibulus insidiator)*, with which it captures small shrimps and crabs in the interstices of branching corals.

esophagi to smooth the passage of rough matter. The results of all these devices can vividly be seen by divers who break up a sea urchin and offer it as food to nearby fishes. Once a Spanish hogfish, for example, senses that the vulnerable underbelly of the urchin is available for eating, it will snatch the entire urchin, spines and all, carry it away, and swallow it. Mucus glands protect the throat, and the pharyngeal jaws crush the urchin shell and spines (see Plate 21).

It should be stressed that although the feeding mechanisms of fishes exhibit an astonishing range of specialization, they are not necessarily limited to related specialized diets. Karel Liem's research has shown that some of the most remarkably adapted fishes are also sometimes jacks-of-all-trades in obtaining a meal.

GRAZERS

Most reef fishes seen by divers during the day are grazers. They include parrotfishes, angelfishes, damselfishes, wrasses, butterfly-fishes, surgeonfishes, trunkfishes (see Plate 22), and triggerfishes. They cruise about just above the surface of the coral or snoop around in its crevices, eating algae, molluscs, worms, and small crustaceans.

Butterflyfishes and angelfishes are members of the Chaetodontidae family, a Greek word meaning "bristle tooth." These grazers have fine, hairlike teeth that enable them to pick out for eating small organisms such as tubeworms, coral polyps, algae, tunicates, hydroids, and (especially) sponges. Perhaps the most striking example of a bristle-toothed fish is the longsnout butterflyfish.* Its delicately extended nose makes possible the extraction of small invertebrates from deep coral crevasses inaccessible to fishes with blunter snouts. It even feeds among the spines of sea urchins, nibbling at their tube feet and other appendages.

Wrasses also have small teeth, but sharper, more protruding ones than those of the longsnout butterfly. Most wrasses cruise along the bottom, grazing on small invertebrates, swallowing a variety of crabs, snails, worms, shrimps, and eggs. With their pharyngeal jaws, they can ingest all manner of gastropods without regard to the thickness of the protective shells, which are later crushed by the rear teeth. Some wrasses, however, have acquired a specialized function: they clean parasites and dead tissues from other fishes (see Chapter 9, on symbiosis). To do this, they use their tweezerlike teeth, which can make precise, surgical incisions enabling them to extract parasites embedded in their hosts' skin. Blennies also have specialized dental machinery, as is suggested by the common names of two kinds: the "combtoothed" and the "sabretoothed."

In sharp contrast to the delicate dentition of the wrasses are the powerful jaws of parrotfishes. Their large front teeth are fused together into a chisel-like structure that resembles a parrot's beak; hence their popular name. This beak can scrape off chunks of hard coral, from which their jaws must extract the algae. To do this, the parrotfishes slide the rocky mass down their throats to what John E. Randall, in his landmark study of the eating habits of West Indian fish, called a "pharyngeal mill." There the hard coral is crushed into a fine sediment that is excreted as sand. During its life a single parrotfish can produce hundreds of pounds of coral sand, some of which no doubt finds its way to the shore and becomes part of the dazzling white beach characteristic of a tropical island. When we sunbathe on that beach, we may be taking advantage, to some extent, of the dietary habits of the parrotfish. These habits seem absurdly inefficient; grinding up massive amounts of hard coral to get at a few bits of algae is a hard way to earn a living, but, as Randall notes, it has the advantage of being a reliable one. The chisel-like front teeth of the parrotfish

---

*In the Caribbean, these are *Chaetodon aculeatus* = *Prognathodes aculeatus;* in the Pacific, *Forciper flavissimus* and *F. longirostris.*

make it a superior competitor to the other fishes that depend on algae for their diets.

In adapting to life as grazers, fishes have developed distinctive body shapes as well as dentition. If they are to graze, they must be able to hover almost motionless above the bottom, to maneuver in and out of tight passages among the rocks, and to back up. All this is made easier if the grazer has a narrow, compressed body, such as that of an angelfish, and flexible pectoral and ventral fins that can function like oars on a small dinghy.

HUNTERS

Most fish hunters, the piscivores, have less specialized diets than the grazers, and therefore their mouths need not be so complex. Since they usually feed on fishes smaller than themselves, their jaws need only be moderately protrusible, just sufficient to enable them to open wide, ingest, and swallow, with a minimum of grinding or crushing.

There are two kinds of hunters: those that pursue their prey and those that take them by deception or concealment. The classic and most commonly encountered pursuers are the jacks (the numerous species of the Carangidae family), some snappers (Lutjanidae), and some sea basses (Serranidae). Lean and muscular, their torpedo-shaped bodies and forked tails are ideal for sustained patrolling and high-speed chases, and their large eyes give them superior vision. Most jacks, snappers, and basses are crepuscular, feeding at dawn and dusk, when their prey are just leaving or returning to the safety of their hideouts. These prey include nocturnal squirrelfishes and cardinalfishes that move out at dusk to feed on crustaceans and diurnal grazers that start at dawn to browse on the coral reefs. It is during these commuting hours that the jacks and snappers are most likely to strike. Apparently small fishes are most vulnerable when they have left the holes in which they sleep but have not yet arrived at familiar territories, perhaps with known sheltering holes, on which they graze, or vice versa. The potential prey know they are vulnerable during commuting hours and often display at these times an anxious, excitable manner. Some hunters are diurnal and will hang about the reef during daylight hours, looking for targets, and a few will regularly prey during the day on the smaller fishes that forage in the open waters for plankton.

One of the commonest jacks of the Indo-Pacific, *Caranx melampygus*, has been studied at length on the atoll reefs of the Aldabra Islands in the Indian Ocean by Geoffrey W. Potts, a British marine biologist. Potts found that jacks tend to hunt in groups when they are on the outer edge of the reef, where drop-offs occur, and alone when working the shallower inshore areas. Their hunting behavior has four phases: *patrolling,* when the jack swims steadily through an area but makes no predatory moves; *quartering,* when it makes a series of zigzag moves at higher speeds; *hunting,* when it has identified a victim and swims faster; and *attacking,* when the jack, now within striking distance, moves in for what it hopes will be the kill. Having a protrusible jaw, the jack's kill may occur faster than the diver's eye can detect it, as the prey is sucked into its mouth. Somehow, fishes that are the jack's prey recognize and adapt to these four stages. Potts found that the prey ignored the jack when it was patrolling but immediately sought shelter when quartering began. Once the kill occurred, the other prey promptly returned to the open reef and resumed their foraging. This helps to explain why divers so often see prey and predator swimming near one another in apparent peace. It is a wary peace, governed by the prey's ability to distinguish patrolling from quartering.

Barracudas are unusual hunters in that they lack a protrusible upper jaw with which to suck up their prey. Instead they have, in evolutionary terms, an older, less advanced jaw that is solidly fused together in order to support an impressive array of large, sharp teeth. What effect the sight of these admirably designed hunting machines may have on other fishes is unknown, but to the novice diver they are unsettling (see Plate 14). Needlessly so, we might add. Barracudas, if in the vicinity when a diver enters the water, will remain as if curious, but habitually maintain a standard distance, perhaps twenty or thirty feet, retreating if the diver approaches and following if the diver moves away. Unless a diver is foolish enough to carry a speared fish close to his body, he need not be apprehensive about swimming among barracudas.

But if the barracuda's fearsome teeth are no threat to the diver, they are to other fishes. Unlike most fishes, the barracudas use their biting ability to capture prey. They cannot expand their jaws to accommodate large fishes, and so they will often bite their prey into two or more pieces, circling back to pick up the chunks. Sharks are the other important hunters that often cut up their meal before swallowing, a matter we shall discuss in Chapter 10.

The sedentary hunters, unlike the pursuers, tend to be fat or awkward and to rely on either concealment or lures to catch their prey. Groupers are piscivores that can grow to great size, but not as a result of their ability to hunt down prey. Their shape does not allow for great speed. Instead, they take cover in holes or behind sea fans, depending on surprise to capture their food, especially during the crepuscular hours. When they retreat from a diver—and unless they have been tamed by repeated hand feedings, they always will retreat —they almost seem to waddle away, displaying thereby an obvious lack of underwater agility. Fishes make up the bulk of the groupers' diet, but eels, crabs, and octopuses have been found in their stomachs. The octopuses are probably taken at night.

The moray eel is also a sedentary hunter. Although they are long and sleek, morays have only a dorsal (that is, back) fin and must move through the water snakelike, in long, slow undulations. They hide in coral or rocky holes, waiting for their unsuspecting prey to come close enough for a strike. Most morays feed on crustaceans, but the West Indian spotted moray *(Gymnothorax moringa)* is a dedicated piscivore. Like barracudas, morays may make the novice diver apprehensive, but this is the result of appearance rather than behavior. Morays shrink from contact with humans and, though they can be lured from their holes with offers of food (Vienna sausage is an irresistible offering), they will only bite a diver who does something ridiculous, such as sticking his hand into the moray's hole.

Although most piscivores are crepuscular, an interesting exception is the solitary trumpetfish.* This elongated fish with its lengthy, underslung jaw hunts by day and retires at night. It eats a great variety of other fishes, including wrasses, gobies, grunts, damselfishes, cardinalfishes, blennies, goatfishes, and squirrelfishes, and also shrimps. To catch them during the day, the trumpetfish relies on camouflage. Special color cells, called chromatophores, enable it to change color at will, from brown or red to blue or bright yellow, in varying patterns of solid colors and stripes. This camouflage is designed to make it blend in, not only with a background of gorgonian coral, but with other fishes as well (see Plate 18). Most divers are familiar with trumpetfishes that hang vertically among the treelike branches of gorgonians, waiting for prey and avoiding predators. Less well known is the ability of the trumpetfish to adopt the color of a nonpredatory blue or yellow tang or a parrotfish and swim close beside it in order to approach the prey undetected. The trumpetfish will even use this technique to sneak into a cleaning station where predation has been suspended in the interest of getting rid of parasites (see Chapter 9).

*Aulostomus maculatus in the Caribbean and *A. chinensis* in the Indo-Pacific.

Voracious and sneaky as it is, the trumpetfish lacks the teeth that would enable it to tear its prey into pieces. Instead, it has an expandable jaw that enables it to suck in other fishes, even fishes larger than its normal jaw opening. The trumpetfish is like a python or boa constrictor in being able to swallow outsize prey. A diver who comes upon a trumpetfish that has eaten a large victim may sometimes observe its distended stomach. Although during the day they are solitary hunters, we have seen scores, adults as well as juveniles, sleeping together vertically, hanging snout down and side by side amidst eelgrass in shallow waters. At first glance, they look like a small stand of seaweed. This nocturnal grouping, a stationary kind of schooling (see Chapter 7), is probably a protective device, since other piscivores prey on trumpetfishes. Randall has found their long bodies, folded in two, in the stomachs of groupers and snappers.

Other predators also use the stalking techniques of the trumpetfishes. The cornetfishes (family Fistulariidae) have been observed by Edmund S. Hobson to use other fishes as shields for approaching prey, sometimes, unlike trumpetfishes, hunting in groups. Jacks have been discovered arriving on a reef from deeper waters and then swimming alongside larger, grazing fish such as parrotfishes and triggerfishes before making their final attack runs. For lack of an accepted term for this behavior, we call it "shadow stalking," as it is similar to the techniques used by a detective following a criminal by trying to blend into a crowd. This blending is easier for some fishes than for others. R. F. G. Ormond reports that in the Red Sea, a yellow surgeonfish *(Zebrasoma veliferum)* is often joined by a slingjawed wrasse *(Epibulus insidiator)*, which can mimic the surgeonfish's color. Since the latter tends to graze in groups, the wrasse can readily conceal itself in the crowd. Small basses, hamlets, and even an occasional grouper *(Cephalopholis argus)* will do the same.

Some fishes use deception not in order to stalk their prey but to conceal themselves from prey that unwittingly come to them. This camouflage strategy has led to a great variety of body adaptations among predators. Flounders, flatfishes with eyes mounted on top to watch for prey, lie motionless on the sandy bottom and employ chromatophores to change their appearance (see Plate 19). Lizardfishes also lie quietly on the bottom and rely on camouflage for concealment, but unlike flounders, the torpedo-shaped bodies of the lizardfishes make them capable of a sudden, brief upward rush to capture their victims. Most species of scorpionfishes (Scorpaenidae) use both coloration and a lumpy, indistinct shape to blend into the rocky bottom where they lie in wait for prey (see Plate 16). Because they have venomous dorsal spines, these sluggish creatures—they can scarcely be provoked into swimming any distance—are a menace to divers, who may inadvertently touch their nearly invisible bodies.

The most elaborate form of deception for eating purposes involves the use of lures. Frogfishes have developed from their first dorsal (back) spine an appendage resembling a fishing pole with what appears to be a piece of bait at the end. In describing the frogfish, James E. Böhlke and Charles C. G. Chaplin were moved to depart from their customary scholarly language: "Frogfishes," they wrote, "are short, fat, lumpy, grotesque." Three-fourths of the frogfish's diet is made up of other fishes; obviously, the lure must work. Randall found a Caesar grunt that was 102 millimeters long in the stomach of a frogfish that was only 97 millimeters long.

Every fish has some sort of defense mechanism to protect it against predators, but hardly any defense is impregnable. There always seems to be at least one predator that has found a way to digest even the most formidable array of spines and venom. Randall found a mushroom scorpionfish *(Scorpaena inermis)* in the stomach of a splitlure frogfish *(Antennarius scaber)* despite the venomous spines that are supposed to protect the former; moreover, this frogfish was only 3 millimeters longer than the scorpionfish it had eaten. Many divers have seen and even handled the slow-moving porcupinefish *(Diodon hystrix),* which will inflate its sharp-spined body into what appears to be an inedible sphere (see Plate 20). Despite this, the porcupinefish has been found in the stomachs of jacks, barracudas, and tiger sharks.

Lionfishes (or turkeyfishes), a branch of the Scorpaenidae family, are marked with bold colors and stripes and long, featherlike plumes that are flamboyantly eye-catching to divers (see Plate 24). One theory is that their fluttering display, although useless for swimming, attracts the attention of the foraging crabs and shrimps that become their dinners. However, many of these crepuscular hunters eat small fishes as well as crustaceans, and the reduced light conditions make them very hard to spot when they are sedentary. When they do move slowly toward prey, their trailing spines and broadly spread pectoral fins effectively shield the motion of their propelling caudal fins. Fishelson has remarked on how lionfishes hide behind dense feather stars and long-spined sea urchins before, with sudden strong gulps, they suck in unsuspecting prey.

Not all hunters look like hunters. Many dwell on the sandy bottom, foraging for small animals. The goatfish has mechanisms specially adapted for this task. Hanging from its mouth are barbels, whiskerlike appendages that sense the presence of prey hidden in the sand. Its teeth are fossorial—that is, adapted to digging. Sensing buried prey, the day-feeding goatfish excavates the sand and eats. Knowing its skills at rooting out meals, small wrasses will often hover about a goatfish, waiting to swallow any escaping morsels. Ormond described the hunting partnership, common in the Red Sea, between the elephant (or bird) wrasse *(Gomphosus varius)* and a yellow goatfish *(Parupeneus chryseredros)*. This wrasse has a long, elephantine snout adapted for exploring crannies and probing into sand and gravel. It combines its skills with the sensory talents of the goatfish. The two fishes work in tandem, sometimes led by the wrasse, sometimes by the goatfish. Food excavated by one will often be eaten by the other. The teamwork seems to benefit both.

Although the best-known predators, such as jacks, groupers, and morays, are crepuscular feeders and some, such as barracudas, trumpetfishes, and goatfishes, are diurnal, there are many nocturnal hunters. For the most part, they feed on invertebrates. Squirrelfishes sleep during the day in holes and caves, emerging at night to feed on shrimps and crabs. Grunts lounge, usually in small groups, during the day; at night, they move out in schools to prey on gastropods, crabs, shrimps, and worms. The ubiquitous yellowtail snapper feeds around the clock, working mostly at night but ready to seize any opportunities that present themselves during the day (see Plate 15). It will eat almost anything: other fishes, crustaceans, eggs and larvae, and even some waste matter. While we were hand-feeding some snappers, one fish, caught up in the frenzy, bit the cheek of one of our fellow divers.

There is one night hunter that could hardly be called diminutive. This is the legendary—and seldom seen—jewfish, *Epinephelus itajara,* the largest tropical reef fish in the western hemisphere. Because it can attain a weight of 700 pounds or more, no guidebook is necessary to identify it. By day, this giant lurks in caves, under ledges, or in large coral crevices. Little is known of its behavior, but it can safely be assumed that it is not distinguished for its swimming ability. Randall investigated the stomach contents of nine jewfishes and found mostly spiny lobsters, with an occasional sea turtle, crab, stingray (!), or porcupinefish. Alex Kerstitch of the University of Arizona reported being threatened by a jewfish in the Sea of Cortez: the predator, encountered in a cave, quivered its body and approached with open jaws. At another time he fended off a jewfish with a blow to the snout. Legend has it that it was a jewfish, not a whale, that swallowed Jonah. Kerstitch will not dispute the possibility.

PLANKTONIC OPPORTUNISTS

A coral community, as we saw in Chapter 1, is sustained by an elaborate food chain that begins with microscopic creatures, the plankton, that drift in the current. Night and day, various reef fishes take turns foraging on these tiny plant and animal organisms. This is best done at the edge of the reef, where currents concentrate the nutrients and where the feeding fishes can quickly retreat to the reef to find shelter from open-water predators. Where plankton are concentrated, plankton feeders often school, possibly because the food is concentrated and possibly to protect themselves from open-water predators (see Chapter 2). Herrings (Clupeidae), silversides (Atherinidae), and halfbeaks (Hemiramphidae), seen near reefs but not reef-based, school while eating. While young, halfbeaks feed on plankton, but on reaching maturity they prey on other schooling fishes, including herring and silversides.

Some plankton eaters feed by straining the water. These fishes have fine gill rakers that sieve the plankton from the water as it passes through their mouths. Because planktonic feeders eat such tiny creatures, most of them do not grow to a large size. A dramatic exception is the giant manta ray (Plate 13). To provide nourishment sufficient to achieve and sustain its great size—from edge to edge, it may cover six to eight feet—it must take in prodigious amounts of food. This it accomplishes with fins situated near its head (cephalic fins) that sweep plankton-rich water toward its mouth. Its awesome size belies its benign behavior.

The typical planktonic feeder, however, is a small wrasse, damselfish, grunt, bass, squirrelfish, or cardinalfish that eats plankton instead of grazing on the reefs or hunting smaller fishes, as do their larger cousins. W. P. Davis and R. S. Birdsong have studied these planktonic feeders at length and have pointed out how convergent evolution has adapted them for this way of making a living. Their body shapes are streamlined and they have forked tails and large eyes; in this way they resemble the fish-eating jacks. But the swimming skills that this shape affords them are used not for pursuit but to cope with the strong currents in which plankton are swept along and to make a quick escape if a piscivore should interrupt their feeding. They tend to have upturned mouths with highly protrusible jaws, tiny teeth, and little in the way of pharyngeal machinery, all well adapted to suction feeding techniques. Some planktonic feeders school in mixed-species groups. One combination familiar to Caribbean divers is that of the blue chromis *(Chromis cyanea)* and brown chromis *(Chromis multilineata),* both of the damselfish family, and the creole wrasse *(Clepticus parrai).* Many of these fishes are bluish in color and thus blend in protectively with the open blue water in which they feed at the reef's edge.

The striped grunt *(Haemulon striatum)* is a planktonic feeder that does not blend in with the open ocean; rather, its color pattern fits in with that of the coral and rocks of the reef where it sleeps by day in small schools. By night, it feeds on plankton. Cardinalfishes (of the family Apogonidae) also feed on plankton at night; they, like the squirrelfishes (Holocentridae), some of which feed nocturnally, are reddish in color. At night, this makes them appear gray and hence hard to see, and so they have less need to school for protection while feeding.

IN SUMMARY: THE FOOD CHAIN

The food chain in the sea begins, as it does on earth, with plant material. Life ultimately depends on the ability of vegetation to synthesize organic compounds. Animal life, including fish life, starts with those species that feed on vegetable matter and proceeds to those species that eat other animals. Biologists call the position a species occupies in this food chain, determined by what the species eats and what in turn preys on it, its "trophic level."

In the sea, the primary trophic level is found near the surface, where sunlight can penetrate the water. Here all manner of tiny plants, the phytoplankton, produce the basic nutrients that enrich the oceans. Small animal organisms, the zooplankton, feed on these plants, as do the larvae of many fishes and invertebrates that begin their lives adrift in the currents. Small fishes, and an occasional large one, feed on the zooplankton. At night, the nocturnal planktonic feeders migrate upward to the shallower depths. After dark, a diver may encounter some plankton feeding on other plankton; together they may number in the millions.

Another trophic level includes the herbivores and omnivores. By day, they are the most visible fishes on the reef as they cruise about, grazing on algae. Yet another trophic level includes the carnivores, both nocturnal and diurnal. Many have specialized jaws adapted for consuming small invertebrate prey: shrimps, crabs, molluscs, and the like. Many of these carnivores fall prey, during their dawn or dusk commuting hours, to the large, crepuscular piscivores.

Fishes that hunt crepuscularly typically engage in straightforward patrol-and-strike techniques, concentrating on those areas where grazers habitually return to their nighttime shelters or where nocturnal carnivores are moving out to look for crustaceans. These crepuscular hunters are the most primitive of the modern fishes, requiring the greatest amounts of food energy and as a consequence constituting the smallest part of the reef population.

Fishes that hunt by day, on the other hand, must rely on deception in addition to patrol-and-strike tactics. Even the strong-swimming, open-water jacks and snappers that usually feed crepuscularly will, when hunting by day, engage in shadow stalking by staying close to large fishes with benign reputations.

Robert W. Hiatt and Donald W. Strasburg, who conducted a systematic survey of the food habits of the fishes of the Marshall Islands, concluded that the more advanced and specialized fishes are usually found in the lower trophic levels, where the food supply is the greatest. These fishes have learned to capitalize on every dietary possibility. Anything and everything—coral mucus, sea urchins, feather-duster tubeworms, filamentous algae, sponges with needlelike spicules, even detritus—has a fish that uses it for food.

There is still much to be learned about the ways reef fishes make a living. The examples in this chapter can only begin to suggest the extraordinary variety and specialization to be found in the ocean. The evolutionary process that has produced this variety continues and varies from place to place. For example, jacks may hunt in small packs in some areas but engage in solitary chases elsewhere. Randall, whose study of West Indian fishes is a standard reference on the food habits of the fishes in that area, found no evidence that a parrotfish eats live coral; it only consumes dead coral on which algae grow. But Hiatt and Strasburg found parrotfishes eating live coral in the waters around the Marshall Islands, as do parrotfishes in the eastern Pacific that eat in particular the *Porites* species. Randall suggests that this difference is perhaps due to the denser coral cover of Pacific reefs, which reduces the availability of algae and causes the parrotfishes to rely on live coral polyps for food. Moreover, with the exception of extremely specialized fishes (such as the manta ray, with its reliance on plankton sieved from the water), a great many fishes—like all hungry creatures —will eat what they can if what they want to eat is unavailable. A grouper, ordinarily a piscivore that waits behind a piece of coral for a chance to seize unwary prey, may, on poor hunting days, settle for shrimps or hermit crabs. Herbivores, such as surgeonfishes, will prey on animal life if starved. Giving an exact catalogue of the dietary habits of fishes is about as unrealistic as giving one for wild dogs.

OMNIVORES

Blennies (many)   (Blenniidae)

Damselfishes   (Pomacentridae)

    Beaugregory—*Stegastes
leucostictus* (Atlantic)

    Dusky—*P. fuscus* (Atlantic)

    Sergeant major—*Abudefduf
saxitalis* (circumtropical)

Gobies (some)   (Gobiidae)

Orangespotted filefish (Atlantic)   (Aluteridae)

Sharpnose puffers   (Tetradon tidae)

Spadefish (Atlantic)   (Ephippidae)

Yellowtail snapper—*Ocyurus
chrysurus* (Atlantic)   (Lutjanidae)

PRIMARILY HERBIVOROUS FISHES

Angelfishes   (Pomacanthidae)

    Lemonpeel
Centropyge flavissimus
(Pacific)

    Potter's, *C. potteri*
(Hawaii)

Blennies*   (Blennidae)

Damselfishes (many)   (Pomacentridae)

Filefishes (some)   (Aluteridae)

Gobies*   (Gobiidae)

Mullets*   (Mullets)

Parrotfishes†   (Scaridae)

Sea chubs   (Kyphosidae)

Surgeonfishes   (Acanthuridae)

Triggerfishes (some)   (Balistidae)

    *These fishes also scavenge detritus.
    †Also eat corals.

CARNIVORES

Primarily Piscivorous Fishes

Barracudas	(Sphyraenidae)
Black Hamlet	(*Hyploplectrus nigricans,* Serranidae)
Coneys	(Serranidae)
Cornetfishes	(Fistulariidae)
Spotted moray	(*Gymnothorax moringa,* Muraenidae)
Frogfishes*	(Antennariidae)
Graysbys (Atlantic)	(Serranidae)
Groupers*	(Serranidae)
Jacks	(Carangidae)
Lizardfishes	(Synodontidae)
Mackerels	(Scombridae)
Scorpionfishes*	(Scorpaenidae)
Snappers (some)*	(Lutjanidae)
Soapfishes	(Grammistidae)
Tobaccofishes	(Serranidae)
Trumpetfishes	(Aulostomidae)
Tunas	(Scombridae)

*Many of these fishes eat crustaceans as well as fishes.

Primarily Invertebrate Eaters

Angelfishes*	(Pomacanthidae)
Bigeyes	(Priacanthidae)
Butterflyfishes*	(Chaetodontidae)
Blennies	(Blenniidae)
Cardinalfishes (some)	(Apogonidae)
Cowfishes and trunkfishes	(Ostraciontidae)
Drums	(Sciaenidae)
Eagle rays	(Myliobatidae)
Filefishes (some)*	(Aluteridae)

Flounders	(Platycephalidae)
Goatfishes	(Mullidae)
Grunts (Atlantic)	(Pomadaysidae)
Hamlets (Atlantic—most)	(Serranidae)
Hawkfish (Atlantic *Amblycirrhitus pinos*)	(Cirrhitidae)
Jewfish (lobsters, crabs, fishes)	(Serranidae)
Moorish Idols (Indo-Pacific)*	(Zanclidae)
Morays (many)	(Muraenidae)
Porcupinefishes	(Diodontidae)
Sand tilefishes	(Branchiostegidae)
Snappers (some)	(Lutjanidae)
Squirrelfishes (most)	(Holocentridae)
Stingrays	(Dasyatidae and Urolophidae)
Triggerfishes	(Balistidae)
Wrasses	(Labridae)

*Including coral polyps.

Plankton-eating Fishes
Found in all Tropical Oceans

Cardinalfishes	(Apogonidae)
Garden eels	(Congridae)
Jawfishes	(Opistognathidae)
Manta rays	(Mobulidae)
Silversides	(Atherinidae)
Sweepers	(Pempheridae)

Primarily Plankton-eating Fishes

Found in the Atlantic

Blackbar soldierfish (squirrel), *Myripristis jacobus*	(Holocentridae)
Damselfishes	(Pomacentridae)
Bicolored damselfish— *Stegastes partitus*	
Blue chromis—*Chromis cyanea*	
Brown chromis— *C.multilineata*	

Creole wrasse—*Clepticus parrai*   (Labridae)
Jawfishes   (Opistognathidae)

Primarily Plankton-eating Fishes

Found in the Indo-Pacific

Butterflyfishes
  Blackface—*Hemitaurichthys*   (Chaetodontidae)
  zoster
  Millet seed—*Chaetodon*
  miliaris
Damselfishes   (Pomacentridae)
  Abudefduf abdominalis
  (Hawaii)
  Blue puller—*Chromis*
  caeruleus
  Scissortail—*C. Atrilobata*
  (Cortez)
  C. Atripectoralis
  C. leucurus (Hawaii and
  Marianas)
  C. vanderbilti (Hawaii)
  C. verater (Hawaii)
  Peacock—*Pomacentrus pavo*
  White-tailed humbug—
  Dascyllus aruanus
Halfbeaks—*Hemiramphidae*   (Exocoetidae)
affinis and *H. laticeps*
Lyre-tail coral fish—*Anthias*   (Anthiidae)
squamipinnis
Surgeonfishes—*Acanthurus*   (Acanthuridae)
thompsoni and *Naso*
hexacanthus
Squirrelfishes (some)   (Holocentridae)
Triggerfishes—Brown-lined   (Balistidae)
triggerfish, *Xanthichthys*
ringens, and *X. niger*
Wrasses—*Thalassoma hardwicki*   (Labridae)
and *T. marnae*

CHAPTER FOUR

Senses

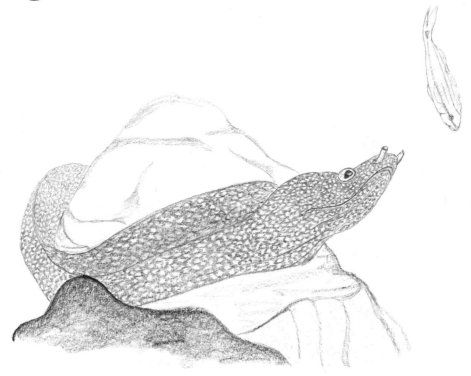

To man, the ocean is the enemy of the senses. Submerged in it, his vision is restricted, his hearing impaired, his sense of smell nonexistent. Without a face mask, he can barely see at all and even with a mask, he often can see only a few yards horizontally and even less when looking down. Exhaust air coming from his diving equipment creates so loud a rattle as to make him wonder why Cousteau ever named his famous underwater film *The Silent World*. But even when the diver holds his breath, he hears little; if a friend nearby shouts at him, the words become little more than an indistinct burble. Indeed, some people otherwise interested in the marine environment never become divers, not because they worry about drowning, but because they think they are claustrophobic, by which they mean that they fear the feeling of confinement and loss of sensory command that they suppose the ocean will inflict on them.

But to fishes, the ocean extends the reach of the senses. They not only produce and respond to an amazing variety of noises, they also can sense the motions made by other fishes and, in some cases, the minute electric charges generated by the beating hearts of their prey. They can detect in the water tiny amounts of various chemicals that tell them not only whether other fishes are nearby, but their sex, mood, and disposition. The social life of some fish species, though by no means as elaborate as that of some terrestrial animals, is made possible in part because these fishes can communicate underwater.

Water has three properties that affect its value as a medium of communication. It is much denser—some 800 times denser—than air, and this means, among other things, that sound will travel much faster through water than through air. It absorbs light, especially light at the red end of the spectrum, and so fishes must be able to adapt to levels of light that are low and of a bluish cast; a few species even generate their own light, though more to be seen than to see. Water also dissolves many substances, and thus chemicals that cannot be sensed at a distance by creatures separated by air can be sensed, sometimes at a great distance, by creatures sharing the same watery environment.

To take advantage of the special properties of water, fishes have developed a far more elaborate array of sensory mechanisms than have terrestrial animals. When man thinks of his senses, he thinks primarily of his eyes, ears, nose, and tongue. He notes that almost all other land animals also have eyes, ears, noses, and tongues and he assumes, rightly, that these animal organs function in much the same way as his own. Little in his everyday experience prepares him for the fact that a fish's sensory mechanisms may not be found in the conventional locations. A fish hears, but sometimes as much with the side of its body as with its ear. A fish can taste, but its taste buds are sometimes in its gills, on its snout, or even arrayed on its skin or along its fins. A much greater diversity of sensory apparatus exists among fishes than among land creatures.

SOUND AND HEARING

Even in the nineteenth century, naturalists knew that marine animals made noises; Charles Darwin wrote about it in the *Voyage of the Beagle*. But it was not until sailors began using sophisticated electronic equipment to listen for enemy submarines during World War II that man became vividly aware of how noisy the ocean is. Since then, researchers have recorded an amazing variety of snaps, grunts, clicks, squeals, whistles, bumps, buzzes, howls, chirps, and rat-a-tat-tats produced by fishes and other marine sources.

Because water is denser than air, more energy is needed to produce a sound of a given volume below the surface than above it, but once produced, the sound waves will travel farther and faster. While diving in Mindoro Strait in the Philippines, where (alas!) some natives catch fish by dropping dynamite into the water, we heard blasts so loud that we thought for a moment the explosions were nearby; in fact, they were miles away. The sound was reaching us at a speed of about 5,000 feet a second, nearly five times faster than it would have in air. The sound waves conserve their energy in water and so make the source of the noise seem very close.

Most of the sounds produced by fishes are at relatively low frequencies, usually well below a thousand cycles per second, and are produced by one or more of three mechanisms: the act of swimming, creating pressure waves; rubbing two bony structures together, making scraping sounds ("stridulation"); and noises made by rapidly contracting the gas-filled bladder used to keep fishes afloat (see Chapter 2).

Just by swimming, fishes set up low-frequency vibrations in the water that are often sufficiently distinct to permit the species to be identified. James Moulton has likened the swimming sounds of the Pacific wrasse *(Choerodon venustus)* to the "thumps of a frenzied squirrel in a boy's wooden box trap." The small, bluespotted boxfish *(Ostracion tuberculatum)* sounds like a tiny one-cylinder putt-putt motor.

Some fishes are noisy eaters. Even divers can hear a parrotfish scrape away with its big teeth at a coral surface. Triggerfishes have powerful teeth that noisily drill through mollusc shells. Other fishes produce sounds when they crush shellfish in their jaws.

But noises that are the by-product of other activities are less interesting than the sounds deliberately made by fishes. One way fishes make sounds involves stridulation, or grinding one hard object against another, much as crickets make sounds on a warm summer's evening by rubbing their legs together. Some fishes grind their teeth together or against special bony surfaces, others rub the spines in their fins together. Pufferfishes (tetradontids), filefishes (monocanthids), and porcupinefishes (diodontids) are among the stridulating reef fishes. Fishes may also make sounds by using the beat of their fins or muscular contractions to cause their gas bladders to emit drumlike sounds.

For example, several kinds of triggerfishes (balistids) beat with their pectoral fins on the skin just behind their gill openings; the sound is amplified by the resonant gas bladder found just under the skin. Other species, such as some squirrelfishes, angelfishes, and groupers, make the bladder resound by contracting certain muscles.

If fishes create sounds deliberately, it implies that the sounds have some behavioral significance. It was not until the twentieth century, however, that scientists established that fishes can hear. And when they did establish it, they learned that fishes "hear" not only with their ears but also with their lateral lines: areas along the sides of their bodies containing pressure-sensitive cells that detect motion in the water and send signals to the central nervous system.

A fish's ear works much like a human's: pressure received by hair-like receptor cells called neuromasts is converted into a signal sent to the brain. The lateral line works in a similar way. A canal running along both sides of the fish contains cup-shaped structures called cupulae, each of which is equipped with a set of neuromasts similar to those in the fish's ear. Water flowing over the surface of these neuromasts stimulates the hairs to generate signals. Although scientists are not certain, it seems likely that the lateral line detects the very smallest and weakest pressure waves, and thus is primarily of value at close ranges, whereas the inner ear responds to stronger sounds and so serves as a longer-range detector.

With its lateral lines, a fish can detect not only a disturbance in the water around it but also the angle from which the disturbance arises. This lateral line sensitivity enables a schooling fish to keep other fish in the school at a constant angle and distance even when the fish has been blinded (see Chapter 7). On most species, the lateral line can be seen as an interruption in the pattern of scales along the fishes' sides, but in some species the line is not lateral at all. In the bottom-dwelling flounders, for example, the line has moved, along with an eye and the pectoral fin, to the top of their backs. Sedentary fishes have abbreviated lines, and in some species, particularly deep-dwelling ones, there are no lateral line canals at all. Rather, motion-detecting neuromasts are situated on special protuberances that wave about. The most actively swimming fishes have the most sophisticated lateral systems.

Not only can fishes hear softer noises underwater than divers, they also are able, unlike divers, to determine the direction from which a sound comes (unless it is very close). Recent research suggests that the orientation of the hair cells in a fish's ear enables it to localize sounds.

What use do fishes make of these ways of detecting sound—that is, of pressure waves—in the water? We know the answer in only a few cases. The distinctive sound signature left by a fish as it swims or eats can attract predators. Moulton made a tape recording of the sound of horseeye jacks *(Caranx latus)* feeding. When he played it back underwater, a barracuda immediately appeared and watched the loudspeaker for three minutes. When A. A. Myrberg, Jr., played back recorded swimming sounds of blue runners *(Caranx crysos),* their prey, the Caribbean slippery dick *(Halichoeres bivittatus),* immediately buried themselves in the sand and became motionless. Similarly, recorded sounds of schooling anchovies stimulated predatory yellow jacks into great excitement.

Sounds also influence courtship behavior. In the Bahamas Myrberg and Juanita Y. Spires tested the response of the bicolor damselfish *(Stegastes partitus = Eupomacentrus partitus)* to sounds and found that the male bicolor damselfish could distinguish between the courting chirps of other bicolor damselfish and the similar chirps of threespot and cocoa damselfishes, in whom the male bicolors had no interest. Playing back recordings of the chirps of their own species produced ritual courtship swimming patterns among the bicolor damselfish.

An even more dramatic confirmation of the reproductive significance of certain fish sounds was supplied by a classic experiment by William N. Tavolga. Male frillfin gobies *(Bathygobius soporator)* can be found in abundance dwelling on shallow, sandy bottoms off Florida and in the Caribbean. Like most gobies, they have no gas bladders but are nevertheless able to make grunting noises by taking in a mouthful of water, snapping their mouths shut, and forcibly ejecting a short, sharp stream of water through their gill openings. When a male frillfin courts a female, he makes his grunting sound while approaching her, all the while fanning the water with his body and tail and intermittently visiting his shelter and cleaning it out. Playing a recording of these noises to female frillfins elicited from them their usual reaction to courtship: a good deal of competitive nipping and butting of one another. However, when an active male, enclosed in a glass flask, was lowered into a laboratory tank of females, they took little notice of him. Merely the sight of a male was not enough to stimulate a courtship reaction. But when the recording was turned on, the combination of sight and sound had an immediate effect: the females scrambled all over the flask (gobies are terrible swimmers) and checked out the loudspeaker as well, nipping and shoving one another in a high state of excitement that lasted for half an hour.

Male frillfins also respond to the sounds of other males. Both in the laboratory and in the open ocean, a recording of these noises would lead them to increase their respiratory rates, inspect the loudspeaker, and clean out their nests.

Many fishes use sound to help defend their territories. The long-spine squirrelfish *(Adioryx rufus = Holocentrus rufus)* is a nocturnal feeder that rests by day in reef crevices. These longspines defend against intruders by a variety of tactics, including displaying erect fins, dashing at the trespasser, shaking their heads, and nipping at the adversary. During all this, they may make one of two distinct noises, each, apparently, for a different purpose. One is a single grunt, which is usually emitted in aggressive encounters when a longspine is chasing away an interloper. The other is a staccato call, a rapid series of rhythmical grunts, which the longspine squirrelfish utters when it is suddenly confronted with a strange fish, especially one that looks too big to chase away. In cavalry terms, the first noise is the longspine equivalent of "charge!" and the latter more like "watch out!" or even "retreat!" The charge call will be directed at other squirrelfishes or at bluestriped and French grunts that pose little serious threat; "watch out" or "retreat" will be directed at big, strange fishes and, apparently, at divers. A similar pair of calls is also characteristic of the longjaw squirrelfish *(Adioryx ascensionis = Holocentrus ascensionis),* and probably of other species of squirrelfishes as well.

The pattern and informational content of these two kinds of squirrelfish noises underscore a general fact about auditory communication among fishes. The sounds are essentially percussive, and thus the information they convey tends to be represented by the frequency, the repetition, and the duration of the noises. But sometimes sheer volume becomes significant, just as one might expect, given our knowledge of when humans yell and animals roar. An anemonefish *(Amphiprion xanthurus),* when it is upset and wishes to threaten a rival, makes a noise that can be heard ten yards away from the aquarium. When a sea robin *(Prionotus carolinus)* was gently stroked by experimenters, it would cluck softly, but if the petting lasted too long or was applied too heavily, the fish would emit a louder burst and break away.

Sounds may enable fishes to communicate in many other ways—while schooling, for example, or seeking food—but the research necessary to show these and other possible connections between sound and behavior has yet to be done. Because birds have been watched in the wild for so long, we know that bird calls can communicate stress, warnings, scoldings, mating desires, and many other dispositions. Fish noises, when they have been observed carefully and long enough, may turn out to convey many of the same bits of information. One striking parallel between bird talk and fish noises is already known: both tend to peak at dawn and dusk.

ELECTRORECEPTION

The lateral lines of sharks, rays, marine catfishes, and certain fresh-water fishes detect electric charges rather than sound waves. These electroreceptor cells, called ampullary organs, are situated not only in the lateral line canals but also in special openings on the head and snout.

The sensitivity of these cells is extraordinary. At the Woods Hole Oceanographic Institution, A. J. Kalmijn buried flounders in the sand and then set loose smooth dogfish sharks *(Mustelus canis)* whose sight, hearing, and sense of smell had been obstructed. Utterly without any conventional sensory organ, the sharks nevertheless located and ate the buried flounders by homing in on the minute electric charges emitted by the flounders' heartbeats. The sharks, in effect, detected the electrocardiogram of their prey. When other buried flounders were covered with an insulating plate through which electric currents could not pass, the sharks could not find them.

In the open ocean off Cape Cod, blue sharks *(Prionace glauca)* were attracted to an underwater apparatus that discharged electric currents that simulated prey. The sharks were initially attracted to the area because of their ability to smell chum that had been pumped into the water, but when on the scene, they attacked the electrical source much more frequently (forty times during one test) than the odor source (twice during the same test).

Sharks may also use their electroreceptors to navigate, much like a compass responds to the earth's magnetic field. In his laboratory, Kalmijn has demonstrated the ability of sharks and rays to respond to electric charges in a variety of experiments.

SMELL AND TASTE

In man, tasting and smelling are two very different processes. We smell with our noses, taste with our mouths. Smells are carried to us by air (and thus we can smell things that are distant from us), but tasting requires physical contact with a substance. Although we know that in our brain taste and smell signals are intermixed, so that food does not taste quite the same when we have a stuffy nose as when we are breathing normally, in general our noses and taste buds perform quite different tasks.

In fishes, all that is changed. There is no air; flavors are all detected from the common medium, water. Since a wide variety of chemicals dissolve in and are transported by water, a fish can "taste" something that is far away. Moreover, tasting can be done not only with organs in the nose but also with cells found elsewhere on the body. The catfish can taste with its mouth but also with its whiskers and even with cells distributed all over its body. Lobsters taste with their feet as well as with their mouth appendages. Under these circumstances, it may not seem that there is any difference at all between taste and smell for a fish. There is a difference, but it is found deep inside the fish's brain.

In all vertebrates, as Jelle Atema points out, the brain cells that respond to tastes and those that respond to smells are quite different. What we call smell is the result of the stimulation of a certain area of the brain called the olfactory bulb (it in fact looks like a bulb), from which many nerves lead to other parts of the brain. In particular, the olfactory bulb is connected to the limbic system, that part of the brain and the central nervous system that, in fish and man alike, is involved in emotional behavior, and to the hypothalamus, a part of the brain that regulates the level of various hormones in fish and human bodies. As Atema writes, "The sense of smell is directly connected to many of the higher brain centers regulating emotions, hormones, and motivation."

The sense of taste in a fish occurs in a very different and more rudimentary part of the brain. The taste center is connected by a few large nerves to those parts of the brain that control simple motions, such as swimming and swallowing, but not, at least directly, to the regions that control more complex forms of behavior. In general, what we call taste is a sensory mechanism that controls certain rather simple reflexes, such as picking up, biting, swallowing, or spitting out, whereas what we call smell is a sensory device that stimulates more complex and subtle forms of behavior, such as, to use Atema's phrase, "home recognition, prey hunting, predator avoidance, and mate selection."

In most fishes, the organs that initiate smell sensations are situated in different places than those that initiate taste sensations (sharks and rays are notable exceptions). As a fish swims along, water flows into its nostrils, situated on either side of its snout, wherein the chemicals dissolved in the water stimulate certain neurons. What man can only taste, the fish can also smell; thus, in a fish, a much greater array of chemicals can arouse emotional behavior than in man. The more a fish depends on its sense of smell, the longer is the nasal groove through which the water flows, the more elaborate are the receptor cells, and the larger is the brain's olfactory bulb. Moray eels, for example, locate their prey largely through their sense of smell, and therefore have long nasal canals with the nostril openings clearly visible at the front of their snouts and the holes through which the water exits the canals situated near their eyes. So sensitive is the moray's sense of smell that Harold Teichman was able to train them to respond to alcohol in the water in concentrations so dilute that he estimated the eel's olfactory receptors had not received more than a few molecules.

Pufferfishes, on the other hand, depend more on vision than on smell and have no nasal sacs and practically no olfactory bulbs. For whatever reason the Caribbean sharpnose puffer *(Canthigaster rostrata)* got its common name, it was not because of its superior sniffing ability.

The airborne chemicals that man smells are but a tiny fraction of all the potential chemical signals that he could detect at a distance if the air could dissolve these substances and carry them to him. A man detects the perfume of a woman from across the room and as a result he may be drawn to her. Suppose his emotion-triggering olfactory bulb could also detect chemicals that, in pitch darkness, could tell him whether a woman, with or without perfume, was present, whether she was in a calm or excited emotional state, and even her size and perhaps her name. Human relationships would be profoundly altered.

Many fishes can do just this. All marine creatures emit amino acids that are the by-products of digestion. These chemicals enter the water not only from excrement but directly through the fishes' skin. Atema describes these released substances, called pheromones, as providing a "chemical picture" of the animal that other fishes can detect and use to identify its species, sex, stress level, and perhaps size and individuality.

This chemical picture will be incomplete in one important detail, however. Chemicals diffuse rapidly in the water, so that, except in unusual cases, it is hard to localize the source of a chemical unless it has been emitted nearby or the currents have formed its molecules into a distinct trail that can be followed.

Despite this limitation, the sense of smell plays an important role in the behavior of many fishes. Much of the pioneering research in this area has been done on a freshwater fish, the bullhead catfish *(Ictalurus natalis* and *I. nebulosus),* but the implications for ocean fishes are clear.

Bullhead catfishes are active at night. Although their vision is poor, they have well-developed senses of taste and smell. Taste buds situated all over their bodies enable them to locate food even when they are deprived of the ability to smell. Smell is used for more complex purposes, especially the management of their social lives, as was discovered in a series of studies by Atema, John H. Todd, and others at the University of Michigan and at Woods Hole.

The sense of smell is used to define who is a member and who is not a member of a bullhead territory. Individual bullheads live in holes and defend the surrounding territory against others. After these neighbors get to know one another, they live in peaceful proximity, often under the supervision of the biggest, strongest bullhead. Violence only occurs when a strange bullhead approaches. If a familiar neighbor is removed and a strange bullhead introduced into a bullhead community established in a laboratory tank, vicious fighting occurs. If the stranger is removed and the original resident returned, peace reigns once again. For several days after such removals and replacements, the mere introduction of water in which the intruder once swam is enough to agitate the tank residents. In one incident several small bullheads were attacked by a larger bullhead that had managed to leap into their tank from an adjoining one. The distress of the smaller fishes was so severe that all but two jumped from their tank and perished. After order had been restored and the bully returned to its tank, the two survivors established territories at opposite ends of their tank. But when water from the bully's tank was introduced into the small fishes' tank, they immediately became frightened, abandoned their separate territories, and hid together. This reaction to water infused with the bully's distinctive pheromones persisted for four months after the initial scare. Water from the tanks of other bullheads of unknown disposition evoked no fear.

The chemicals a fish emits and that other fishes detect change with changes in its social status. When a catfish that once dominated its community was removed to another tank containing an even larger catfish, the original dominant was defeated in combat. When the now vanquished fish was returned to its original home, its old neighbors immediately noticed, with the aid of their noses, that something had changed. They were now no longer afraid of it.

Sometimes catfishes that ordinarily live in a hierarchical community dominated by one powerful member abandon that life—for reasons not yet understood—and live close together. They spend so much time sprawled all over one another that Todd has called their behavior a "love-in." Water bearing pheromones from a love-in tank that is pumped into a tank containing two aggressive, territorial bullheads will, in time, convert the antagonistic bullheads into docile, communal fishes. Two once hostile bullheads that had been pacified by several days of bathing in water from a love-in tank would resume their combat if the love-in pheromones were withheld for even a day. If the love-in water was then reintroduced, the combatants would once again become pacified, and on this, the second trial, much more rapidly than during the first experiment.

When catfishes had their olfactory organs blocked, anarchy reigned: they could neither settle into a communal, love-in life nor engage in systematic efforts to establish a dominance hierarchy.

The sense of smell is important on the ocean reef, although no research has yet been published reporting findings for marine fishes as dramatic as those obtained from freshwater catfishes. Obviously, many reef fishes use their sense of smell to locate food; in addition, smell plays a role in reproduction. The frillfin gobies that employ sound as a part of courtship also respond to chemicals. When water in which a sexually ripe ("gravid") female frillfin had been bathing was introduced to male gobies, they began their court-ship ritual. Blind gobies *(Typhlogobius californiensis),* which live in bur-rows in the sand constructed by ghost crabs, are monogamous and recognize their mates by smelling their chemical signals. Simi-larly, two closely related species of blennies, the mussel blenny *(Hypsoblennius jenkinsi)* and the tidepool blenny *(H. gilberti),* recognize their own species for mating purposes by chemical, not visual, signals.

Olfaction also plays a role in schooling behavior and in homing. It is the sense of smell that helps to explain the mystery of how salmon find their way back to their home stream in order to spawn. Salmon returning from the open ocean will encounter dozens of freshwater streams, each with countless branches and forks, flowing into the sea. How do they know which is the right stream and right branch? One way is that the water of the correct stream smells right. A distinctive odor has been fixed in the minds of the juvenile salmon years earlier; if they are unable to smell, they are lost. There are indications that other migratory fishes, including some that live on coral reefs, also rely on smell to find their way about.

Taste plays a simpler and more obvious role in behavior. Fishes can find food with their sense of taste and use that sense to discriminate between things that are or are not worth eating. A blinded bullhead catfish can still easily find food. When the taste buds on one side of a bullhead's body were surgically destroyed, the fish had to swim with a looping, side-to-side motion in order to locate its food. But it is smell that is involved in the more complex behaviors of fishes.

Atema summarizes the differences with only slight exaggeration: "Taste acts—smell thinks."

VISION

Divers know they need a face mask in order to see underwater, but they may not know why. The reason they can see clearly in air and hardly at all underwater is that the eye must refract, or bend, the rays of incoming light so that they will focus on, and thus create a sharp image on, the retina at the back of the eye. Air has so little density that this bending of the light rays can be accomplished for man by the thin, watery cornea, situated on the outermost edge of the eyeball. The light passing through the cornea is naturally bent because the light has crossed from one medium, air, to another medium, the watery cornea. The differences in the refractive indexes of the two substances make light change direction. The curve of the human cornea further helps to focus the light. A bit more focusing is still required for a good picture, and this can be accomplished by the small lens behind the cornea, which is operated by relatively (compared with those of fishes) weak muscles.

Underwater, all this changes. Now light is passing from one watery substance (the ocean) into another watery substance (the cornea). There is very little natural bending. The curve of the cornea is not great enough to make up the difference and the lens is too small, and its range of movement too slight, to handle the large focusing job remaining. The result is a blurry image. When we put on a face mask, we are trapping some air between our corneas and the sea, and this once again makes the incoming light pass through two mediums, air and water (in the cornea), thereby restoring the natural bend to the light.

Fishes solve the problem of vision differently. Their corneas, having the same refractive index as water, are of little value in bending light rays. Instead, their eyes have large lenses operated by powerful muscles that can bend the light rays in order to produce a usable image. But then a new problem arises. Since the ocean absorbs daylight, the level of natural illumination declines rapidly with depth. To compensate for this, the fish eye must be larger in order to gather in more light.

Reef fishes that swim and eat at night, such as squirrelfishes and cardinalfishes, have abnormally large eyes (see Plate 60), as do fishes that live at great depths where there is little light. (Some fishes that live in the total darkness of the deep sea have given up the struggle to see; their eyes are mere vestiges.) Because fish eyes tend to be large and because they tend to protrude from the body, fishes have a larger field of vision than do many land animals. Humans, like cats and dogs, have relatively small eyes and so we must turn our necks from side to side to widen our field of vision. But the large, bulging eyes of many fishes enable them to see a large area without moving—a good thing, since, having no necks, they would have to turn their entire bodies to change their angle of vision.

The field of vision is also enlarged by the way certain fishes' eyes are mounted. Hammerhead sharks have their eyes mounted far apart, at the ends of their bizarrely shaped heads. Bottom-dwelling sting-rays have eyes mounted on the tops of their heads for looking upward and to the sides. Both eyes of peacock flounders are placed atop their flat heads at the end of stubby but flexible tubes so that, with their bodies buried in the sand, they can still see up and to all sides (see Plate 19).

Most reef fishes have one eye on each side of their face. Some, such as many wrasses, can operate one eye independently of the other: one eye watches where the fish is swimming, the other moves about following some action occurring elsewhere in its field of vision. Fishes, such as these wrasses, that have their eyes set well back from their snouts do not have good binocular vision—that is, the fields of vision of each eye do not overlap very much—and as a result their depth perception is impaired (see drawing on page 73).

Angelfishes, butterflyfishes, and triggerfishes have especially good vision. Their flexible eyes, supported by powerful and complex muscles that provide excellent focusing ability, are set well forward and close together on their heads. As a result, these fishes have both a wide visual field and good binocular vision, with its attendant depth perception.

A fish's eyes are also adapted to the color of the light they encounter in the ocean. That color changes with variations in the depth of the water and with the amount and kind of organic matter floating in it. Blue light penetrates the deepest, and so things observed at depth tend to appear blue. Near shore, the water may become yellowish from dissolved organic matter or green from the reflection of light off the shallow bottom. Freshwater streams running to the sea from forested areas may bring into the ocean water that is tinted brown or black with decayed organic matter.

Most fishes can recognize colors. Among vertebrates, this ability is shared, so far as we know, only by primates (man, apes, and monkeys), birds, lizards, and turtles. Most mammals, including dogs and

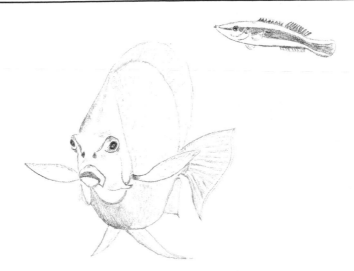

The French angelfish *(Pomacanthus paru)* has eyes set well forward on its snout, giving it excellent binocular vision; the cleaner wrasse *(Labroides dimidiatus),* in profile, has eyes set farther back and has good peripheral sight but not as much binocular vision.

cats, are color-blind. Many biologists believe that the existence of color vision among fishes has persisted because its absence in the ocean environment would be fatal.

Consider a pelagic fish (one that lives in open ocean waters). To find food, it must be able to distinguish its prey, often colored blue, from a background that is also blue. Color vision makes recognizing subtle differences between fishes and a similarly colored, monochromatic background easier. Scientists have discovered that the eyes of deep-dwelling fishes are most sensitive to the blue end of the spectrum. For every offensive advantage there is, of course, a defensive counter-measure. For open-water fishes attempting to avoid predators, it is called countershading. Almost all fishes that swim in open waters during daylight hours are darker on their backs than on their bellies. When a predator looks down at them from above, their bluish or dark backs blend in well with the deep blue of the surrounding ocean; when it looks up at them from below, their whitish bellies blend in well with the sun streaming down from the sky. Even reef fishes that ordinarily stay close to their protective coral crevices tend to be countershaded, especially if they venture out from the reef in search of food. The blue chromis and the creole wrasse are countershaded to blend in with the blue of the open ocean.

But these defensive color patterns can be employed by predators as well, and even turned to their advantage. Sharks, tunas, and mackerels mostly have dark backs and light bellies, and, in addition, tend to attack their prey from below. By coming up at them, these predators are hard for their prey to see, whereas the prey, sometimes silhouetted against the surface light, are a bit easier to spot.

It is obvious that many fishes use their eyes both to find food and to avoid becoming food, but only recently have scientists begun to learn how fishes tell whether another fish is or is not a predator. In a series of experiments, Ilan Karplus and his co-workers in Israel have found that certain common reef fishes, such as the chromis, use two cues to tell them whether another fish is a predator: the size of its mouth and how far apart its eyes are. By exposing fishes to stylized drawings of other fishes seen head on, Karplus was able to show that of the two cues, the size and shape of the mouth was the most important. The chromis's rule of thumb seems quite plausible: if another fish looks as if it can swallow you, assume it will try.

Vision can also help certain species navigate by using the sun. Two kinds of parrotfishes, the rainbow parrotfish *(Scarus guacamaia)* and the midnight or purple parrotfish *(Scarus coelestinus),* migrate from the coral caves where they hide at night to daytime feeding grounds as much as 400 to 500 yards away. Howard E. Winn, Michael Salmon, and Nicholas Roberts studied these migrations in Bermuda waters by releasing captured parrotfishes in unfamiliar areas under varying conditions of sunlight, cloudiness, and darkness and with the fishes' eyes either covered or uncovered. Those with covered eyes became completely confused; those with uncovered eyes were confused (they would stop swimming or circle about) whenever clouds covered the sun or darkness fell. When the sun came out again, those with uncovered eyes would promptly resume their swimming in the correct direction to reach their customary habitats.

The most interesting aspect of fish vision, however, involves the uses to which fishes put their color vision. The most brightly colored fishes are those that inhabit the brightly lit and brightly colored coral reefs. Studies of these fishes show that those that swim about during the day have eyes that are well-equipped with cones, the retinal devices that enable fishes to recognize colors. Of what value is knowing the color of another reef fish? Indeed, on the reef, of what value is it to be colored oneself? In the next chapter we shall take up that puzzle.

CHAPTER FIVE

Color

*I*t is color that the novice diver sees first and remembers the longest. If reef fishes were not marked with hues and patterns of such extraordinary brilliance and variety, it is unlikely that the first trip with mask and snorkel out over the coral would be so unforgettable an experience, one whose memory draws us back again and again to tropical waters. The diver soon wants to know the names of the fishes he has seen and, in time, may become curious about their behavior, but if the fishes had no names and did nothing but swim about, the iridescent beauty of these darting and flashing creatures would suffice to make watching them an irresistible activity. To us, the color of the fishes is an unalloyed delight.

But if one thinks about color from the fishes' point of view, it no longer seems so splendid. They are struggling to survive in an environment teeming with predators. Many swim slowly and lack any defensive armor. Jacks, groupers, and barracudas hover about, ready to pounce. Hiding in coral niches is often the only way many fishes can survive. Under these circumstances, anything, such as a bright color or distinctive marking, that makes it easier for a predator to spot prey would seem to work to the latter's disadvantage. How is it that reef fishes have been able to survive by advertising rather than concealing their presence? What possible benefit can a brightly colored fish derive from its brilliant display?

Compounding the puzzle is the fact that open-water—that is, pelagic—fishes have evolved color patterns that are obviously well-adapted to the problem of survival in this environment. In the open ocean, one rarely, if ever, sees a brightly colored fish with distinctive, highly visible markings. Most of these fishes are, as we noted in the last chapter, countershaded: their backs are dark, to make them hard to see from above, and their bellies are light, to make them hard to see from below. In this way, the pelagic species blend in with their monochromatic background: from above, they are as dark blue as the surrounding water; from below, they are as light as the descending sunlight.

Early in this century, scholars recognized that many reef fishes can rapidly change color. For example, a flounder will blend almost instantly into its surroundings, changing color to match the surface over which it glides, even duplicating on its skin the texture of the sand, coarse or fine, on which it comes to rest (see Plate 19). At least one species of flounder *(Paralichthys albigutta)* has even been able, in a laboratory experiment, to match the pattern of a checkerboard. Other fishes will change colors at twilight to conceal themselves from crepuscular feeders. When the sharpnose pufferfish beds down, its bright spots retreat, its mascaralike eye markings fade, and the bars of color on its snout and tail disappear. Perhaps this ability to change color means that color exists primarily to protect fishes. Perhaps the patterns of bars, stripes, and spots that we see on damselfishes and sergeant majors help them to harmonize with their backgrounds by making their fishlike shapes less distinctive. Biologists have called these markings aspects of "cryptic" or "disruptive" coloration. Perhaps, in short, the bright colors of reef fishes are not so great a disadvantage after all—some patterns serve as camouflage, and others can be changed for purposes of concealment.

But it soon became evident to observers that concealment cannot be the primary reason for the gaudy colors of the reef fishes. Although some species may use hue and pattern in this way, others, such as butterflyfishes and angelfishes, stand out vividly from their backgrounds and do not change color at dawn or dusk. Recall that what we see on the reef is the result of millions of years of evolutionary adaptation. If there were even the slightest disadvantage to having a blue spot on the tail, a red blotch on the snout, or a yellow stripe down the body, and if some members of a given species were born without the spot, blotch, or stripe, then these mutants would be somewhat more likely to survive and mate. Over the eons, the spot, blotch, or stripe would disappear. If pelagic fishes have evolved dull colorations, why haven't reef fishes also evolved in this way?

It was Konrad Lorenz, one founder of the science of ethology (that is, the application of biological methods to the study of animal behavior), who proposed in the early 1960s the first important modern theory to account for the bright colors and vivid patterns of reef fishes. Lorenz suggested that these colors and patterns existed, not in spite of the fact that they drew attention to the fishes, but because they drew that attention. Their purpose was not concealment, but advertisement. He argued that the reef fishes that are brightly colored were the territorial species. Their bright colors—which he called "poster colors," to indicate their role in advertising—were useful to territorial species because they identified who was and who was not a member of that species. A territorial fish would attack and drive off any other member of its species that intruded into its territory and so potential intruders would be warned off by the sight of these poster colors. The bright colors of a territorial species thus served to space out the members of that species and to prevent unnecessary aggression between noncompeting fishes of different species.

The only difficulty with this theory is that it is wrong. Lorenz had studied fishes chiefly in laboratory aquariums; in these tanks they tend to be more territorial than in the ocean, where Lorenz saw them only briefly during a snorkeling trip on the shallow reefs of the Florida Keys. With the spread of scuba equipment, it became possible to observe fishes in their native habitats and in deeper water. It soon became evident that many highly territorial species are not poster-colored at all and that many territorial fishes do not direct their aggression only toward other members of their own species ("conspecifics") but toward other species as well. For example, it is hard to find more resolutely or fiercely territorial fishes than the damselfishes, yet far from being poster-colored, most adult territory holders are among the dullest-colored creatures on the reef. And they will attack almost anything, including divers, not just conspecifics. Some butterflyfishes are quite peaceable during daylight hours, when their colors are the most vivid, and will defend their resting territories only at dusk and dawn, when their colors are the least vivid and thus have the smallest advertising value. We also know that many aggressive fishes normally display quite unremarkable colors, intensifying or changing hues only when they are aroused. Finally, poster coloration is often not a permanent feature of a fish; it may change colors during its life cycle or in response to certain situations. To make sense of the relation between color and behavior, it is first necessary to make some distinctions.

There are two kinds of fish coloration. The first is the color pattern that is characteristic of the fish during most of its active hours. This is the color typically presented in field guides and used, along with shape, for species identification. Scientists call this a fish's *morphological* coloration. Although it may change during different stages of life, as happens with many birds and terrestrial animals as well, it will change gradually. Morphological color changes come about when the color pigment cells, called chromatophores, increase or decrease in number or in the amount of color granules they contain.

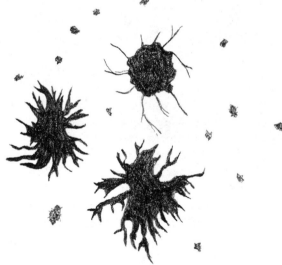

Color cells (chromatophores). Three are expanded, dispersing color over broad areas, and the smaller ones are retracted.

The second coloration consists of those rapid color alterations that enable a fish to imitate its background or to express its emotional status; it is termed *physiological*. This quick-change artistry possessed by so many fishes, as well as by some other cold-blooded vertebrates such as amphibians and reptiles, is made possible by the elastic quality of the chromatophores, which can concentrate color granules in a small area, thereby intensifying them, or disperse them over a larger area, thereby producing paler shades. These changes are in response to hormonal or central nervous system signals (see drawing on page 78. Chromatophores come in several types, each able to produce certain hues according to its chemical content. One type, the iridophore, breaks up and reflects light with its opaque white crystals, containing guanin, thereby producing an iridescent sheen. The layering of different types of color cells in the skin, together with their ability to expand and contract, makes possible not only color change but also pattern change.

MORPHOLOGICAL COLOR STAGES

In the mature lives of many fishes their "normal" or identifying color patterns are quite stable. Once we learn them, a queen angelfish, a foureye butterflyfish, or a rock beauty is not going to differ much from another of its species, at least not enough to fool our eyes. Juveniles of the same species are another matter.

Juveniles

Young queen angelfish *(Holacanthus ciliaris)* resemble mature ones in body shape but not in color. The two-inch young queen angels have four narrow bright blue curved bars on a dark background. The bars increase in number as the fish grows and then fade away altogether. Their eyes, set in a dark band between the blue bars, are rather obscured and their snouts are bright yellow. As the fish becomes an adult it develops an arresting dark ornamental nape spot (on the forehead) dotted and ringed in electric blue—the queen's crown—plus a seductive-appearing blue eyelid and blue lips. In place of the bars an iridescent effect is achieved with scales blue-green in front and yellow behind (see Plate 26). Juvenile foureye butterflyfish *(Chaetodon capistratus)* are really "six-eyed": they have an additional pair of false eyespots above the permanent spot by the tail fin as well as darkish bands that disappear in adulthood. Baby rock beauties *(Holacanthus tricolor)* are yellow all over save for a small black spot near the rear tip of their dorsal fins; as they become adults, their lips become bright blue. Similar juvenile-adult changes could be catalogued for angelfishes and butterflyfishes worldwide. Some surgeonfishes and damselfishes change color from babyhood to maturity and some do not.

No one is quite certain why some fishes experience such dramatic color changes between their juvenile and adult stages. Hans Fricke has suggested that, at least in the case of butterflyfishes, juveniles are masking their species membership. By looking radically different from adults they can live within the territories of mature individuals without being attacked. A similar consideration may explain why juvenile garibaldis *(Hypsypops rubicundus)* have blue dots but adults do not. T. A. Clarke, who studied the life history of this California coastal damselfish (see Chapter 8, on territoriality), noted that juveniles are tolerated within carefully guarded adult territories only so long as the dots endure. When young fishes assume the solid orange adult hue, they are chased away.

Juveniles may also have a distinctive coloration in order to camouflage them during the vulnerable period when they are growing up. Murray Itzkowitz, among others, has advanced this theory, noting that several species of juvenile damselfishes living on Jamaican reefs are adaptively colored to match the background of variously colored corals, rubble patches, and sand. These damselfishes include the threespot, dusky, and beaugregory damsels, all fiercely territorial when mature. Threespot and dusky adults in particular are noted juvenile chasers. Perhaps both functions—concealment from predators and masking from territorial adults—work to the advantage of some juvenile species.

Just the reverse of this process may be at work among Caribbean blue tangs *(Acanthurus coeruleus)*. With them, it is the juvenile that is territorial and the adult that is sociable. The tang begins life colored a plain pale yellow and gradually changes, as it grows, to intense yellow, thence through stages of gray and blue-gray, and finally to a deep blue. The oldest individuals are the darkest blue ones and are quite sociable, schooling fishes that often join mixed-species groups to forage for algae. The young yellow-phase tangs, by contrast, are strongly territorial, at least toward other yellows. According to Ronald E. Thresher, they may occasionally feed together with wrasses and young parrotfishes but will not tolerate other yellow tangs in such groups. As the yellow tang matures and becomes blue it seems to calm down and abandon territoriality. Is its early yellow color a communication signal advertising its behavioral habits to its own species?

Male, Female, and Sex-Change Colors

In the next chapter, on reproduction, we shall find many examples of rapid but temporary color changes that are used to indicate sex differences. A male damselfish, for example, may suddenly flash a nuptial coloration to a female as a way of telling her, "I'm male and I'm ready to spawn!" Many species of fishes, however, are hermaphrodites, a subject also discussed in the next chapter. They begin life either as males or females and, when their population biology requires, some change sex. In many species individuals that change sex change color patterns as well (see Plate 25).

The related families of wrasses (Labridae) and parrotfishes (Scaridae) are hermaphroditic fishes. Over their life cycle, these fishes may go through five or six color pattern stages, with gradations in between. In some species the terminal male, or "supermale," has a different shape as well as color. The supermale blue parrotfish *(Scarus coeruleus)* has a prominently humped nose; the supermale lyretail coralfish *(Anthias squamipinnis)* has a long, trailing, threadlike dorsal fin (see drawing on page 113). Color differences are so pronounced among some species of wrasses and parrotfishes that not too long ago scientists believed they were dealing with many more species than was actually the case. Indeed, reclassification and consolidation of these species is still taking place.

The social lives of hermaphroditic fishes tend to be complicated with hierarchies that may include two kinds of males: initial-phase, or "intermediate," males and terminal-phase males, or supermales, or, in some cases, two kinds of females. Each of these phases is usually denoted by quite distinct color patterns (exceptions include the Spanish hogfish, *Bodianus rufus,* and the cleaner wrasse, *Labroides dimidiatus*). Supermales are not only the biggest fishes in their group, they are usually the most vividly colored as well. Occasionally, as is the case with the bluehead wrasse *(Thalassoma bifasciatum),* females and initial-phase males are indistinguishable in pattern, although the supermale is dramatically different. Since social status in the species community is affected by whether a male is an intermediate or a dominant supermale (many of the latter dominate harems or are territorial or both), color probably helps these fishes to identify who belongs where in the hierarchy. In fact, color may be more important in establishing one's position in the hierarchy than in signifying one's sex. (Fishes can tell sex by smelling pheromones.) If a distinctive color permits each fish to recognize and honor every other fish's rung on the social ladder, then stressful aggressive acts can be minimized so that making a living and producing young can take place in an orderly society.

QUICK COLOR CHANGES

In Chapter 1 we emphasized the diversity, complexity, and stability of the coral reef community, where every niche is filled with life and where to a much greater degree than anywhere else in the sea fishes have developed complex social systems. Because reef fishes need to make use safely of every available space, and need refuge as well as hunting backgrounds, instant color change can be an invaluable biological tool. Moreover, living as they do in such close proximity with neighbors, it is understandable that social reef fishes have need of more sophisticated methods of communication than do their roving pelagic cousins. Expressive physiological color changes provide this unique capacity; for some fishes, such changes function in the same way that facial expressions do for primates.

Mimicry and Camouflage

Mimics, discussed in Chapter 9, make use of form and behavior as well as color for all manner of purposes. While many of them use color morphologically, meaning they more or less permanently resemble something else in color, some are accomplished temporary mimics. We noted earlier the sneaky, shadow-stalking trumpetfish (Chapter 3). Its shape is quite distinctive (a trumpetfish cannot be mistaken for anything else), yet it self-confidently imitates a variety of flora and fauna by means of its talented chromatophores, which are capable of changing colors and patterns (see Plates 17 and 18). So completely can it change color that many novice divers return to the boat excitedly reporting that on one dive they saw a green, a blue, a yellow, and a brown trumpetfish. In fact, there is only one species of trumpetfish in the Caribbean and one in the Pacific; thus, it is quite possible that the diver has seen one trumpetfish displaying four different color phases. Ann Hartline, an observer in the Tektite Habitat program carried out in the Virgin Islands in 1970, reported a camouflaged trumpetfish that aligned itself with the loops of a coil of yellow, plastic-covered wire she was carrying. It swam for more than fifty yards in this way and departed only when the wire was placed on the reef.

Camouflage is a widespread underwater practice. Flounders, which habitually use camouflage to make a living, are the most adroit at concealing themselves with color changes; they are aided in this by their flat shapes. The blobbish shapes of scorpionfishes and frogfishes make it easier for them to employ color camouflage to resemble a pink sponge, a patch of greenish algae, or a mottled lump while lurking in coral rubble (see Plate 16).

However, many fishes of brighter patterns, even poster-colored fishes, achieve degrees of camouflage from time to time. The redband, yellowtail (also called redfin), and bucktooth Caribbean parrotfishes *(Sparisoma aurofrenatum, S. rubripinne, and S. radians)* have all been observed avoiding predators by freezing on the bottom and becoming pale or mottled in an attempt to blend in with the background. The redband has also on occasion developed two black stripes extending the length of its body when posing vertically against sea whips. Most gaudy fishes become paler or change patterns when retiring for the night. The foureye butterflyfish, for example, bleaches out its dark eye bar considerably when it goes to bed.

Less noticeably, a good many rather plain denizens of the reef routinely change color intensities to blend in with their backgrounds. These include many of the planktivores that school off the reef in open waters by day: blue chromises, gray nasosurgeonfish, and the like. In their exposed habitat they blend in with the monochromatic background of endless water. Returning to the reef for shelter they darken to match coral patches. Similarly, fishes that are bottom feeders tend to be sandy colored or of a drably muted pattern and bleach out or darken as is appropriate to the terrain they frequent. Many dull-colored damselfishes make subtle alterations in color intensity that help them to blend in with light conditions and surroundings.

Color Communication

The use of color for camouflage is obvious; its use for communication, though no less important, is harder to describe. It is by no means clear what the range of these signals is or their effect on other fishes. The scientific journals are replete with fascinating observations of color changes, followed by guesses as to their significance. As Wolfgang Wickler has pointed out, we still do not know the complete significance of coloration and color change for even one species. Fishes are hard to interview.

In the Tektite Habitat program one team kept careful notes on species behavior for weeks. They found that the graysby *(Epinephelus cruentatus)* has a row of three or four spots near the base of its dorsal fin that are sometimes white, sometimes black. On one graysby, the spots changed from white to black almost instantaneously as daylight faded into dusk. One might easily surmise that this was done to provide protective camouflage, but the observers found the spot coloration changing in the opposite direction in other graysbys and could discover no correlation between spot color and time of day.

Finding one night a sleeping red hind *(Epinephelus guttatus)*, the Tektite observers tweaked its tail. Startled, it fled to a nearby hiding place, blanching except for the part of the tail that had been tweaked, which became black. A nocturnal bigeye *(Priacanthus cruentatus)* was seen being cleaned of parasites by a pair of sharknose gobies *(Gobiosoma evelynae)* one dusk. As the gobies worked it over it changed from light gray with a dark bar under its eyes to dark all over. Are these two instances merely a result of tactile stimulation or is there a more significant reason? We do not know. Adult purple chromises *(Chromis scotti)* are able to turn the reflective blue spots on the fronts of their bodies on and off. Why? We do not know. The cocoa damselfish *(Stegastes variabilis = Eupomacentrus variabilis)* sometimes has a spot on the base of its tail and sometimes does not. The reason? Again, we do not know.

In addition to the difficulties of assessing the meaning of color changes, observers must deal with the difficulties of vision underwater: light conditions change depending on the time of day, cloud cover, and the turbidity of the water and the particulate matter in it. A fish may seem dark under one condition and light under another. Moreover, some fishes change more rapidly than others and some may vary individually one from another. Some may be affected by an observer's presence and others may be so engrossed in a predatory strike or a compulsion to spawn that the observer makes no difference. Finally, fishes that change color have a finite pattern of chromatophores and thus a limit to their color repertoire. It is likely that a fish may use the same color costume for more than one reason. We are confident that color is important in communication among reef fishes, but the contents of the communication are still largely a matter of guesswork.

One message that is communicated by color changes has to do with sexual intentions; that was mentioned earlier in this chapter and is discussed further in the next chapter. Another message seems to involve hostility. Several researchers have remarked on the surgeonfishes' habit of accompanying their aggressive threats, chases, and territorial displays with profound color expressions. G. W. Barlow noted that the tang, *Ctenochaetus hawaiiensis,* usually black, sometimes has a brilliant blue face while chasing another fish. The lavender tang *Acanthurus nigrofuscus* when angry develops a dark profile around its head and body, outlining a pale center. Other surgeons change in a similar fashion under similar circumstances. The brightest-colored species, *Naso lituratus,* undergoes the most spectacular change, producing a canary yellow forehead and pectoral fins when fighting. Sometimes, Barlow reported, its entire body turns sky blue and back to black again in an instant. J. R. Nursall, who studied the bluelined (or bluestriped) surgeon, *Acanthurus lineatus,* described how in fight situations its central caudal fin patch turns from black to white as the overall coloration darkens and its erected dorsal fin displays a blue margin and stripes. Barlow found that the least aggressive surgeonfish, the convict surgeon, *A. triostegus,* does not change colors when being assertive, although juveniles, which are more combative than adults, do show such changes.

Parrotfishes, butter hamlets, and some butterflyfishes also change color during aggressive behavior. The drab Pacific damselfish *(Pomacentrus jenkinsi),* apparently lacking in chromatophore versatility, conveys its aggressive intentions by darkening its typically yellow eyes to gray. For many of these fishes, especially the territorial ones, color changes probably aid in lessening violent conflict and perhaps the need for chases, signaling as they do that the aggressor means business and will, if necessary, follow up with sterner measures.

Research with freshwater cichlid fishes, which are akin to damselfishes, suggests other possibilities of color communication. It may be involved in parental care as a signal to young fishes to follow or close ranks. The ability to deploy bars and stripes, Barlow hypothesizes, may, among other purposes, facilitate grouping and socializing among friendly species. Many observers of both marine and freshwater fishes speculate that color change may sometimes signify that food has been found. Temporary spots and bars on the tuna, *Euthynnus affinis,* while it is feeding may communicate to other tunas in the school that food is available, although the displaying fishes may not intend to convey such a message. Perhaps the spots and bars appear involuntarily or perhaps they are meant to say, "hands off."

THE ROLE OF PATTERN

Bars (the vertical markings on a fish's body) and stripes (the horizontal lines) seem to play distinctive roles in helping fishes to conceal their presence. Bars help a stationary or slow-moving fish to blend in with the crazy-quilt pattern of corals, vegetation, and encrusting growths to be found on the reef. Stripes, on the other hand, accentuate the "now you see me, now you don't" effect of a fast-swimming fish.

If marked at all, most fast-swimming fishes have stripes. Barlow observed that cichlids that wear rows of spots when on their bottom breeding grounds change to a single long stripe when swimming up into open water. Jack P. Hailman reported how a Pacific goatfish, *Parupeneus porphyreus,* effectively camouflaged itself under an overhang. While motionless, it maintained a deep brick-red color all over except for a whitish saddle at the base of its tail. When it moved out from its shelter into open water, it turned purple and developed a black stripe outlined in white, which emphasized the stripe. Slender fishes tend to be striped, and in general they are also the fastest swimmers.

Deep-bodied fishes such as butterflies, angelfishes, and trigger-fishes tend to be barred. Barlow observed that the deep-bodied fishes usually stick close to the reef, threading their way through its intricate, narrow passages. As discussed in Chapter 2, these fishes are not particularly fast or strong, but they are skillful in maneuvers, able to pivot quickly. Bizarre patterns of bars disrupt their body's outline and presumably make a confusing visual target during such movements. Seen sideways they produce an entirely different impression from that made when they wheel about and flee, suddenly presenting only a thin vertical image. Many scientists have remarked on the camouflage value of such shape and pattern combinations. This combination of ability to pivot and a confusing visual pattern seems to work: angelfishes and butterflyfishes are much less likely than other prey fishes to turn up in the stomach contents of predators.

Such camouflages, to be effective, must be very good, because some animals readily learn to identify other species. Terrestrial creatures that have never seen a fish can be trained to recognize one from just a few visual clues. In his laboratory at Harvard University, Richard J. Herrnstein showed pigeons a series of our underwater reef photographs, some of which included fishes and some of which did not. When rewarded with food for a correct choice, the birds rapidly learned to peck at a lever when they viewed a photograph in which a fish was present. Even though they were shown a wide variety of scenes with divers, turtles, invertebrates, corals, and vegetation as well as a diverse group of fishes, they soon were able to respond correctly most of the time and to apply their newly learned general concept of fishes to new sets of underwater pictures. As might be expected, they had the least difficulty in identifying as fishes those photographed from the side. Deep-bodied fishes viewed head on or while retreating proved more challenging, as did small striped gobies camouflaged against grooved coral backgrounds.

Although bar markings may at times be useful to fishes for camouflage or at least to confuse their predators, how is it that these same fishes seem to be the very ones that, with their bright colors, catch our eyes first and endure in our memories the longest? A strong case can be made for the possibility that their color is also in some circumstances valuable for its very conspicuousness. Many butterflyfishes are monogamous. When pairs greet each other, they often tilt their showy bodies toward each other, an action some theorists believe helps them to recognize their partners, as well as their species (see Chapter 7, on social life). Like brightly plumaged tropical birds living in a highly populated, visually confusing, tree-canopied habitat, the colors of fishes help them to single out their kind. They also help them to recognize other species. Social fishes of varying species that school together while feeding are sometimes called feeding "guilds." Their color patterns may be used as guild marks, signifying fishes that are safe to associate with or, conversely, fishes that compete for their resources.

Other fish markings are thought to protect fishes from predation. The best-known example is probably that of the foureye butterflyfish, perennially cited in Caribbean tourist literature as illustrating the theory that false eyespots enable some fishes to avoid a predator by confusing it. This theory holds that predators zero in on the eye for attack. The foureye butterflyfish has a large false eyespot (termed an "ocellus" by scientists) near the base of its tail. This effect is heightened by a bar line running through the fish's true eye, making it look less eyelike. These false eyespots are common in many fishes, including several of the damselfishes, angels, and wrasses as well as butterflyfishes, and they are especially widespread among juvenile fishes, which sometimes have more than one. The juvenile spotfin butterflyfish *(Chaetodon ocellatus)* bears three ocelli, retaining only the topmost one at the rear of its dorsal fin, for which it is named, when it matures.

But the theory that false eyespots confuse a fish's predators may not always explain their presence. The ocellus may have a very different function, as suggested by Ilan Karplus and Daniel Algom. They tested the reactions of small pomacentrid (damsel) fishes to potential predators by presenting them with various two-dimensional models painted with eyes and mouths in various patterns. They found the size of the mouth to be the most telling cue, as reported in the previous chapter. The bigger the mouth on the model, the more frightened the small damsels were. In addition to mouth size, the next most important cue was the distance between the eyes. The combination of a big mouth and wide-set eyes (think of a grouper) was enough to send the damsels scurrying for cover without hesitation, whereas the combination of a small mouth and close-set eyes, such as a herbivorous surgeonfish might have, failed to scare. Since many false eyespots are about the same size as the fish's true eyes and are often situated on the same axis, the researchers hypothesized that many small reef fishes with these ocelli may be mimicking the appearance of predators. Turned broadside at a sufficient distance, fishes with these markings may fool predators into thinking they, too, are piscivores (see drawing below).

False eyespots on two-eye coralfish *(Coradion melanopus)* and spotcheek blenny *(Labrisomus nigricinctus)* and frontal views of wide-mouthed piscivore with wide-set eyes and small-mouthed herbivore with close-set eyes. (Adapted from Karplus and Algom, 1981.)

We have to temper all these speculations by reminding ourselves that the brightly colored reef fishes are active during daylight hours, a time when predation is at a minimum. Only those predators that hunt by stealth have much daytime success. The eyes of most predators are adapted to seeing best at dawn and dusk, when most poster-colored fishes have retired. Eyespots that decorate adult fishes in a conspicuous way may well serve one or several defensive purposes, but in a crowded reef habitat such markings are probably primarily useful in signaling species recognition. Observing butterflyfish pair behavior both in the field and on film, Christopher D. Kelley and Thomas F. Hourigan noted that these fishes frequently view each other from behind, one following another. Their compressed body shapes afford minimal surface area for viewing from a posterior position. Kelley and Hourigan hypothesize that conspicuous posterior markings help pair members to identify each other (see drawing below).

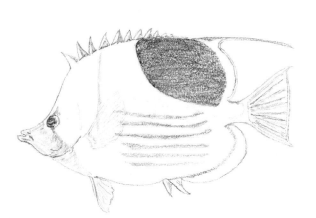

Conspicuous posterior markings of saddled butterflyfish *(Chaetodon ephippium)*. (After Kelley and Hourigan, 1983.)

Many fishes have eyelines that follow a distinctive pattern, depending on the shape and posture of the fish. Eyelines on deep-bodied fishes are, without exception, vertical and tend to repeat the slope of the forehead; on slender-bodied fishes eyelines run longitudinally; on bottom-dwelling blennies and gobies that spend their time gazing upward, eyelines, when present, are set at an angle, corresponding with the posture of their heads (see drawings on page 90). Stripe lines completely disguising the eyes of slender fishes probably help to camouflage them. Barlow pointed out that the closer to the bottom slender, active fishes live, the more stripes they tend to have. If one of the stripes runs through the eye the background blending is more effective.

The barred patterns, including eyelines, found on deep-bodied fishes disrupt the body outlines of these fishes and may give them protection from predators while at the same time serving as social signals. It is the many species of the butterflyfish family (Chaetodontidae) that most consistently have eyelines. Although many of the eyelines seem to conceal the eye, some enhance it (Tinker's coralfish, *Chaetodon tinkeri*, has a dark eye on an orange bar line; Klein's coralfish, *C. kleini*, has a light-colored iris that interrupts prominently its dark eyeline) and others seem to have minimal effects (for example, that of the yellow-headed butterfly fish, *C. xanthocephalus*). Eyelines, it is

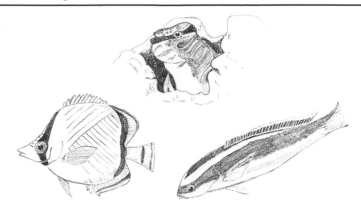

Eyeline pattern variations on hole-dwelling, deep-bodied, and slender elongated fishes. (*Blennius pavo* male after Barlow, 1972; butterflyfish, *Chaetodon lineolatus,* after Carcasson, 1977; Cortez rainbow wrasse, *Thalassoma lucasanum,* after Thomson, Finley, and Kerstitch, 1979.)

tempting to say, simply come with butterflyfishes, and it is unclear whether they have a protective function. Butterflyfishes are not much subject to daytime predation, nor are they piscivorous themselves.

Eyes are camouflaged in many other ways besides eyelines. A quick check of a field guide reveals the possibilities. Eyes may be lost in a pattern of all-over spots (such as in the wrasse, *Coris angulata,* and the female boxfish, *Ostracion lentiginosum*), blend into a mottled maze (clown or whiteblotched triggerfish, *Balistoides niger*), be hidden in a mask (foxface, *Lo vulpinus,* and the imperial angelfish, *Pomacanthus imperator*), or be obscured by bodily appendages (lionfish, *Brachirus zebra*).

The problem with the theory that it is advantageous for a fish's eyes to be camouflaged is that just as many if not more species have conspicuous eyes. Indeed, some have outrageously conspicuous eyes. The queen triggerfish *(Balistes vetula)* and the sharpnose pufferfish *(Canthigaster rostrata)* appear at times to have tried every eye cosmetic on the market. Thresher categorized eighty-five species of twenty-five families of Caribbean fishes and concluded that a majority of them have ornamented eyes. Eye rings, eyebrows, contrasting color backgrounds, and all sorts of other ancillary markings heighten one's awareness of many fishes' eyes. Furthermore, the color contrast of their dark pupils and lighter irises attracts attention. Finally, the colors most often combined in eye colors and surrounding ornamentation are blue and yellow—the very colors that are the most visible underwater. Besides, many fishes with disguised eyes are predatory, notably many groupers. Their markings probably serve to disguise them from prey rather than to provide protection.

Other pattern markings are thought to serve at times as warning coloration. The surgeonfishes, mentioned earlier in the chapter, that intensify colors to signify aggressive intent are called surgeons because they bear small scalpel-like knives on either side of the base of their tail. Normally the scapel lies flat, but sometimes it is used in aggressive encounters. (We had a territorial yellow tang in our saltwater aquarium that slashed a newly introduced butterflyfish with its scalpel.) Only three species of surgeons inhabit Caribbean waters, and their scapels are not particularly distinctive in appearance. But many species abound in the Indo-Pacific, and of these a good proportion have an ornamental pattern around their scalpels. The Achilles tang *(Acanthurus achilles)* has perhaps the most conspicuous mark, a triangular orange spot set on a dark body. The wedgetailed or flagtailed surgeons *(Paracanthurus hepatus)* have scapels set in bright yellow tails that contrast with their blue and black bodies. The green unicorn surgeon *(Callicanthus lituratus)* has double scapels, each set in bright orange circles superimposed on green. Sometimes a fish's entire body pattern is thought to serve as warning coloration. Lateral displays commonly signal aggressive intent among fishes and necessarily present the pattern of a fish. David Coates experimented with the small, boldly marked black-and-white barred humbug damselfish *(Dascyllus aruanus)* in the Red Sea. This fish lives in large groups in and near finger corals, where it takes shelter when threatened. Studies of humbugs have demonstrated that they distinguish between predators and friendly fishes. Repeated fright provocations by Coates indicated that rather than disappearing from sight when entering coral shelters, the humbugs typically turned sideways and conspicuously erected their dorsal and pelvic fins. Coates interpreted such behavior as an attempt to warn predators away, possibly communicating to them the folly of their efforts.

The sheer diversity and spectacle of color patterns in reef fishes both invite speculations and frustrate their confirmation. We are on firm enough ground in identifying the many behavioral uses of physiological color change, such as courtship displays, aggressive encounters, and protection against background, and those morphological patterns that clearly are for purposes of camouflage or mimicry, such as are found on stonefishes and frogfishes. But it is difficult to generalize with certainty about the functions of many patterns. Our best guess is that they serve, as many have suggested, primarily as social signals in both intra- and interspecies identification. In addition, some of the whimsical variations may simply result from evolutionary accident.

CHAPTER SIX

Reproduction

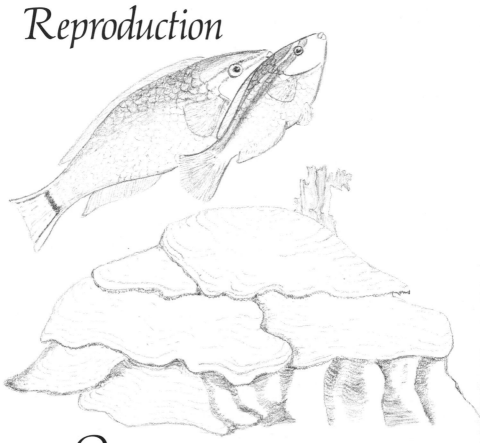

Occasionally, a diver may see a fish behaving as if its central nervous system had gone awry. The fish may be quivering while performing a headstand (bicolored damselfish), engaging in a series of high-speed jumps (blue puller), swimming in jerky zigzag patterns (lyretail coralfish), undulating frantically against the sand (frillfin goby), or alternately rubbing its body hard against the side of a rock or coral cavity and nipping at these surfaces (sergeant major). These fishes have not taken leave of their senses. They are preparing for, or are engaged in, courtship by readying a nest site or signaling to prospective mates. Even when engaged in apparently aggressive behavior toward another member of the same species, the fish may in fact be courting rather than defending a territory or displaying its irritation. Rapid head-to-head circling or nose-to-belly nuzzling may signify that spawning is about to take place. Any of these out-of-the-ordinary performances may be accompanied by dramatic changes in the patterns or intensity of colors or both.

These imaginative ways by which reef fishes signal their readiness for procreation are accompanied by another trait that suggests the perpetuation of the species is a matter of overriding concern for fishes. Fishes, virtually alone among all vertebrates, are often hermaphroditic (that is, they can change sexes); it is as if fishes have taken every precaution to ensure that males and females will be available when they are required for mating. But after going to such great lengths to make reproduction easier, most fishes release their eggs into the water and forget them. Only a few protect or care for their offspring. Nature, it would seem, has attended carefully to the act of procreation but left what happens after procreation almost entirely to chance.

But not quite to chance. Although most fishes fail to protect their eggs, many release them in ways that appear designed to improve the odds that the eggs will survive, and a few even guard the eggs.

PELAGIC SPAWNERS

The coral reefs abound in egg-eating creatures. In addition to the many varieties of plankton-feeding fishes and bottom scavengers that delight in egg finds, the corals themselves, as we have seen, feast on zooplankton diets, including eggs and larvae. Even other members of the dense zooplankton community of which eggs and larvae become a part are enthusiastic egg eaters. Studies indicate that half or more of the zooplankton in shallow coral communities are consumed within a few hundred meters of the reef. For nonterritorial fish species to survive, therefore, it is helpful for each member to produce as many eggs as possible as often as possible and to send them into the relatively safer open waters.

The great majority of saltwater fishes spawn pelagically; that is, they release their eggs where currents will carry them away from the reef and its greedy populace. Moreover, since the upper layers of the ocean have the fewest planktonic feeders, fishes that spawn pelagically have equipped eggs with some means to make them buoyant, such as a globule of oil or a watery fluid less dense than salt water, to keep them at the surface while they grow from eggs into larvae and finally into juvenile fishes. These young fishes then, somehow, find their way back to a protective and nurturing reef.

The compulsion to send their eggs into open waters means that for pelagic spawners the time of day, the phase of the moon and its consequent effect on tides, and the direction and intensity of the current become important in the timing of mating behavior. For many fishes even the physical act of spawning seems designed to get their fertilized eggs up and away from planktonic nibblers. Biologists repeatedly speak of the "spawning rush" of many small species. The final mating climax is often a dash toward the surface by both male and female; at the highest point, eggs and milt (fish sperm) are simultaneously released.*

The down-current edges of the forereef are favored spawning spots. As we shall see in Chapter 7, fishes that live away from the best currents sometimes form migratory schools. This affords them protection en route to the chosen spawning sites as well as access to mating partners. Most of these fishes spawn at dusk or at night when plankton predators are usually resting in their protective crevices. Traveling at dusk means, however, that they must balance their drive to reproduce against the risk of encountering larger fish that feed at dusk.

Experienced tropical fishermen have long known that certain reef locations are always used by fishes as spawning stations. When Robert E. Johannes of the Hawaii Institute of Marine Biology studied this phenomenon in the waters of Palau in the Caroline Islands of the central Pacific, he was puzzled by the fact that the best-known spawning area had prevailing currents that led south, *away* from the archipelago. Although eggs and fry might escape planktonic predation by taking advantage of such currents, they then face the problem of where to find a reef when they grow up, for south of Palau are hundreds of miles of empty ocean. The answer to the puzzle was provided by local fishermen, who reported that there exists at the spawning area a "gyre," a spiraling current perpetually returning its contents back to their point of origin. The nearby shore had become known as "Bloody Beach" after being the site during World War II of a violent amphibious battle between the Americans and the Japanese. The circling current was tragically illustrated when the waterborne blood of dead troops moved offshore and remained visibly stationary in the gyre for several days.

Studies of currents used for spawning in other locations support the

---

*Some marine biologists have speculated that the spawning rush serves to expand the fishes' gas bladders and thus aids in the expulsion of eggs and milt. Others dispute this explanation, pointing out that this behavior has developed in many species with differing anatomies.

hypothesis that in striving to get their eggs delivered away from the reef, pelagic spawners select currents that eventually return their progeny to the reef habitat. Philip Lobel notes that the peak in reproductive activity for pelagic-spawning reef fishes in Hawaiian waters occurs when a shift in ocean currents keeps the plankton near the islands. Somewhere deep within their genetic makeup, fishes know to spawn just prior to a full moon, when the evening tides sweep outward from the shore. They can then derive safety from the darkness and transport from the tides, while their offspring are later brought back to the reef by the returning currents.

BOTTOM SPAWNERS

A few reef fishes build nests and lay their eggs on bottom surfaces. They are called "demersal" spawners and include damselfishes, triggerfishes, gobies, blennies, pufferfishes, and a few others. Many of these species care for their eggs. They place them in protected nests, on the undersides of rocks, in crevices, or in burrows and nip defensively at intruders in the nursery area. The larvae of many of these species hatch during the relative security of nightfall and make their way quickly toward the surface away from the hazards of bottom predation. Larvae of demersal eggs develop in the plankton. Studies in Hawaiian waters indicate that most tend to remain in inshore areas, where they undergo a direct development. Demersal hatchlings, for the most part, are more mature than pelagic larvae, which often are specialized for long periods of floating existence. More research will probably confirm the theory that in many cases the timing of hatching, as well as of spawning, is correlated with the phase of the moon and thus with appropriate tides: either returning ones that aid young fishes ready to settle into reef homes or outgoing tides that help those needing time to develop away from the reef.

THE TIMING OF REPRODUCTION

The moon seems to play a major role in fish reproduction, but the exact connection is only partially understood. Peter H. Pressley has pointed out that although tidal influences are the most commonly accepted reasons for lunar timing, reproductive behavior is also influenced by the lunar cycle even in places where tidal fluctuations are insignificant. It seems that the moon's light may be as important as its gravitational pull. Some fishes may use periods of maximum moonlight for effective nest guarding during the week or so it takes for many demersal eggs to incubate. Since the larvae of many demersal-spawning species are light-sensitive, bright moonlight may help to orient them toward the water's shallows after nighttime hatching. In addition, if fishes use the phases of the moon to time their spawning, they will produce their progeny in so concentrated an amount as to swamp potential predators. Many larvae may get eaten, but many will escape if such an "all at once" strategy is used. It has also been theorized that larvae might have greater opportunities of finding food sources in moonlight plankton. As Pressley put it, the moon "may prove to be the ultimate pacemaker of tropical reef communities."

In temperate and arctic oceans, fishes generally procreate on a predictable seasonal basis, strongly linked to temperature changes. For tropical fishes, however, the timing is more complex. On the reef, variations in water temperature are minimal and their influence on reproduction questionable. Johannes has pointed out that the peak breeding period for Jamaican reef fishes occurs during times of lowest water temperatures but occurs for Great Barrier Reef fishes during periods of the highest water temperatures; in Hawaii and Madagascar, there are two intense breeding periods during times of intermediate temperatures. Other factors besides temperature must be at work.

Regional weather patterns, such as monsoons and periods of high wind velocity, and major current shifts affect procreation. Extreme weather and fierce currents make it difficult for young fishes ready to assume reef niches to find their way out of pelagic waters. In southern Micronesia, for example, which is bathed on either side by the Pacific equatorial countercurrent and the north equatorial current, spawning peaks in the spring, when these currents are at their weakest. Studies at Heron Island and One Tree Island off eastern Australia show that spawning coincides with the period between high monsoon winds. Individual reefs can be expected to have idiosyncratic variations influenced by particular local geographical features.

Within the constraints of tides and weather, reef fishes breed according to their own individual seasonal patterns. A few fishes, such as some jacks and grunts, seem to spawn around the calendar. Groupers, at least in the Caribbean, concentrate their spawning between January and March. Some fishes, such as blueheads, wrasses, and lyretail coralfishes, will spawn daily during the season, some between the full and new moon, others between the new and full. And during any given day, some fishes will procreate in the early morning, some at high noon, some in the midafternoon, many at dusk, and a few in darkness.

SPAWNING PATTERNS

There are at least four major spawning patterns among reef fishes. Some fishes migrate to spawn, some remain on the reef and spawn in pairs, some build reef nests where they guard their eggs, and a few actually protect their eggs in their mouths.

Migratory Spawners

Fishes that do not normally make their living at the down-current edges of the forereef but spawn pelagically must somehow get there. Some travel alone over considerable distances to form schools at the site with their own kind, and others migrate in schools from their territories to search out proper places to build nests for demersal egg-laying.

Groupers   When not spawning, most groupers are solitary, rather stationary creatures about whose reproductive habits rather little is known. On occasion, however, they will come together in vast schools. An enormous spawning aggregation of Nassau groupers *(Epinephelus striatus)* was reported in the Bahamas off Cat Cay by C. Lavett Smith, who estimated that between 30,000 and 100,000 fishes, probably most of the mature grouper population for several miles around, congregated near the edge of the deep water in January, just as predicted by local fishermen, who regularly take commercial advantage of the groupers' courtship schooling. While in the school, the normal head color pattern was reversed in about one-third of the fishes, with dark bars becoming white and white ones turning dark.

Sergeant Majors   The familiar sergeant majors of the genus *Abudefduf* are common in tropical and subtropical shallows all over the world. They are fishes that sometimes school and sometimes are solitary. In the Red Sea, Lev Fishelson kept track of a population of about 500 sergeant majors *(A. saxatilis)* for a year. Although the fish led their lives in the same general area year-round, their social lives differed according to the season. In the winter months, from October to March, they were generally solitary or swam in small groups, with rarely any evidence of breeding. From April to August, however, they formed schools of varying sizes and participated in monthly cycles of colonial nesting, the sites for which were sought by mature males leading schools along predictable migratory routes.

During the reproductive season the sergeant major population spent the early morning hours of each day feeding in the upper layers of plankton. Feeding was regularly interrupted at about 10:00 in the morning and again at about 4:30 in the afternoon when several small groups formed larger schools of 150 to 200 fishes and streamed out behind the leading males along the edge of the coral wall, moving back and forth for distances of up to 500 feet. Ripe males, a few at a time, were attracted to eroded areas of the coral wall and would leave the main body of fishes to inspect choice places with many bare crevices and holes. The entire school would then halt and mill about; some ripe females would be attracted to the males. If the inspected site seemed not quite right, the males would rejoin the school and the search would continue. If the site proved attractive, however, the lead males, usually in numbers of from eight to twenty, would separate from the school and other males would assume the migratory leadership to keep the school moving.

The colonizing males would change color from their habitual pattern of vertical black bars on a yellowish background to a dark blue coloration that blurred the bars and was the most intense on the back of the head. They became aggressive and touchy, closely inspecting eroded places for potential nests and claiming territories within the general colony area. There would follow a period of territorial fighting with chasing and biting; any late-coming males that tried to squeeze into the chosen spaces would be summarily ejected. Once order seemed established, individual territory holders began scraping clean their nest sites with their mouths and violently fanning water toward the site. Within one-and-a-half to two hours after establishing a breeding colony, the males were ready to court passing females with inviting displays of swimming jumps. Typically, they would swim upward in a zigzag pattern, turn abruptly at the apex and dive straight back to the prepared nest, but increased excitement brought variations. Females attracted from the parade of passersby paused and swam in small groups toward the colony. Courtship intensified and pairs were formed, with intruding males being chased away.

Spawning in the nest was accomplished with much tail trembling, head-to-tail circling, and fanning. The female pressed her swollen abdomen against the nest surface and deposited eggs, circled about her mate, spawned more eggs, and slowly became disinterested. This waning of activity seemed to trigger aggressiveness again in the male and she was usually chased away. Males would then invite other females to add to the egg masses in their nests and occasionally would entertain a new partner before the prior one had departed. In this way, individual males accumulated dense masses of perhaps 200,000 eggs, which they proceeded to guard night and day until hatching. They kept the area around them clean and chased away all fishes. During the four days or so it takes for the eggs to mature, the males gradually changed back to their normal coloring. When the little hatchlings were able to school protectively in the spines of *Diadema* sea urchins or in small crevices and holes, their male guardians returned to the general sergeant major population.

After such a reproductive effort about three weeks elapsed before the migratory searching initiated a new procreative cycle and colonies were reestablished. Some individually recognizable fishes were observed to return to their prior breeding grounds. This pattern continued throughout the summer to the end of August, but in September no more schooling occurred. Fishelson's census at that time showed the sergeant majors under study to have increased in numbers from 500 to 800 fish. After winter was over, the number had dropped back to 500.

Parrotfishes and Wrasses   The common Caribbean bluehead wrasse *(Thalassoma bifasciatum)* migrates daily at midday to down-current reef edges in order to spawn. Many parrotfishes include in their daily schedules blocks of time to meet and procreate in forereef areas favorable for egg dispersal. The yellowtail (or redfin) parrotfish *(Sparisoma rubripinne),* for example, has been observed spawning at deep reef areas in the Caribbean only from the middle of the day until late afternoon. Early morning finds them feeding elsewhere. Divers hoping to witness their spawning must be patient and quiet, for yellowtail parrotfish, thought to spawn year-round, are edgy during mating bouts and apt to discontinue their efforts if disturbed.

Reproductive action begins for these fish while they are in large, milling groups. A small subgroup within the crowd suddenly seems to take on a purpose and move as a unit, rowing with their pectoral fins, rising higher in the water, and appearing erratic in their behavior, with many changes of direction. Abruptly the subgroup turns toward the surface and the yellowtail parrotfish burst speedily upward, propelled by caudal fin thrusts. This nearly vertical dash may cover several meters and culminates with the simultaneous release of a cloud of eggs and milt at the peak of the rush. Stimulated by this example, other small groups form and repeat the same behavior. Several spawning rushes may occur over a period of from one to three minutes, and then a lull of five minutes or so takes place while the yellowtail parrotfish feed and loaf about. Then the aggregation may move off to another vantage point and resume the introductory milling that initiates another spawning session.

Pair Spawners

Migratory spawners tend to procreate in groups. Some fishes, such as the redband parrotfish *(Sparisoma aurofrenatum)*, spawn in pairs formed briefly as a result of male courtship display. Several males within a small area might display at the same time, erecting all their fins and acting aggressively toward one another. This seems to impress the females, and when one chooses a specific male the couple rushes toward the surface in a spiraling manner, rotating closely around each other and releasing their gametes—their eggs and milt—at the surface. Sometimes a female initiates pairing by swimming up from her habitual bottom-grazing habitat, remaining stationary, and becoming "available" a yard or so up in the water column where a male might join her for a gyrating rush.

Angelfishes and Butterflyfishes Potter's angelfish *(Centropyge potteri)*, a common reef fish in Hawaiian waters, engages in an elaborate courtship to form a temporary spawning pair. Between December and May, about an hour before sunset during the weeks before full moons, the male Potter's angel starts his courtship by swimming with fluttering pectorals and erect median fins toward the female in a distinctive heads-up undulating style. If she shows interest, he tries to lead her upward over the highest coral projections in his reproductive territory; if she is hesitant, he returns to her and flutters around, always undulating, and then resumes his upward leadership until she is persuaded. Both fishes change from blue coloration to reddish, and at about one meter above the apex, very close to the time of sunset, the larger male appears to nudge the female's bulging abdomen with his snout, thereby triggering spawning (see drawing on page 101). Immediately afterward the pair heads for coral cover, the female chasing and nipping at the male's caudal fin.

Potter's angelfish assumes different reproductive demeanors depending on its habitat, apparently due to differences in the ratio of males to females. Lobel noticed that on patch reefs where there were two to four or more females per male, the male spawned with each female consecutively, one at a time. These males were territorial about their relatively small reef areas. On larger reefs, however, where travel

Spawning behavior of Potter's angelfish *(Centropyge potteri).* (After Lobel, 1978.)

back and forth among continuous stretches of corals is less risky than in the open areas between patch reefs, male Potter's angelfish mated only once per evening. Presumably, females on extensive reefs have a broader choice of partners.

Several species of butterflyfish pairs engage in temporary pair formations in a manner similar to that of Potter's angelfish, although sometimes the female may lead the male. Like Potter's angelfish, they select the water space above the highest coral peak in the neighborhood. Probably these locations serve to protect spawning fishes by affording ready places to take shelter, while at the same time enabling the fishes to broadcast fertilized eggs as close as possible to surface currents.

Lionfishes Lionfishes of at least three species *(Pterois volitans, P. radiata, and Dendrochirus brachypterus)* form temporary pairs for spawning. The male courts the female, inducing her with distinctive swimming motions toward a surface release of eggs and milt. The males are unusually possessive of their partners, engaging in fierce defense of their mating privileges should another male approach. If ritual agonistic display does not deter a rival, a defending male may finally grasp his adversary's head and shake him vigorously, despite the risk of being badly stung by, or even impaled on, the intruder's erect venomous spines.

Anemonefishes   Some fishes form pairs not just for the momentary purpose of spawning, but for life. Monogamous fishes are, of course, the ultimate in pair spawners. They are represented by some butterflyfish and angelfish species, several kinds of gobies, such as those described below in the section on nest builders, a few damselfishes, and the anemonefishes of the genus *Amphiprion,* which live symbiotically with anemones in Indo-Pacific waters.

The black clownfish *(Amphiprion melanopus)* breeds twice monthly on a lunar schedule during the first and third quarters of the cycle. A year-long study of the spawning behavior of five black clownfish couples was carried out off Guam by Robert M. Ross. The spawning habits of the black clownfish are typical of several *Amphiprion* species. First, a pair prepared a nest site at the base of its anemone home and within its protective radius by nipping at the bottom surface and biting at the anemone tentacles, which served to expose the nest, sometimes shaking their heads while doing so. The next day, always between the second and third hour after sunrise, the fish spawned for an hour and a half, the female fluttering across the nest and the male following closely, again and again, resulting in a clutch of from 200 to 400 fertilized eggs. The proximity of the anemone's protective tentacles (see Chapter 9, on symbiosis) makes predawn or nocturnal spawning unnecessary for anemonefishes. On the appearance of a predator they need only hurl themselves headlong into their hosts.

The eggs incubate for from seven to eight days, and the male during this period fans and mouths the eggs. Hatchlings emerge during the periods of full and new moons, when the highest and swiftest reef waters occur. Ross theorized that the breeding cycle is adapted to take advantage of currents that facilitate the escape of planktonic larvae.

Nest Builders

Some fishes, like the black clownfish described above, do not immediately commit their offspring to the fortunes of ocean currents but instead build nests in which the eggs can be guarded, often by the male, occasionally by the female, and sometimes by both parents taking turns.

Damselfishes Most species of the large damselfish family (Pomacentridae) guard their fertilized eggs in nests. Usually the male guards the eggs. Indeed, some female damselfishes have been suspected of egg cannibalism and, in any event, females are often chased away by males at the conclusion of courtship activities. Almost all tropical reef divers have noticed the territorial assertiveness of damselfishes and may remember that some seem more aggressive than others. It is a good guess that an extremely ferocious damselfish is one that has a clutch of eggs to worry about.

Some damselfish species prepare algae nests for their eggs, and others clear algae away from the surfaces of dead coral. Some use empty shells. One such is a small Pacific sergeant major, *Abudefduf zonatus*, whose mating behavior has been described by Miles H. A. Keenleyside. *A. zonatus* males and females maintain separate territories and do not form pair bonds. At Heron Island in the southern Great Barrier Reef, where Keenleyside observed these fish, males initiated the breeding cycle by cleaning out empty clamshells. They used several methods. Most frequently, a male tried to dig out debris by settling his body on the bottom of the shell and plowing through sand with sidewise wiggling and vigorous tail beating until he created a depression and some of the sand had been carried off by the current. He then continued excavating by carrying coral fragments away in his mouth and depositing them elsewhere. Large coral fragments were pushed away, if possible, by his swimming against them with his wide-open mouth pressed against the obstacle. Once the nest was prepared, the male kept it tidy with daily digging while he sought to entice a female into it.

Normally both male and female *A. zonatus* are dark gray to black fish with yellowish shadings on their cheeks, gill covers, and bellies and a vertical white bar just in back of the yellow pectoral fins. But when the male is ready to court, he suddenly darkens to deep black with large yellowish-white blotches along his dorsal spine forward of the white bar and white speckles and spots alongside the posterior portions of the dorsal spine (see drawing on page 104). In this nuptial raiment he spreads his median fins wide to impress a ripe female and swims toward her with a violently trembling body, turning from side to side and swimming around her, and then abruptly spins about and swims toward his clam nest with his median fins now folded but his body still trembling, hoping to lead the female in. If she is hesitant, he pauses and waits for her and then resumes his nestward direction. Immediately when the nest is reached, the male's behavior intensifies as he flusters about his mate with compulsive quivers, nipping gently at her head and snout, and swims in and out of the nest persuasively until she is induced to enter and deposit her eggs. During the three or four minutes it takes to accomplish her task, the male swims in circles about her, pausing beside her on each round, presumably releasing milt. When the female leaves the nest, the male may court her again and reenter with her or he may decide to lower his head at her and chase her away. When she leaves, he immediately reverts to his ordinary coloration. She may go off and accept courtship from a different male and the original male may, in the same day and with the same nest, court other females.

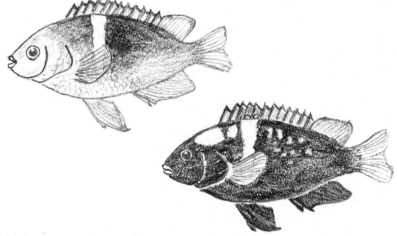

Male damselfish, *Abudefduf zonatus,* in normal (above) and spawning colorations. (Adapted from Keenleyside, 1972.)

Breeding males tend their egg masses, which are attached to the shells' interiors, by nipping at them, perhaps to remove dead or diseased eggs, and fanning them with their tails, probably to aerate them. They guard the nests for a few days until the eggs are hatched and the larvae enter their planktonic stage. A brief period of relaxation may ensue during which the nest fills up with sand and coral debris, but the cycle eventually will be repeated as the territorial *A. zonatus* reexcavates his clam shell and readies the nursery.

Triggerfishes   Triggerfishes use their undulatory swimming style, described in Chapter 2, to excavate large nests in the sand as well as to displace sand in search of food. They turn on their sides just above the bottom and alternately flap their dorsal and caudal fins until this fanning activity creates a sufficient depression. In this they lay, with lunar rhythm, a fist-sized cluster of eggs. One species, *Pseudobalistes flavomarginatus,* weight their nearly buoyant eggs down with pieces of coral and rubble. Nests are guarded by one or both parents, who drive away egg eaters, particularly wrasses.

Field studies in the Red Sea established that the female brown triggerfish *(Pseudobalistes fuscus)* is the parent responsible for egg care, a sex role unusual in fishes. Females maintain permanent year-round territories within the protection of a larger territory-holding male. The size of his superimposed territory would make it impractical for him to do the egg guarding. He has many females to court and long borders to patrol against intruding males. In the Red Sea habitat the brown triggers court only between June and September. First the female builds a sandpit for a nest, starting just before sunset and choosing a site not far from her sleeping hole. She removes coral rubble and shells with her mouth and blows sand away; within ten minutes she is ready to invite a male to her nest with flutter runs, fanning motions, and more pit building. Spawning is believed to occur shortly before sunrise, when thousands of tiny translucent eggs can be found.

Egg-tending lasts only one day for the female of this species, but it is extremely energetic. She fans the eggs and vigorously attacks would-be egg predators. Hans W. Fricke reported that two divers venturing near a clutch of eggs were bitten in the legs badly enough to be hospitalized! A half hour or so after sunset the female blows currents of water into the nest from various angles, removes any stones with her mouth, and in less than twenty minutes empties the nest, blowing away the eggs as well, apparently into the open water for further development. This unusual behavior has not been reported in any other species.

Gobies   Most, if not all, gobies tend their eggs. Many of these small, droll-looking bottom-dwelling fishes, some of which are among the smallest-known vertebrates, are pair-bonding creatures. Many nest in burrows. Both sexes of the Indo-Pacific monogamous goby, *Signigobius biocellatus,* cooperate in the excavation of elaborate burrows for nurturing their eggs. They remove large pieces of shells and corals with their mouths, deliver mouthfuls of sand to the sides or top of the tunnels and spit it out, and expel clouds of sand with energetic tail beats while they hover head down in their holes. This tail-sweeping technique is also used to maintain the burrow, which is commodious enough for the gobies to enter head first, turn around, and exit head first. R. C. L. Hudson, who watched these fishes on the

FISHES THAT SPAWN IN AGGREGATIONS

Bluehead wrasses (Atlantic)	(Labridae)
Groupers (some)	(Serranidae)
Hamlets (some) (Atlantic)	(Serranidae)
Lyre-tail coral fishes—*Anthias squamipinnis* (Indo-Pacific)	(Anthiidae)
Parrotfishes (some)	(Sparidae)
Damselfishes (plankton-eating species)	(Pomacentridae)

FISHES THAT TEND NESTS

Damselfishes (most)	(Pomacentridae)
Clownfishes (anemonefishes)	(Amphiprionidae)
Gobies	(Gobiidae)
Triggerfishes	(Balistidae)

Great Barrier Reef, reported that during a two-week period each of five pairs of gobies dug, redug, remodeled, and concealed up to six burrows. A gravid female (one sexually ripe) was observed to nibble at the body of her mate whenever he fell idle during excavation work!

After spawning the male is sealed inside the burrow for three to four days. The female, who closes it up, may periodically reopen it, whereupon the male emerges and they both fuss about removing sand from the interior for five to ten minutes and then begin to fill in the entrance once more. Before the entrance is completely filled in, the male reenters and the female again seals him in. This behavior is repeated several times during the three-to-four-day period. Meanwhile the female remains nearby, feeding and cleaning other burrows. On the fourth or fifth day after spawning the male leaves the burrow for good, and for a day or two both parents tend the burrow, opening, sweeping, and resealing it. When it is open, the fishes change the water inside by directing their tail beats toward the entrance.

Inside the burrow the fry develop in safety from external predators, but not, apparently, from one another. When the parents open the burrow, a single juvenile emerges, the sole survivor. More observations need to be made, however, to determine if this is an invariable pattern.

Brooders

A few fishes go beyond nest building to protect their eggs: they carry them about in their mouths. This reproductive technique is more widespread among certain freshwater fishes, but marine mouth brooding occurs among the cardinalfishes (the family Apogonidae). These secretive fishes hide deep in coral nooks by day and feed nocturnally; their reproductive acts are thus difficult to observe. Typically, and perhaps always, the male has the job of incubating the eggs in his mouth and often the task of carrying about the newly hatched fry for a time as they develop, sometimes for as long as two weeks. In some cardinalfish species, the male has a longer head than the female, thereby making his brooding task easier. Cardinalfish eggs vary in size, so that some egg clutches may number only a few dozen and others range well into the thousands. The Mediterranean cardinalfish, *Apogon imberbus,* swallows as many as 20,000 tiny eggs and keeps them in his pharynx, managing to turn them about continually so that they are aerated. Some jawfishes and catfishes are also mouth brooders.

Sea horses and pipefishes (both of the family Syngnathidae) have perhaps the most sophisticated apparatus for brooding their young. As usual, the male is in charge, receiving the eggs directly from the female. Some pipefishes attach the eggs to the underside of their bodies near the tail. Other pipefishes, and all the sea horses, share a convergent evolutionary feature with the kangaroos, wombats, and opossums: they have pouches. The fish pouches nourish the developing eggs with placental linings and after hatching provide a haven for further development.

HERMAPHRODITES

One of the fascinating ways in which certain fishes have come to terms with the problems of procreation in the oceanic environment is the development of hermaphroditism. Hermaphroditism, the condition of coexisting male and female sex organs in one individual, is better known in plants, which, being stationary and (sometimes) isolated, can more efficiently produce progeny if all the reproductive equipment is self-contained. Hermaphroditism is virtually unknown among the vertebrates except for fishes, where it is found in many forms. It has evolved independently in widely disparate families whose reproductive needs it serves. Identifying a hermaphrodite is not easy, because in some species the sexes are markedly distinct in pattern and color—that is, they are sexually dimorphic—and thus the casual observer can be misled into thinking that the fishes are permanently and from birth male or female (see drawing below).

Simultaneous Hermaphrodites

Some fishes are simultaneous (or synchronous) hermaphrodites. They have the mature reproductive organs of both sexes and can reverse their sexual functions at will, performing either as a male or a female as the situation requires. This is the case, for example, with hamlets, the Caribbean harlequin bass *(Serranus tigrinus)*, and the belted sandfish *(S. subligaris)*, a small bass inhabiting Floridian waters.

A terminal male blue parrotfish *(Scarus coeruleus)*, a female that has changed into a male and has characteristic bump nose, and two other adult blue parrotfish, which may be either male or female.

Many adult harlequin basses live in pairs and defend territories against others of their kind. Their spawning peaks near the time of the full moon, when, at sunset, each member of a pair alternates in spawning as a male and a female. The sequence begins when one fish, playing the female, displays its body in an "S" shape with its exposed belly turned to the other fish, which might be as much as three yards away. If so inclined, the invited partner approaches and the two proceed with a spawning rush. Often a role reversal takes place soon afterward, with the opposite fish assuming the "S" position. Occasionally a pair member tries to spawn with a solitary harlequin bass in the area, and this may result in a group spawning. These lone harlequin basses always take advantage of the opportunity to replace a pair member if one disappears. Eugenie Clark studied the similar "S" displays of pairs of the belted sandfish, small members of the bass family, and found their sexual role reversals accompanied by immediate color changes as well. The beckoning "S" formation, assumed also by the courted fish at the climax of the spawning rush, served to snap the fishes' bodies at the surface, releasing eggs and milt. After several snaps Clark reported that the surface of the water was covered with eggs derived from both fish.

Simultaneous hermaphroditism may have some evolutionary advantage, Pressley suggested, because such fishes occupy large territories distributed in a narrow band around reef edges, making the search for a mate at the brief sunset spawning hour a major undertaking. The ability to change sexual roles maximizes the genetic value of any nearby potential mate.

Sequential Hermaphrodites

Around the reefs, the typical mode of hermaphroditism is sequential rather than simultaneous. These fishes begin their lives as members of one sex and may change into the opposite sex. This is accomplished in a variety of patterns. In some species all individuals begin life as females and later on some of them change permanently, as the need arises, into males. Or, some may begin as males and change into females. Then again, both male and female juveniles in some species may develop from embryonic stages and only a few individuals later on switch sexes. These fishes undergo complete physiological changes in their reproductive organs; they are termed *protogynous* if they begin as females and *protandrous* if they are first males. Wrasses, parrotfishes, and some species of anemonefishes and angelfishes are sequential hermaphrodites. Although the change is physiological, it occurs in response to social signals.

Wrasses   One of the first species in which social control of sex reversal was clearly demonstrated was the Pacific cleaner wrass, *Labroides dimidiatus*. At Heron Island on the Great Barrier Reef, D. R. Robertson kept field records on eleven male-dominated harems for two years. During that time he recorded forty-eight sex reversals in those and an additional eight groups. The males of this protogynous species are highly aggressive in controlling their females and employ a distinctive display when threatening them. Females, though in a less feisty manner, have a little dominance hierarchy of their own, as might be expected in a harem society.

On the death or removal of a male, the dominant female, usually the largest in her group, responds with a sex change. This takes place quickly. In one to two hours' time she is using the male aggressive display toward other females and is patrolling the territorial borders. Within two to four days her sexual metamorphosis is complete and she—now he—is capable of male courtship and spawning behavior. In harems where females of nearly equal size struggle for dominance, the disappearance of the male overlord may result in a split of the harem, with each of the two rival females switching sex and assuming leadership of part of the former group.

In such a tightly controlled social system, in which the male mates only with females in his harem, there is little opportunity for interbreeding with other cleaner wrasse harems. The terminal male, produced only when needed and derived as he is from the strongest, largest female, probably will carry the best genetic material for fertilizing the eggs of all his mates and thus maximize the quality of their offspring.

Anemonefishes   As far as is known, all anemonefishes, including the black clownfish described earlier in the section on pair spawners, are protandrous (that is, male-first) hermaphrodites. It is the female that is the larger member of the fish couple in these species. An adult pair may tolerate a few juveniles in a commodious anemone but not other adults. Unless an anemone is extraordinarily large (an unusual occurrence) juveniles on reaching maturity must make the hazardous search for an unoccupied anemone. In the interim, however, should something happen to the adult female, the adult male transforms into the breeding female and the largest juvenile quickly becomes, at this social signal, the breeding male.

Lyretail Coralfishes   The beautiful, diminutive lyretail coral-fishes *(Anthias squamipinnis)* live in large colonies in the protective branches of table coral throughout the Indo-Pacific, as is described in Chapter 7, on social life. Protogynous hermaphrodites all begin life as females and later on some change into males (which some researchers term bachelors), and a few, as opportunities arise, become supermales, with definitive color markings and special trailing dorsal fins. Most colonies have a ratio of one male for every fifteen to twenty females. They have been studied on several widely dispersed reefs as well as in field and laboratory experiments in which males were removed from groups to reveal the social mechanism for the switchover to male from female. The change occurs on a precise timetable: during a period of several weeks, male coloration and behavior are gradually developed, the ovaries degenerate, and testes mature.

Divers who descend at dusk on Indo-Pacific reefs where table coral flourishes can look for lyretail coralfishes in mating swarms. They engage in reproductive activity year-round just before sunset, intensifying it seasonally depending on the region. Reproductive activity begins when the supermales simultaneously initiate courtship display for the entire colony (which may number in the thousands), performing speedy U-shaped swims in a zigzag pattern (see drawing on page 113). The U-swims gradually take place on a higher and higher plane and stimulate the whole population to follow along, including the "bachelor" males, which during interruptions in the U-swim are frantically bitten and pushed away by the supermales. The displaying males, their fins tautly spread, end their upward climb with zigzag circling and return to the table coral surface, again followed by the excited colony. Several repeats of this up-and-down mass movement

SOME HERMAPHRODITIC FISHES

Simultaneous

Hamlets (Atlantic)	(Serranidae)
Harlequin basses (Atlantic)	(Serranidae)
Groupers	(Serranidae)

Sequential

Angelfishes (some)	(Pomacanthidae)
Clownfishes (anemonefishes)	(Amphiprionidae)
Lyre-tail coral fishes—*Anthias squamipinnis* (Indo-Pacific)	(Anthiidae)
Parrotfishes	(Scaridae)
Wrasses	(Labridae)

take place and culminate at the top of each ascent when ripe females and supermales pair up and, in an excited quiver, swim side by side for a ways with their bodies touching and their mouths agape. Eggs and milt are released and float away in the current. During these sessions supermales may spawn in turn with many different females. Whether or not the bachelor males release milt in this milling crowd is not really known. Just before dark everyone retreats back down into the coral.

The Advantages of Hermaphroditism

The adaptive value of simultaneous hermaphroditism is not hard to imagine. Such fishes are frequently members of small species with short life spans, and they often live as solitary or relatively isolated individuals. Many are territorial and thus are disinclined to explore widely for a mate. If they were not hermaphroditic, they might well become extinct—the odds against an isolated, short-lived, territorial fish finding a suitable mate are very high. For these fishes, hermaphroditism, as illustrated by the harlequin bass, makes possible the mating of any two mature fish that happen to come together.

Explaining sequential hermaphroditism is more difficult. Because it is characteristic of so many species—wrasses, parrotfishes, anemonefishes, sea perches, and some angelfishes, among others—this kind of hermaphroditism must provide widespread benefits. For monogamous pairs, such as those of anemonefishes, the benefits are clear. Confined for protection to an anemone, the largest juvenile anemonefish can quickly assume a breeding vacancy should anything happen to one member of the adult pair. Among most sequentially hermaphroditic fishes, it is the largest male that finds the best opportunities for breeding; thus, it is possible that the ability to change sexes enhances the quality of the species by conserving the optimal pool of genes. And should a species experience some disaster that upsets the balance of males and females, the correct balance can be quickly restored without any perilous migratory search for mates.

The social systems of sequentially hermaphroditic fishes are remarkably stable. Whether they live in pairs, small harems, or large colonies of coexisting harems, these fishes as a whole behave as if they were made up of fishes that were permanently of one sex or another even though in fact they can change. There is always the right number of males and females to maintain a stable social structure. This stabil-

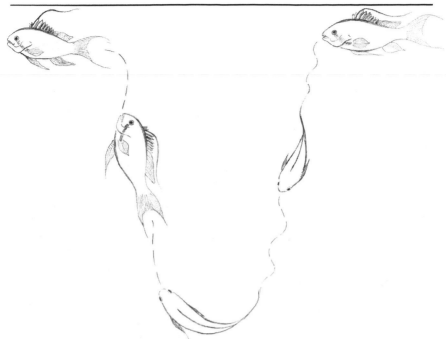

Courtship U-swim display of supermale lyretail coralfish *(Anthias squamipinnis).* (After Popper and Fishelson, 1973.)

ity reduces the energy that must be expended on competition for mates.

Similarly, the behavior of the simultaneously hermaphroditic fishes suggests a stable pattern. Even when one fish has both male and female organs, it apparently does not fertilize itself. For example, the belted sandfish, although it is capable of self-fertilization, courts other sandfish and spawns in pairs. C. Lavett Smith has suggested that, from an evolutionary standpoint, sequential hermaphroditism may be a more advanced development than simultaneous hermaphroditism. The belted sandfish may be in the process of slowly transforming itself from a simultaneous to a sequential hermaphrodite. And we know that the kelp bass *(Paralabrax clathratus)* is now a separately sexed (that is, gonochoric) species that developed from hermaphroditic ancestors.

Of course, what is to the long-term advantage of the species is not likely to be of much interest to the individual fish. It goes about its business, leaving us to speculate about whether, and how, that business is beneficial to the species. As Karel Liem has emphasized, the element of chance has always been at work in the development of hermaphroditism. Differing environmental conditions, such as tropical swamps subject to droughts and the peculiarities of individual reefs, have shaped the evolution of hermaphroditic answers to the problem of survival.

FISHES AS PARENTS

As parents, fishes cannot compare with terrestrial vertebrates in the length and quality of the care they give their offspring. Most parental activity is exhibited by the nest builders, which, as we have seen, guard and tend their eggs. Once hatched, however, their progeny are on their own. A few, such as the mouth brooders and the burrowing gobies described earlier, are a bit more advanced. A variation of that technique is employed by a frogfish of Philippine and northern Australian waters, *Antennarius caudimaculatus.* Frogfishes are sluggish creatures that attract their prey with a fishing-pole-like lure, a part of their anatomy modified from the most anterior dorsal fin. Many young frogfishes hatch from rafts of floating pelagic eggs. *A. caudimaculatus,* however, cares for her eggs until they become fairly mature by keeping them attached to her side just below the dorsal fin. She may not in fact be all that devoted, however, for one theory is that a fish that makes its living with lures may be all the more alluring when it has a cluster of appetizing eggs as a part of its camouflage.

There is, however, a remarkably advanced level of parental care behavior exhibited by the spottytail humbug *(Acanthochromis polyacanthus),* a feisty little damselfish abundant on the reefs of the East Indies, the Philippines, Melanesia, and northern Australia. Spottytail humbugs pair up for a four-month-long breeding season each year. Part of the courtship process is the selection of a well-hidden nest, usually a small cave in dead coral. This activity involves a style of slow waggle-swimming when the fish approach the nest from a yard or so away.

Both sexes clean and prepare the nest, both defend it against other spottytail humbugs and predatory fishes, and both are involved in caring for the eggs—unusual at all in ocean fishes, and even more unusual in that they devote a full month to the task. The fry, numbering between 100 and 150 juveniles, grow from a tiny quarter-inch size to just over an inch in length during this period, schooling in tight bunches near their parents and nest. As they mature they school more loosely and may wander farther and mix with similar-size fry of neighboring clusters. Meanwhile, the parents chase away predatory wrasses and snappers and larger spottytail humbug juveniles but tolerate benign species unless they approach very close.

While swarming about their parents, spottytail humbug fry have been seen repeatedly bouncing off the adult bodies. They may be feeding on mucus covering the parental skin, a practice, called glancing, of fry of some freshwater fishes of the cichlid family, which are closely related to the damselfishes.

Perhaps this extended parental care is a natural development in species that lay demersal eggs and defend their nesting territory. We may possibly be seeing the beginning of a trend in the direction already taken by many of the cichlid fishes, which are demersal egg spawners and which have more complex patterns of parenthood.

OTHER CURIOSITIES

Divers will encounter some marine creatures that reproduce in ways wholly dissimilar to those of the fishes we have discussed so far. Unlike almost all other fishes, many sharks bear their young alive. Sharks and rays spawn, not by bringing eggs and milt into close proximity, but by actual copulation. And octopuses and cuttlefishes use their tentacles for mating.

Sharks

Most sharks likely to be encountered by a diver on a reef are of the family Carcharhinidae, which includes the bulk of shark species. Carcharhinids bear their young alive, fully formed. They are viviparous (able to nourish their fetal young internally) or ovoviviparous (developing their eggs for internal hatching and further maturation). Male sharks have a pair of claspers, formed from the inner sections of their pelvic fins, which transmit their sperm to the oviducts of the female. As might be expected, not a lot is known about their courtship habits, but a few descriptions exist and some courtship has been observed among captive sharks. Some male sharks chase females around tanks and grab them by their pectoral fins with their teeth. Other sharks follow each other closely and may swim side by side.

Two biologists who have devoted much of their attention to shark studies, Richard H. Johnson and Donald R. Nelson, have reported the mating of both the blackfin and the whitetip reef sharks *(Carcharhinus melanopterus* and *Triaenodon obesus)*, commonly seen around Indo-Pacific reefs. Probably attracted by scent, the male blackfin swims closely after the female with his nose pointed under her up-tilted tail while she leads him low over the sand in a deliberate, sinuous course. In one observation copulation followed when the male pushed the female from behind and she lay passively on her side in the shallows. Similar nose-to-tail orientation occurs with the whitetip before the male grasps the female's pectoral fin with his teeth during copulation. Plate 31 is one of the few photographs in existence of sharks mating at sea; it was taken by Eric Le Feuvre.

Nurse sharks *(Ginglymostoma cirratum)* court with a synchronous parallel swimming display for a period of a few seconds to several minutes. Then the male grasps the female's pectoral fin in his mouth, a signal for her to pivot her body and roll onto her back on the bottom surface. There she remains motionless and cooperative. The male may nudge her a bit with his snout and then swims into a position atop her for copulation, which may last several minutes and during which the positions may change somewhat.

Stingrays

The rays, related to the sharks, have similar reproductive systems and, though rarely observed, apparently have similar courtship behavior as well. A recent report described the copulation of the Sea of Cortez bullseye stingray *(Urolophus concentricus)*, during which the male lay on its back below the female, holding her clamped in position by biting her pectoral fin. This clamping is made easier by the sharply pointed, backward curving teeth in the upper jaw of the male, a dental feature also characteristic of male sharks in species that grasp females with their teeth during mating.

Octopuses and Cuttlefishes

Octopuses and cuttlefishes, of course, are not fishes at all, but molluscs. They are invertebrates that are classed as cephalopods, a word meaning that their feet derive from their heads. In male octopuses, one of the long tentacles, the third right arm, is modified to transfer sperm, which is produced in the mantle cavity, to the mantle cavity of the female, where her oviducts (and all the rest of her organs) are situated. Octopuses can swim about by a jet-propulsive method, but they spend most of their time scuttling about on bottom surfaces, and that is where their courtship occurs.

Plate 1. Shallow-water Caribbean elkhorn coral *(Acropora palmata)*. Grand Cayman.

Plate 2. Pacific table or umbrella coral. Ponape, Caroline Islands.

Plate 3. An abundant variety of life clusters about a small section of the superstructure of a sunken cargo ship: encrusting and projecting sponges; pastel soft "tree" corals—some retracted and one, pink and white at center, expanded; "rooster comb" oysters; small blue damselfish and smaller schooling baitfish. Truk Lagoon, Caroline Islands.

Plate 4. Soft corals, punctuated with bright-red encrusting sponges, flourish on the deck railing of a sunken fishing boat in Mindoro Strait, Philippine Islands. The two round leather corals, bottom center, are of the genus *Sarcophyton*.

Plate 5. Shallow-water Caribbean staghorn coral *(Acropora cervicornis),* with damselfish protecting its territory. Bonaire, Netherlands Antilles.

Plate 6. Tubastrea coral with tentacles extended for night feeding, with two Christmas tree worms (serpulid polychaetes of the genus *Spirobranchia*). Bonaire, Netherlands Antilles.

Plate 7. Brain coral at night, with its feeding tentacles projecting from its grooved skeleton to trap plankton. Grand Turk, Turks and Caicos, Bahamas.

Plate 8. Large-cupped boulder or star coral *(Montastrea cavernosa)* feasting on nocturnal zooplankton attracted to its sweeper tentacles by underwater lights. The zooplankton are the pale-pink and lavender wormlike animals. Grand Cayman.

Plate 9. Pacific alcyonacean soft "tree" coral. Note the needle-like spicules that strengthen its body walls. When expanded to feed, as here, its body is inflated with water, but it can pump the water out and collapse its body walls to a small, blobbish shape. Truk Lagoon, Caroline Islands.

Plate 10. Atlantic gorgonian soft coral with its polyps extended for feeding. Bonaire, Netherlands Antilles.

Plate 11. A coral predator, the crown-of-thorns sea star *(Acanthaster planci)*, curled around a branch of finger coral. It has devoured the coral's polyps and laid bare its skeleton. Ponape, Caroline Islands.

Plate 12. Caribbean fingerprint snail *(Cyphoma signatum)* feeding on gorgonian soft coral. Grand Cayman.

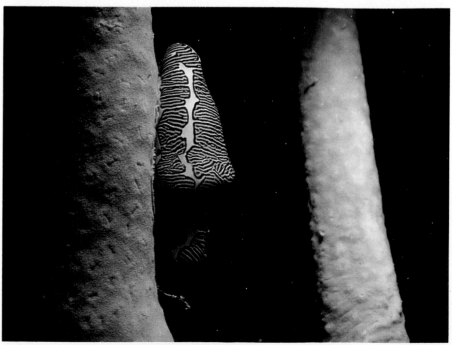

Plate 13. Manta ray with remoras above Apo Reef, Philippine Islands.

Plate 14. Barracuda *(Sphyraena barracuda).* Grand Turk, Turks and Caicos, Bahamas.

Plate 15. Yellowtail snapper *(Ocyurus chrysurus),* an opportunistic feeder. Andros, Bahamas.

Plate 16. Camouflaged scorpionfish, a lie-in-wait hunter. Bonaire, Netherlands Antilles.

Plate 17. Pacific trumpetfish *(Aulostomus chinensis)* hoping to find a fish to eat while shadowstalking with a coral-eating foxface *(Lo vulpinus).*Ponape, Caroline Islands.

Plate 18. Atlantic trumpetfish *(Aulostomus maculatus)* camouflaged among soft coral sea whips. Grand Turk, Turks and Caicos, Bahamas.

Plate 19. Peacock flounder *(Bothus lunatus),* a lie-in-wait camouflaged hunter. Roatan, Bay Islands, Honduras.

Plate 20. Closeup of porcupinefish *(Diodon hystrix),* inflated for defense against predators. Belize Barrier Reef, Caribbean.

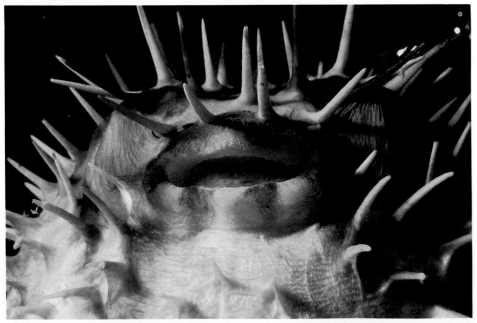

Plate 21. Spanish hogfish *(Bodianus rufus)* eating Diadema longspine sea urchin, with yellowtail snapper above and rock beauty *(Holocanthus tricolor)* below. Bonaire, Netherlands Antilles.

Plate 22. Smooth trunkfish *(Lactophrys triqueter)* feeding on coral surface. Bonaire, Netherlands Antilles.

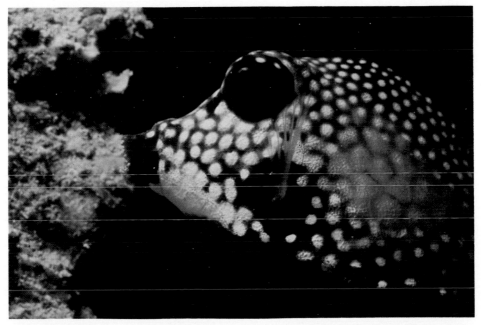

Plate 23. Clown, or white-blotched, triggerfish *(Balistoides niger)*. Apo Reef, Philippine Islands.

Plate 24. Lionfish *(Pteropterus antennatus)*. Its eyestripe, which seems to function as camouflage, extends through the armored spines (supraorbital tentacles) on its head. Apo Reef, Philippine Islands.

Plate 25. Terminal male coloration of stoplight parrotfish *(Sparisoma viride)*. British Virgin Islands.

Plate 26. Queen angelfish *(Holacanthus ciliaris)*. Bonaire, Netherlands Antilles.

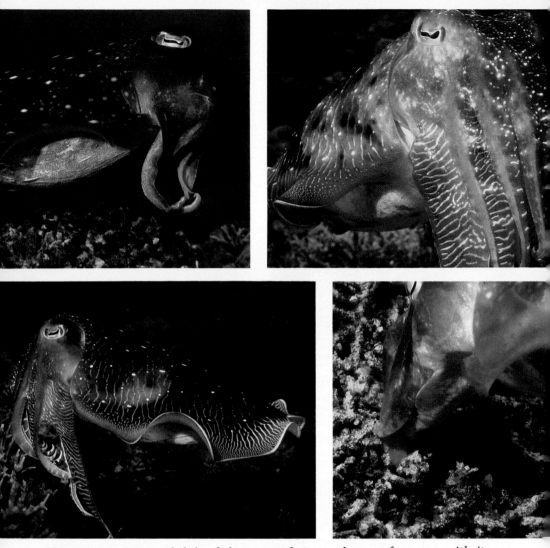

Plates 27–30. A cuttlefish of the genus *Sepia* gently transfers eggs with its tentacle tips to a secure place in the coral rubble. Brown Rocks, Busuanga, Mindoro Strait, Philippine Islands.

Plate 31. Two whitetip sharks *(Triaenodon obesus)* mating in about 20 feet of water in Molokini Crater, off Maui in the Hawaiian Islands, June 1982. The male, right, grasps the female's pectoral fin in his mouth; with the female thus stabilized, the mating continued for about 20 minutes. (Photo by Eric M. Le Feuvre.)

Plate 32. Banded butterflyfish pair *(Chaetodon striatus)* above star coral. Grand Cayman.

Plate 33. Gray angelfish pair *(Pomacanthus arcuatus).* Belize Barrier Reef, Caribbean.

Although procreation of octopuses has often been seen in aquariums, rarely has it been observed in the ocean. One pairing of a common reef octopus, *Octopus horridus,* has been reported by an English biologist, J. Z. Young, who watched for half an hour a mating couple off the reefs of Singapore. The male displayed a dramatic pattern of vertical bars that were the most intense on the side of his body facing the female, his right side, as they sat side by side at tentacle length from each other. She appeared in a normal, blobbish octopus way, whereas he drew himself up tall, and, after about five minutes, inserted his third right arm into her mantle, remaining this way for about ten minutes. During this time both animals showed color fluctuations, but the male more so, with his color sometimes fading altogether on the side away from his mate and the barred pattern on the side near her always distinct. The female moved off at this point, slowly dragging the male by his attached tentacle for about ten feet. Then, his arm withdrawn, he followed her another twenty yards until she stopped. Another ten-minute copulation ensued, broken off by the female and followed by the male's withdrawal into a hole.

Seventy-six aquarium matings of *O. vulgaris* were observed by M. J. and J. Wells. All these courtships occurred when a female was put into a tank already occupied by a male. Immediately on her introduction, the male invariably would emerge from his shelter, approach the female with extended arms, and sometimes make a jet-propelled rush and pin her down. Copulation soon followed, the male stretching tall in an arched posture and transferring his sperm from his mantle through his specially grooved arm in a manner similar to that of *O. horridus.*

Female octopuses are devoted parental caretakers. They lay their eggs in a protected shelter and guard them zealously, using their siphons to aerate them continuously with pumped water currents and lifting the egg clusters about with their tentacles, constantly inspecting them and fretting over them. Depending on the species, the incubation period may take as much as six weeks, and the maternal care extended is the final act in the life of the mother. Her life span is just long enough for her offspring to get their start in life. She ceases feeding shortly before or at the time of spawning, gradually loses weight, and dies soon after her young are produced. The photograph in Plate 46, taken of a motionless octopus off Cozumel, an island near Yucatan in the Caribbean, is probably of a mother whose spawn have hatched and who has begun to die. Spawning is accompanied by a dramatic decrease in the enzymes necessary for digestion in the octopus. Males stop eating at about the same age and body weight as their mates and die as well, apparently also as a result of the reproductive cycle.

Cuttlefishes of the genus *Sepia* mate swimming above the substrate, forming temporary pair bonds while displaying vivid courtship colors. The male presents the most intense color patterns, with dark brown and white zebralike stripes on his mantle and on his fourth pair of tentacles, which he keeps on the side near the female he courts. He also uses his color intensity to threaten and compete with rival males. The losing male, usually the smaller one, pales and withdraws. Mating involves an intertwining of tentacles while the cuttlefishes hover head to head. The female deposits her eggs in coral rubble one by one in a solemn, almost ceremonial way, the male keeping vigil nearby.

One mid-March morning we spent over two hours in Mindoro Strait (the Philippines) near Brown Rocks off Busuanga Island watching a trio of cuttlefish involved in what seemed an imperturbable egg-laying trance. In about forty feet of water the female slowly produced egg after egg from within her mantle and with her long arms carefully transferred each one to a niche in a tangle of dead coral surrounded by a thick forest of fire coral. Each egg was about the size and color of a ping-pong ball, slightly pointed on one side, opposite which was a short cylindrical stem with which it was attached to the coral (see Plates 27, 28, 29, and 30). The male attended closely, hovering parallel to the female and alternately displaying blotches, dots, and stripes. We were never sure what the role of the third cuttlefish was. It hovered during the entire ritual several yards off. Perhaps it was a rejected male. Near noon the cuttlefish departed.

REPRODUCTION AND EVOLUTION

The reproductive habits of fishes are those that have survived the process of natural selection. We know that the reef environment and its constraints have shaped the strategies developed by different reef species, but we are only beginning to understand how the many aspects of that environment fit together. Much of what we know permits only intelligent guesses about how and why fishes behave as they do. About some of the more secretive species, such as eels, which live in crevices, and nocturnal fishes, which are rarely observed, we have very little basis even for guessing. Still, it is clear that much of the organized life of fishes is addressed, in more complicated ways than one might think, to the problem of successful reproduction. Closely linked to reproductive methods are the social systems of the fishes. In general, the greater the level of parental care of the young, the more elaborate and complex the social system. In the next chapter we shall explore other facets of social life.

CHAPTER SEVEN

Social Life

*T*he reproductive habits of fishes, described in the last chapter, would seem to make the development of any social life on reefs impossible. Land animals that have social lives—birds in nests, lions in prides, or elephants in herds—do so in large measure because their offspring are dependent on parental nurture to survive. The more protracted the dependency of the young, the more elaborate the social structure that arises for their protection. A newborn elephant, for example, is not weaned from its mother until it is four or five years old, and during this period it is carefully guarded by the herd. The social insects, such as ants and bees, are alike in that they care cooperatively for their young. But as we have seen, parental care among fishes is extremely rare. Most fishes release their spawn into the current, where it becomes part of the plankton. The larvae survive largely by chance. Even most offspring of fishes that guard their eggs in nests pass through a planktonic stage in which they are utterly without adult protection.

Nonetheless, fishes do create social systems, the most obvious of which is the school. As Hans W. Fricke has pointed out, the ability of fishes to develop a kind of society despite the absence of parental care is one of the most striking, and most difficult to explain, aspects of marine life. Although biologists differ in their explanations of underwater communities, most agree that, partly because of communal living, the populations of reefs are remarkably stable. No two reefs, of course, are alike, but allowing for variations in region and terrain, most have similar population structures. Barring disasters, what one sees on a given reef on one occasion—certain fishes living in certain niches and regular traffic patterns along predictable routes to and from feeding and sleeping areas—is what one will see a year or three years later. This stability both promotes and is reinforced by social living. Reef animals recognize and adapt to one another's habitual behaviors and act cooperatively for certain purposes.

SCHOOLING

The most striking example of social living among fishes is schooling. Although the vast schools of open-ocean (that is, pelagic) fishes, such as anchovies and herring, will rarely be seen by a person diving on a reef, he will see enough examples of schooling among jacks, snappers, and silversides to encounter a problem that has vexed marine biologists for decades.

Dozens, hundreds, even thousands of fish swim about in a large mass. As a diver draws near, the fish line up in formation, each moving in the same direction at what appears to be the same distance from its neighbors. If the diver moves closer, the entire school turns as if in response to a spoken command, wheeling about to travel in a new direction. If a barracuda approaches, the school of potential prey senses whether it is in a hunting mood and, if it is, the school separates in an instant, splitting apart into two groups that circle back around behind the predator; if it strikes, they explode outward into a larger sphere. Although hundreds of fishes are moving simultaneously, there are no collisions and apparently no confusion. As Brian A. Partridge wonders in his recent review of research on schooling, How do they do it?

That research has not yet fully answered his question, but we know more today than we did even ten years ago, thanks not only to the advent of studies in natural settings by scuba-equipped scientists but also to the invention of laboratory tanks in which schooling can be studied under experimental conditions. The first thing we have learned is that some distinctions are in order. There is a difference between a *school* and an *aggregation*. Evelyn Shaw of Stanford University urges scientists to use the word school to refer to fishes mutually attracted to one another and the word aggregation to refer to those fishes that come together in response to an external stimulus, such as chum thrown into the water by a fisherman or a sea urchin cut up by a diver. The evidence of mutual attraction, according to Partridge, is that in a true school each fish constantly adjusts its speed and direction to match those of other members of the school. Some schools are regularly polarized (that is, made up of fish all headed in the same direction at the same time), others are normally nonpolarized, and still others display polarity at some times and not at others (see drawing below).

Polarized schooling formation. Fish are of similar size, are oriented in the same direction, and maintain fixed distances from one another.

Moreover, it is a mistake to think that we can easily divide fishes into those that school and those that do not. Although there are some species, such as sharks and groupers, that are almost never found in schools and others, such as silversides (family Atherinidae), that always are, some species will school at some points in their life cycle and not at others, at particular times of the day and not at others, and on some reefs and not elsewhere. Finally, schooling does not invariably involve fishes of the same species. Although most schools are made up of one species, mixed-species schooling is quite common on the reef.

Schooling is a more widespread phenomenon than most divers may realize. Shaw has estimated that out of the 20,000 known fish species, about 80 percent school when they are juveniles and about 20 percent school throughout their lives. The species that always school are composed disproportionately of smaller fishes.

Since schooling cannot be learned by juveniles imitating the behavior of their parents, its development must result from some combination of innate instinct and trial and error. Shaw and Madelaine M. Williams studied this process by hatching the eggs of some silversides *(Menidia menidia)* and rearing the young fish in laboratory tanks. Very early in their lives, the silversides began approaching one another, either head on or at an angle, and then suddenly veering away. The fish were clearly drawn toward one another, but avoided coming closer than a certain distance. Partridge later estimated that this "minimum-approach distance" is equal to about 30 percent of the length of a fish's body. As the silversides grew, they began to approach one another head to tail. Partridge was able to show that, at least among minnows, when there are only two fish in a tank, they swim in a line, one leading and the other following. But when three or more fish are in the tank, they school as a group, swimming parallel to their nearest neighbor, with no leader.

The evidence is beyond dispute that, for some species, schooling is innate. But circumstances can influence how quickly and smoothly schools are formed. Shaw and Williams raised some of their silversides in isolation and others in groups. When they were finally brought together with other fish, the fry reared in isolation took much longer to learn how to school than did those reared communally, and they never achieved the ease of the latter.

As fish come together into large groups, they establish a certain distance from one another. At least in the minnow schools studied by Partridge, each fish, on the average, stayed about one body length from its neighbor (this is somewhat greater than the minimum-approach distance of fish who are learning to school). Moreover, each fish, on the average, tried to keep its neighbor at a particular angle from itself.

To maintain these distances and angles among themselves while swimming in large schools, fish must meet several conditions. First, they must swim at the same speed; otherwise, they would become separated and, as we shall soon see, becoming separated from the school can be fatal. For this reason (and perhaps for others as well), schools tend to be composed of fish of the same size. This in turn means that schools of juvenile fish are age-graded; to avoid swimming at different speeds, younger juveniles do not mix with older ones.

Second, each fish must have some way of measuring the distance and angle to its neighbor. The obvious way to do this is by sight, but scientists have discovered that fishes can school even when blinded. When Partridge, at the Department for Agriculture and Fisheries in Scotland, fitted opaque contact lenses to pollocks swimming in a tank, they were still able to swim in a school but they could no longer swim quite as close to one another as they had when their vision was intact. They stayed parallel to their neighbors, but farther apart. We know that a fish can also detect other creatures and measure distance to them with the sensory organs in its lateral lines. When Partridge severed these lines, the fish were still able to school, but now they swam closer to one another than they formerly had. Only when they were both blinded and deprived of their lateral lines were the fish unable to school at all. Apparently, eyesight is the most important in measuring the distance to a neighbor and the lateral lines are the most important in measuring a neighbor's speed. Partridge was also able to show that when the information reaching a fish from its eyes is at variance with that reaching it from its lateral lines (as it is when two fish are turning in parallel arcs), then the fish relies chiefly on its eyes.

Third, the fish must have some way of knowing when to change direction, as when they rush outward to evade a predator. Research in tanks has shown that each fish in a school that has been attacked will accelerate in only a *fiftieth of a second* from a standing start to a speed of from ten to twenty body lengths per second. The fish farthest from the predator move out as quickly as do those closest to it, giving to the school the appearance of what Partridge has described as a "bomb burst." There is no way that each fish could communicate to its neighbors (by, for example, flicking its tail) that it is time to move out, or instruct it in the direction it should move to both evade the predator and avoid bumping into a member of the school. Scientists do not know how this is done. They are coming to understand, however, what value schooling has for fishes.

Schooling for Speed

One advantage of schooling may be that it makes swimming easier for its members. Just as bicycle riders or automobile drivers in a race will try to stay right behind the bike or car in front of them in order to take advantage of the reduced wind resistance (racers call it "drafting"), a fish will discover that if it swims in a certain position behind and to the side of another fish, it can take advantage of reduced water resistance. Since water is a denser medium than air, the energy that can be conserved in this way is substantial. The drag of the water increases with the square of the speed, and so the advantage of "drafting" is particularly great at high speeds. Various scientists have estimated the theoretical advantage of swimming in a school to involve energy savings of from 10 to 60 percent. This gain, it turns out, does not accrue to a fish that swims directly behind the one in front of it; in that position, the wake of the lead fish would actually slow the follower down. Rather, the gain is greatest for a fish that swims behind and to the side of the one ahead of it. This may help to explain why the members of so many schools position themselves in a kind of staggered checkerboard pattern, rather than in a nose-to-tail formation. The evidence on these matters, however, is still sketchy. In any event, it is not likely that reef fishes find much speed advantage in their schools, since in and around the reef they rarely move quickly for any great distance. For these fishes, schooling has persisted primarily because it offers other advantages, chiefly in safety and feeding.

Schooling for Protection

Most fishes school in order to avoid predators. That is probably why fishes that school all the time tend to be the smaller, defenseless species, or to be made up of juveniles, just as many of the land animals that form herds, such as zebras, gazelles, and impalas, tend to be those least able to defeat an attacking lioness or leopard.

It is not obvious why fish in a school would be safer than each fish swimming alone, just as it was not obvious at the start of World War II why merchant ships steaming from the United States to England would be safer from submarine attack if they moved in groups, or convoys, than if they traveled singly. Some admirals thought that a lone merchant ship would be harder to find than a big convoy, and hence safer. But experience showed the overwhelming advantage of the convoy. Given the vast size of the ocean, it was about as difficult for a submarine to find a convoy as it was to find a single ship. But with a convoy, it was easier to detect an approaching submarine (there would be many more sonar units and many more pairs of ears listening to them) and cheaper to destroy one (a navy could afford to send destroyers with a convoy but not with every lone ship).

Some scholars think that oceangoing fishes school because a school is as hard for a shark or a tuna to find as a single fish, and thus each individual fish in the school is safer than if it traveled alone. Others doubt this, and in any event the theory does not explain why some reef fishes school since, by being on or near the reef, they are in effect staying at a fixed address that any predator worth its salt can easily find. Moreover, unlike the convoys of merchant ships, schools of fishes cannot hire destroyers or frigates to protect them.

On a reef, and perhaps in the open ocean as well, the chief advantage of the school is that it makes it harder for a predator to carry out an effective strike. There may be three reasons for this. First, a tightly packed school presents no obvious single target. The barracuda or the jack literally may not be able to make up its mind. Second, even if the barracuda should pick out one fish and strike, the ensuing movement of the other fishes in the school will distract the attacker (what Partridge calls "sensory confusion") and reduce its chances for a kill. Third, fish in a school can keep under surveillance a wider area of ocean than a fish swimming alone; given their uncanny ability to communicate the presence of a threat, any given fish would be well advised to join a group that can so greatly expand its own early warning system.

In any case, experiments have confirmed the fact that the more fish there are in a school, the harder it is for a predator to kill any given fish. Sean Neill and Michael Cullen at Oxford University have shown that gradually increasing the number of prey from one to twenty proportionately reduces the chances of a successful kill.

If this is true, then obviously a fish has a powerful incentive not to do anything that will make it more identifiable (and thus more readily a target) than any other fish in the school. Hence, both lagging behind and moving too far out in front are risky; this risk leads almost inevitably to a tendency to maintain a more or less constant distance to one's neighbor. Moreover, if the fish in a school are milling about feeding on plankton, they have a strong incentive to form up into a tight, often polarized school whenever a predator approaches. Many observers have noted that fishes tend to bunch up more closely when predators are about. Some have suggested that, in doing so, each fish merely wants to hide behind its neighbor (W. D. Hamilton called this tendency among land animals that of the "selfish herd"), but close motion-picture analyses of fish do not not reveal any evidence of hiding in schools. Each fish gets into its regular parallel formation when a predator is around, apparently relying for its survival on the advantages of better surveillance and sensory confusion.

The relationships between hunter and hunted have been carefully studied in natural settings by, among others, Peter F. Major of the University of California at Santa Cruz. Major watched the predatory jack, *Caranx ignobilis,* try to feed on Hawaiian anchovies *(Stolephorus purpureus).* When a marauding jack first appeared, the anchovy school would condense into a compact mass and begin to swim in a weaving pattern. If the jack got too close, the school would part, each half swimming around the jack and rejoining the other to the jack's rear. In this way, they took advantage of the jack's inability to make quick changes in direction or to back up. This parting maneuver was less successful if more than one jack was around, because inevitably some anchovies would lag behind or get too far ahead. These would often be eaten by the second jack. The jacks were more successful in capturing isolated anchovies than ones in schools; the bigger the school, the safer the anchovies. As we shall see in the next section, these facts provide a reason for jacks and some other predators to form their own schools for hunting purposes.

Groupers, which are poor swimmers, sometimes hang about waiting for a schooling fish to make a mistake and lag behind the pack. E. S. Hobson watched a grouper for two hours as it lurked beneath a herring school. During that time, it made exactly three strikes, each one immediately after a diving pelican plunged down from the sky and scattered the school. Lev Fishelson observed lionfish *(Pterois volitans)* at dusk, hanging motionless in open water just beneath the surface. At this hour other crepuscular hunters chase schools of small fishes that jump frantically across the surface. When they fall back into the water they may fall prey to the ambushing lionfish.

Schooling fishes can distinguish between greater and lesser threats. During Project Sea Lab II off La Jolla, California, observers noticed that schools of mackerel *(Trachurus symmetricus)* would ignore attacks by scorpionfishes (only the victim would react) but go into polarized formation and flee when attacked by sea lions or bonitos.

A familiar sight to divers is a group of fishes resting during the day in a protected coral setting. These schools are often composed of several different species and are drawn together, despite their differences, out of a common concern for safety. Usually, they are nocturnal or crepuscular feeders and sleep during the day. French grunts *(Haemulon flavolineatum),* which feed on worms, crustaceans, sea cucumbers, and other creatures active at night, frequently form the nucleus of these mixed-species schools. Their companions, naturally, are fishes that neither threaten nor feel threatened by the grunts, such as yellow goatfish *(Mulloidichthys martinicus)*, white grunts *(Haemulon plumieri)*, and various snappers. Being generally of the same size, these fishes are capable of maintaining a school (they do not swim at different speeds) and will occasionally take on the polarized form of a true school. At other times, they will appear to be nothing more than a casual aggregation.

Another mixed-species school involves the blue tang, a common Caribbean surgeonfish that grazes in schools on algae, and the blue midnight parrotfish *(Scarus coelestinus)*, a herbivore from another family. A distinctive fish when seen alone, the midnight parrot becomes quite inconspicuous when mixed in with blue tangs. W. S. Alevizon, after watching these mixed schools for many months in several locations, concluded that the parrotfish are too few in number to form protective schools of their own, and so they join the populous tangs to travel safely through open patches in the reef area.

When night comes, many reef schoolers will break formation and head for their feeding territories alone or in small groups. The Pacific sweeper *(Pempheris oualensis)* dozes by day in large schools under ledges or in caves but hunts at night in small groups away from the reef. When researchers tagged some on a Red Sea reef, they learned that the sweepers had quite regular habits, always returning to the same shelter areas at about the same time: between 3 and 4 A.M., well before dawn brings the risk of predators.

The same routine is followed by certain common snappers such as *Lutjanus monostigma*, studied by G. W. Potts on the Aldabra reefs off the coast of east Africa. During the day, these resting schools might include 1,000 to 2,000 fishes, all facing into the current. Like most schooling fishes, the snappers can tell the difference between dangerous big fishes and just big fishes. The snappers would warily follow barracudas and sharks in order to keep an eye on them, but rarely felt obliged to take evasive action. They displayed greater apprehension when various groupers appeared: the school would become compacted, parting in the pattern already described to keep the predator in front of them. But when a dangerous jack, *Caranx melampygus*, arrived, the snappers would become extremely agitated and make intense evasive moves. A sudden attack by the jack would send them scattering, so suddenly and with such force as to create a shock wave perceptible to a diver. An impartial justice rules here: the snappers that prey on schools of smaller fishes at dawn and dusk must themselves form schools during the day to evade those fishes that prey on them.

Schooling for Food

Some fishes form schools not to rest on the reef but in order to leave it. Ocean surgeons apparently feel secure living and moving about on the reef as individuals, but when it comes time to go into the open ocean to feed in sandy and grassy areas, they will hang about at the edge of the reef until they are joined by others. Like merchant ships in wartime, they form up into convoys before entering the sea lanes. Bluehead wrasses *(Thalassoma bifasciatum)* behave in a similar fashion.

Many fishes that feed on plankton form schools for the obvious reason that the plankton, being concentrated in one spot, draw fishes together at that spot. The blue chromis *(Chromis cyanea)* eats plankton in the open water, often as part of a mixed-species school, but sleeps on the reef. The unicorn fish, a familiar sight to Pacific divers, feeds on plankton found near the deep edge of the reef, but unlike the chromis, it prefers its own kind. Most species of butterflyfishes are ordinarily found in pairs, nipping at coral polyps, tubeworms, and the like, but a few gregarious Pacific species school in order to feed on plankton. These include the blackface butterfly *(Hemitaurichthys zoster)* and the milletseed or lemon butterfly *(Chaetodon miliaris)*, both of which, like the blue chromis, scatter at night to individual reef bedrooms.

If schooling fishes were always successful in evading predators, the number of predators in the ocean would be greatly reduced. But they are not always successful, in part because some make mistakes and in part because some predators have adopted schooling tactics of their own.

Aerial photographs of giant bluefin tunas show them hunting cooperatively. When hungry, a school of tuna may separate into smaller attack groups of from ten to twenty fish, each forming a precise, concave formation (see drawing on page 130). In these patterns, they could search more efficiently for prey and, when spotted, move to break the prey's school up into smaller units, thereby generating confusion and increasing the number of isolated fish that could readily be attacked.

We have already seen how several jacks were more successful at capturing Hawaiian anchovies than one jack working alone. The major value in the jacks' forming a school is that they, like the tunas mentioned above, can more easily break up the schools of prey.

Schooling can also improve the chances for getting food, not by capturing prey but by overcoming the defenses of territorial fishes.

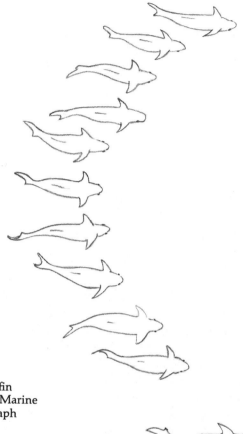

Cooperative, concave hunting
formation pattern of giant bluefin
tunas. (Based on U.S. National Marine
Fisheries Service aerial photograph
in Partridge, 1982.)

The convict surgeonfish *(Acanthurus triostegus)*, known in Hawaii as the manini, is a timid algae-eater that would like nothing better than to be left alone while grazing. But the highly territorial lavender tang, or brown surgeonfish *(Acanthurus nigrofuscus)*, has other ideas: it wants the exclusive use of its algae fields. It bullies an invading manini by rushing at high speed and ramming it. The manini will not defend itself and moves away. George W. Barlow of the University of California at Berkeley noticed that the maninis would eat alone when few or no tangs were about but would form schools when their rivals were numerous. They typically assembled in long lines of (sometimes) several hundred fishes. As the lead manini descended to graze on a tang's algae field, the tang would promptly attack. The first manini would rise up, move off a short distance, and begin to graze again. Meanwhile the tang would ram the next manini in line (see drawing below). Unless the tangs were present in very large numbers, this linear invasion would enable each manini to eat, though obviously not in the most relaxed circumstances.

Schooling convict surgeonfish, *Acanthurus triostegus,* overcoming territorial defenses of lavender tang, *A. nigrofuscus,* in order to feed on algae.

Similarly, striped parrotfish *(Scarus iserti = S. croicensis)* often form the core of mixed-species schools in order to overcome the pugnacious threespot damselfish, whose stubborn defense of algae fields is described in detail in Chapter 8, on territoriality. The damselfish can drive away larger fishes, even when outnumbered, but not when overwhelmingly outnumbered. The school of parrotfish, in effect, saturates the damselfish's defenses.

Some of the other species mixed in with the parrotfish, such as trumpetfish *(Aulostomus maculatus)* and butter hamlets *(Hypolectrus unicolor),* are not there in order to eat algae but in order to sneak in to prey on smaller fishes, including the damselfish. As with human crowds, fish schools, especially when agitated, can attract pickpockets and muggers.

Thus schooling serves many purposes, particularly for those fishes that live on or near the reef. Schools afford protection, make possible cooperative hunting, combat territoriality, and (especially for those species that always school) facilitate reproduction. But schooling is not the only form of social life on the reef. Fishes also form colonies and enter into monogamous pairs.

FISH COLONIES

Not all gregarious fishes display their affinity for one another by schooling. Some live together in more or less stationary reef communities, where they share the protection and food supply of a coral head. They are territorial fishes, but unlike most of the territorial species discussed in the next chapter, they willingly tolerate the presence of many—often hundreds—of other members of their species. Indeed, they more than tolerate them; they create, through their reproductive habits and social structures, a kind of extended family, or colony.

Among the colonial species are various damselfishes, including humbugs and blue pullers, certain wrasses, lyretail coralfish, and the bluelined surgeons. Not all of these colonies are identically organized, but all have in common group living in a more or less fixed territory. The whitetailed or banded humbugs *(Dascyllus aruanus)* and the lyretail coralfish *(Anthias squamipinnis)* are plankton feeders that live in the protective niches of branched coral, such as table coral (of the Acroporidae family), which is situated where nutrient-rich currents bring food directly to the fishes. At Apo reef in the Philippines we have seen fragile sheets of table coral ten to fifteen feet in diameter growing like delicately balanced umbrellas on the edge of the reef drop-off and supporting colonies of small humbugs and lyretail coralfish that easily number in the hundreds, perhaps thousands. The fishes hover motionless like a flock of tiny birds just above the surface of these tables, eating from the water flow and dropping back down into the coral interstices at the first sign of danger. In this way they can feed on plankton without running the risk of migrating to the edge of the reef, where large predators lie in wait.

The social structure of lyretail coralfish colonies resembles that of a harem. These fish are "sequentially hermaphroditic," that is, a single fish may change during its life from one sex to another. All the juvenile are females, delicately colored in shades of pinkish orange. At about the age of one year, some of these female juveniles will become males and a few will become supermales. A supermale is much larger than the other lyretail fish, with dramatic eye markings and a spectacular violet dorsal fin from the end of which threadlike filaments trail. Spaced out in contiguous horizontal territories and hovering just above the rest of the colony, the supermales vigorously defend the areas around them against rivals. Just below them and sometimes at the front of the colony, one finds the ordinary males; at the center of the group are the females and the juveniles. The evening hours are devoted to ritual swimming dances executed by the supermales, leading to mating, as described in Chapter 6. As the light fades, the lyretail coralfish descend as a group into their coral home. Often mixed in with the lyretail coralfish are various alien species. D.

Popper and L. Fishelson observed lyretail colonies in the Red Sea that included groups of sergeant majors *(Abudefduf azysron)* and schooling damselfish *(Chromis dimidiatus),* usually found in the upper front area of the lyretail coralfish school and headed into the current. Not having an elaborate social structure of their own, perhaps these sergeant majors and damsels found it advantageous to attach themselves to fish that had evolved a system of colonial living.

The clown wrasse *(Halichoeres maculipinna),* widely found in the Caribbean, also lives in a colonial harem. It, too, is sequentially hermaphroditic, but unlike the lyretail coralfish, which invariably begins life as a female, the clown wrasse may begin life as either a male or a female. Some females, however, will in time turn into males. For some reason, these late-blooming males become the dominant ones and take responsibility for defending the colony against challengers. Subordinate to them are the males that have been of that sex from the beginning. The wrasses form herds, composed of females and initial-phase males, each watched over by a supermale. A supermale moves about among the herds in his territory, courting females as he goes. When an intruder is encountered, the supermale displays an aggressive manner by standing on its head, swimming parallel to the challenger, and gaping at it. And as if all this were not enough, the supermale must from time to time bully the initial-phase males to remind them of their subordinate status.

The cleaner wrasse *(Labroides dimidiatus)* is organized into smaller harems. The male cleaner wrasse tends only one herd, rather than several, each composed of a half dozen or so mature females. There is a clear pecking order among these females, with the more dominant ones assigned the choicer feeding spots. The larger male supervises this dominance hierarchy and mates with each female, with sexual activity occurring each day shortly before high tide.

Apparently not all colonies are composed of solely hermaphroditic fishes. The whitetailed humbug, a widespread Indo-Pacific species, inhabits finger corals in stable communities within which several kinds of social units flourish. In one Red Sea study of eighty social units, 56 percent were estimated to live in small harems dominated by males, assisted by the highest-ranking female, 6 percent in larger polygamous groups, and 38 percent in heterosexual pairs. Group members were, of course, closest to one another but able to live in close proximity to other whitetailed humbugs.

As with almost all of the distinctions made in this book, that between social and isolate fishes is not exact. The bluelined surgeon *(Acanthurus lineatus),* found throughout the Indo-Pacific oceans, is partly individualistic and partly gregarious. It lives in colonies with a social structure, but unlike some other communal fishes, it has its own individual territory within that structure. In its territory, defended vigorously against other surgeons, it feeds on algae. But these individual territories are contiguous, so that in a given area many surgeons will coexist peaceably, with the strongest adults having the best, centrally located algae crops to work and the weakest ones living on the periphery and subsisting on the poorer crops. These colonies will act cooperatively to defend the area against intruding algae-eaters; when the threat has passed, each member will return to its individual territory. Similarly, the whitebellied sergeant major *(Abudefduf leucogaster)* will defend its own territory, typically found in the branches of fire coral, but for some reason will periodically join in groups of ten to sixty individuals to school temporarily before returning to its home.

PAIRS

The novice diver who notices no other aspect of underwater social life will almost always observe the tendency of butterflyfishes and angelfishes to live in pairs (see Plates 32 and 33). Not all butterflyfishes (family Chaetodontidae) live in pairs, but the majority do. By tagging them, the habits of a given pair can be followed over a long period. With this method Fricke has found that such pairs will endure for at least three years. Since male and female butterflyfishes are identically marked (in scientific terms, they are not sexually dichromatic), it would be possible for these stable pairs to be of the same sex, but Ernest S. Reese has captured and examined a great many pairs and verified that they are invariably male-female couples. So tight is this pair bond that if its members become separated, one member will stop feeding, rise above the coral head to look for its mate, and swim quickly in a straight line to rejoin it, celebrating the reunion with a greeting ceremony in which the two fishes swim around each other at very close range for a few minutes, frequently tilting toward one another. Some observers have suggested that this tilting may be intended to reflect sunlight off their bright, posterlike colors as a way of sending a recognition signal.

Reese, who has studied butterflyfishes on Eniwetok atoll, off Johnston Island, and in the Great Barrier Reef, has classified them into species that are solitary, weakly paired, strongly paired, or schooling. In general, seven species are strongly paired, including the familiar saddled butterfly *(Chaetodon ephippium)* and the onespot *(C. unimaculatus)*. However, the percentage of any given species that is strongly paired varies from one reef to another, suggesting that environmental conditions influence this behavior to some degree.

Other butterflyfishes are hard to categorize since they seem to lead solitary lives at some times and to swim in small groups at others. Occasionally, a pair will form between two members of different species. Fricke suggests that this mixed pairing is more likely to occur among species that habitually form strong pairs that are found in locations with sparse butterfly populations. Beggars can't be choosers.

There is no well-accepted theory explaining why some fishes form pairs. To a degree, the tendency is no doubt innate, but the fact that this tendency has survived suggests it serves some adaptive function. For example, saddled butterflyfishes eat coral polyps by day. Since many corals are nocturnal, only a few will have their polyps extended during the day; hence, a butterflyfish will have to cover a large area to find enough polyps on which to dine. Being dependent on scarce food supplies, the saddled butterfly is not numerous; roving so widely, it cannot be territorial. Early pair formation helps it to solve the otherwise great problem of finding a mate.

For other species, their habitat may make pair formation advantageous. The clownfish that lives throughout its life amidst the protective tentacles of an anemone (as described in Chapter 9, on symbiosis) cannot risk leaving its host to look for a mate. Early pair bonding enables the species to survive without taking those risks. Similarly, pair bonding is useful to the blind goby *(Typhlogobius californiensis)* that lives symbiotically in burrows with a shrimp; having mated for life, it need not leave its burrow to search—blindly—for a mate. Not only does pair bonding conserve on the time and energy needed to find a mate (a gain that is, as we have seen, more important for some species than for others), it also facilitates the cohabitation of a territory shared by the same species: having already formed pairs, the members of such species need not go to war with one another over sexual claims.

SOCIAL LIFE AND ADAPTATION

Fricke contends that fish species that have developed social lives, whether by schooling, maintaining colonies, or forming pairs, have taken an important evolutionary step. They have made it easier to achieve reproductive success, and so have increased the chances for their own survival. He speculates that social animals may begin by being merely territorial and then create out of this attachment to a site more complicated patterns of interaction, including pair bonding, harems, and dominance hierarchies.

What is remarkable about fishes is that this development has occurred despite the general absence of any nurturing of the young and thus in the absence of both an incentive (to protect the young) to create social systems and an opportunity (a period of dependence on parents) for learning how the social system operates.

However it is achieved, the complex social lives of fishes help to explain why to the diver a reef so often seems to be a peaceable kingdom. Most reef inhabitants go about their routine business without apparent concern. Much of this orderliness stems from the knowledge reef neighbors have about one another. A schooling fish relies on its neighbor to warn it of danger and to confuse, by its movements, an attacking predator. An opportunistic fish, such as a yellow goatfish, will know with which species it can forage and with which it cannot. The territorial fishes are well known to their neighbors, which will either observe the territorial boundaries or figure out how to circumvent them. Dominance hierarchies among colonial fishes permit each member to know its assigned place; if a disagreement breaks out, it is quickly settled by ritual displays or an occasional bump or bite.

Knowing the rules of a reef community permits the dense and diverse population found there to live together with a minimum of energy devoted to defense and conflict. And this in turn means that the resources of a reef can be parceled out in the most economical way among the inhabitants of its various niches.

CHAPTER EIGHT

Territoriality

A diver watching fishes will soon discover a puzzle. He will search long and hard for a big fish—a grouper, for example—but often without success, and when he finds one, it will quickly move away, often a great distance. If pursued, the grouper will retreat into a hole in the reef, where it will cower, obviously fearful of the diver. But the diver will have no difficulty finding the small damselfishes (see Plate 34). They are abundant on most reefs, racing about over a small area and holding their ground before the advances of even the largest diver. If the diver gets too close, the damselfish will attack, darting at the diver, nipping at his body with what, by damselfish standards, must be regarded as extraordinary bravery and ferocity. Only when the diver is close enough to touch the fish will it move away to a hiding place, but even then its refuge will be temporary and only a foot or so away from the diver.

The grouper may weigh thirty or forty pounds (indeed, the larger the fish, the more fearful it seems to be) and is capable of inflicting, should it choose to attack, a nasty wound. Even the barracuda, though more willing to linger in the presence of divers, will move away if the diver approaches, despite its awesome jaw with rows of razor-sharp teeth. The damselfish, by contrast, weighs only a few ounces and is incapable of inflicting any injury at all. Despite this, it is fearless.

Every diver has seen this sharply contrasting behavior, and most divers offer the same explanation for it. The damselfish is territorial; the grouper is not. But to use the word "territorial" is merely to describe the behavior we have seen, not to explain it. What we want to know is why one fish clings, at great risk to itself, to a fixed territory and why another, much more able to defend a territory if it chose, flees from an intruder. Nor is that the whole of the puzzle. Why is it that the damselfish is able to drive off other fishes that approach its territory even when those others are much larger and stronger than itself? We might discount the bravery of the damselfish confronting a diver on the grounds that divers rarely, if ever, harm or capture damselfishes and the damselfish knows this. But if it knows this, it cannot be ignorant of the fact that other fishes are not so benign and regularly eat smaller fishes. Yet the damselfish stands its ground, successfully, against almost all comers. A single dusky damselfish *(Stegastes dorsopunicans = Eupomacentrus dorsopunicans)* has often been observed to turn a foraging school of hundreds of surgeonfish, striped parrotfish, blue tangs, goatfishes, hamlets, and others by advancing sideways and blanching its color.

To explain this puzzle, we must begin by getting a clearer idea of what is meant by territoriality. A good place to begin is with our own sense of territory as it is manifested in everyday life. We are territorial in the strictest definition of the term when we stake a claim to a particular area and are willing to defend it against intruders. Say the area is a homesite. If it is small—perhaps a city lot—we know very well its precise boundaries, and they are usually also obvious to neighbors and passersby, delineated by fences, driveways, hedges, or the like. If the homesite is larger—perhaps a farm or ranch—we still are quite aware of the extent of our ownership, although now the outer limits may not be so obvious to others. Generally, if someone camps on our property without permission or digs a well to take water from our land, we are not pleased. Transgressions violate our sense of property. Still, we welcome friends and neighbors on our own terms, and whereas we might not look kindly on a stray cow treating our lawn as pasture, we do not take seriously the intrusion of a wandering cat or two. We make distinctions, usually, between well-meaning intruders and those whose intentions are suspect or run counter to our own interests. While abroad, we might stake out temporary territories for, say, a picnic on a crowded beach and look askance at later comers with less "legitimate" claims. Or we might join with others in sharing a seasonal recreational area such as a country club golf course, but tolerate winter sledders and skiers when it is not in use. With varying degrees of intensity we are apt to entertain territorial feelings about our communities and our countries. Of course we may disagree with one another about the meaning of those feelings and ways to maintain them, but for the most part we are able to agree enough on substantive matters of territory so that in our ordinary lives we have a certain stability to our expectations.

Beneath the waters—down on the reef—life is not so different for a great number of creatures. Since snorkel and scuba have brought us face to face with the coral world, we now know that most, if not all, reef fishes attach themselves for one purpose or another and for varying lengths of time to particular spaces. Many spend their entire adult lives attached to relatively small sites of a cubic meter or two in which they find food, take shelter, and reproduce. Some defend these sites with impressive tenacity and with a broad range of behaviors: behaviors sometimes ritualized in complicated patterns. Others loosely defend larger areas. Most, perhaps all, territorial fishes recognize what are to them benign neighbors and reserve their aggressive actions for known competitors, either of their own or another species or both. Depending on their ecological niche on the reef—their particular combination of biological needs—they are permanent or seasonal territorials and their concept of property, like ours, may vary from strict definitions to apparently loosely held opinions, according to the situation.

A body of scholarly literature is slowly growing as reef studies worldwide yield monograph after monograph about the observed behavior of territorial fishes. The accumulated data support various hypotheses about the function territoriality serves for its practitioners, what biologists call "adaptive significance." In the beginning, before scuba made observation more accurate, territoriality in fishes was often thought to be primarily intraspecific, that is, practiced among members of the same species. Competition was thought to be a cutthroat evolutionary race for Darwinian survival. If, for example, one is a bluehead wrasse *(Thalassoma bifasciatum)*, one's best efforts ought to be directed to making sure one is *the* bluest-headed, fattest-bellied, strongest, handsomest, most reproductively desirable blue-head in the neighborhood. But that explanation, though it accounts for much of fish behavior, does not account for all. The damselfish defending its territory is not in any obvious way enhancing its chances for mating, because much of its defensive behavior is aimed, not at other damselfishes, but at other species. Moreover, this explanation would include the grouper in the category of territorial fishes; after all, though it flees quickly to the shelter of a coral cave, it will defend that cave, if not against man, then against other fishes that might want to use it.

To understand territoriality among fishes, we must first understand that it is much commoner than we first supposed (damselfishes are obviously territorial, but other fishes are territorial in ways that are harder to observe) and that it serves several different functions. For some fishes, a territory is important as a source of food, for others as a place of refuge, and for still others as an aid to reproduction. For many fishes, territoriality may serve all three of these functions, and for some especially interesting ones, the need for a territory and the purpose it serves change over the life cycle. Since the study of fish behavior in natural settings is still in its infancy, we cannot be confident that we know all the various uses to which fishes may put a territory. Even with what we already know, it is clear that any rigid classification of fishes based on types of territoriality would be mistaken. But to explain the puzzle with which we started and to simplify for the reader the bewildering variety of behavior he will encounter while watching fishes, it is useful to discuss three functions that territory may serve: protecting food, providing security, and aiding reproduction, illustrating each with examples drawn from fishes commonly encountered while diving. Then we can consider how some fishes use territories for one, two, or all three of these purposes and how others change, over the course of their lives, the uses to which territory is put. Then we may be in a position to offer some educated guesses as to why territoriality works—why, that is, a small fish can drive off a larger, stronger one.

FARMING

Threespot damselfish *(Stegastes planifrons = Eupomacentrus planifrons)*, among the most abundant species belonging to the damselfish family and frequently encountered throughout the Caribbean, are farmers.

They eat algae that grow on or amidst coral, especially staghorn *(Acropora cervicornis)* and star coral *(Montastrea annularis)*. Each threespot cultivates a small algal crop about one-tenth of a square yard in size. It vigorously defends this crop against intruders, especially sea urchins, which move slowly about on rocks and coral, bristling their protective spines and digesting the algae in their paths. Both the male and the female threespot are territorial, but not chiefly against each other. Although, as we shall see, territory may serve a number of functions for them, its chief value is as a source of food, which must be protected (mostly) against nondamselfishes.

A threespot spends much energy patrolling its farm. Like most species of damselfishes, it will move around the boundaries of its territory, turning sharp corners and unflaggingly retracing its route over and over again. A diver might wish to use the techniques of marine biologists and mark the edges of a damselfish territory with small colored weights (painted nuts or bolts, for example) so as to get an exact sense of what the fish regards as its property lines. Constantly alert, the damselfish will react to the presence of an intruder with frontal or lateral displays: by erecting its fins, striking postures, making popping or clicking sounds, and swimming rapidly parallel to the route of the invader. If these displays do not produce a retreat, more drastic measures are employed: the intruder is attacked and bitten. During all this, the damselfish may change color. The intruder almost always yields.

These defensive maneuvers, according to Ronald E. Thresher, a longtime observer of threespots, are directed at other species about 95 percent of the time and occur about once every six minutes. None is more impressive than the attacks of the threespots on sea urchins. Ann Houston Williams spent a year at the Discovery Bay Marine Laboratory in Jamaica watching threespots deal with urchin intruders. As the urchins advanced, waving spines that, as every diver knows, will easily pierce not only skin but protective clothing, the threespot damselfish attacked, biting off the spinal tips. In dealing with short-spined urchins, the fish sometimes grasped the sturdier tips and carried them out of their territories.

The territory defended by the threespot damselfish is quite small. But its relative, the cocoa damselfish *(Stegastes variabilis = Eupomacentrus variabilis)*, will exercise some degree of control over a much larger territory. This fish, extensively studied in Florida waters by Ann Gronell White while at the University of Miami, is called home ranging because it ranges out from a stoutly defended core territory to larger grazing territories along pathways that it also defends. The whole range may encompass seven square yards or more. Its size reflects the diet of the fish. Unlike the threespots, the cocoa damselfish does not maintain an algal lawn but instead harvests algae where it finds it and feeds on small, soft-bodied invertebrates such as sponges, anemones, tunicates, and polychaete worms as well. This diet necessitates a large feeding range, which cannot be defended as intensely or as successfully as the core territory where the cocoa damselfish lives and breeds. As a result, the cocoa damselfish has to be content with defending the pathways to the grazing areas (as well as the core). If threespot damselfish are farmers, cocoa damselfish are hunters and gatherers for whom free passage is as important as secure home boundaries. The great enemy of the cocoa damselfish is the blue tang because it, along with some other surgeonfishes and porgies, competes with the cocoas for food.

Although both males and females will engage in these protective efforts, in the case of the threespots a dominance hierarchy emerges with the males on top and the strongest males at the very top, so that these preferred males get to work the best farms and inhabit the choicest niches. The less preferred males are always looking for a chance to upgrade their resources. Thus, intraspecific territorial disputes will occur, but since dominance hierarchies tend to be stable over time, most display posturing and fighting behavior will be directed at other creatures, especially the sea urchin.

These dominance hierarchies are part of a larger and more complex social organization. Although damselfishes create and patrol individual boundaries, their proximity to and relationship with other damselfishes seem to be important to them. Wherever one damselfish is found, other damselfish are almost surely nearby. This tendency to live in colonies has been described by Murray Itzkowitz and by Thresher, who have done extensive field experiments with them, as have other marine biologists. While threespot territories are unmistakably individual in their boundaries, the fish prefer group living and dwell in populous colonies, often among protective staghorn branches. Field experiments by Itzkowitz in which staghorn patches were artificially moved near existing colonies of threespots demonstrated that individual adults homesteaded a new territory only if it were sufficiently close to an established colony, preferably within a yard or so. As the artificially created habitats were gradually moved farther and farther away, willingness to occupy new territories quickly declined to zero. The threespots' preference for colonial living and the consequent familiarity of neighbors enables them to conserve energy in defending their sites against one another, saving strength for dealing with intruders of other species, particularly food competitors and also wrasses, some of which are infamous egg eaters.

Periodically individual threespots engage in what Itzkowitz terms forays, leaving their own niches and swimming relatively long distances around their colonies at a leisurely pace, apparently looking for more desirable spaces. In this way smaller fish—juveniles ready to claim territories—find vacant areas and establish themselves. Stronger, more mature subadults on a foray may find a poorly defended territory and test its occupant. In this ritualized way they attempt to better their position in the colony, working their properties inward, if possible, to safer shelters. Peripheral dwellers, more vulnerable to competitors and predators, were observed to be more nervous about their domains than the more secure inner residents of the complicated staghorn growth, attacking would-be intruders at as much as three times as great a distance as elicited a chase from dominant threespots.

In experiments exploring the ability of threespot damselfish to recognize other species, Thresher concluded after testing the role of hearing, vision, and smell that visual cues were by far the most critical for the fish. Territorial defense has to be rapid and consistent if it is to be effective, and the dynamics of odor and sound in a fluid world, affected as they are by surge, current, and noise, would render quick responses uncertain. Further tests led Thresher to hypothesize that threespots probably respond primarily to form rather than color, since many closely related fishes vary considerably in color but have similar shapes (the role of color remains in question).

In the Sea of Cortez lives a damselfish for which the communal element of territoriality is particularly important. The Cortez damselfish *(Stegastes rectifraenum = Eupomacentrus rectifraenum),* like their Caribbean cousins, are algae farmers that vigorously defend their crops. But unlike the threespots, their defensive maneuvers are not entirely individual. Thresher has observed a phenomenon he calls clustering. Periodically, up to a dozen Cortez damselfish leave their territories and mill about together, engaging in a pattern of short chases, parallel swimming, and mild displays but never during clustering exhibiting more extreme aggressive behavior such as frontal displays and biting. Nor did Thresher ever observe any courtship activity involved at these times. Clustering usually was accompanied by a color change: the damselfish assumed a bicolor pattern, paling from a normal gray-brown to a vertical division of a light anterior and dark posterior, a change that occasionally affects individuals at other times, for example when being pursued by attackers.

Most clusters are apparently of spontaneous origin, starting when one Cortez damselfish assumes a bicoloration and rises one or two feet off the bottom, swimming in a jerking motion toward a neighbor. This stimulates several other nearby fish of its species (conspecifics) to do the same, and a cluster results. Thresher found that Cortez damselfish within a meter of the initiator always join in and those up to three meters away usually do, but beyond such distances damsels are unlikely to participate. An artificial stimulus can sometimes produce a cluster, such as a rock dropped or a snorkeler passing over. Lasting about 90 seconds, clustering is always more intense during crepuscular periods—just after dawn and at dusk—and seldom occurs during the middle of the day. (The deeper the water, the longer the peaks of activity observed around the crepuscular periods, suggesting that bright light levels may inhibit clustering.) Miles Keenleyside reported similar clustering behavior among the Great Barrier Reef damselfish, *Abudefduf zonatus.*

Not enough research has been reported to make possible strong conclusions about the function of clustering, but it seems to serve as a kind of mild boundary-defining and exploratory behavior similar to the solitary foraying expeditions of the threespot damselfish. Thresher suggests that its major benefit may be in providing an opportunity for aggressive neighbors to become and remain familiar with one another, a habituation resulting in what has been termed "dear enemies": fishes that can reserve their energies for attacking strangers while still making clear on the home front that they are established property owners.

A larger underwater farmer is the bluelined surgeonfish *(Acanthurus lineatus).* Although most of the surgeonfishes a diver will see are found in schools, some are territorial, defending feeding areas from four to twelve yards square. Found in Indo-Pacific waters, the bluelined surgeon has specialized dietary requirements that render it dependent on high-density algal mats. Such mats grow in exposed areas, but are not all that common, and they appeal to a wide range of fishes. The bluelined species has evolved a territorial strategy that, like that of threespot damselfish, has a colonial basis. Bluelineds maintain continuous territories, which they ritually defend against one another but which as a colony apparently make defense against foraging groups of other species more effective.

J. R. Nursall has described blueline territorial behavior. This surgeon regularly patrols against intrusions of other species as well as by its conspecifics and maintains a well-developed scale of aggressive actions to discourage trespassing. All these actions are accompanied by color change, a substantial darkening of their normally blue and golden shades. If routine patrolling and watching are inadequate measures in discouraging others of its species, the bluelined surgeon engages in circling, involving close-range head-to-tail chases with each fish trying to nip the tail of the other, often resulting in satisfactory separation and a return to individual property. Circling between two bluelines might also terminate in a parallel run over neutral territory. Parallel swimming is one of the most notable aggressive rituals, involving high speeds, raised dorsal fins, intensified coloration, coordinated directional turns, and rapid shaking of tails and fins, perhaps with the sharp caudal spines (the "scalpels" that give surgeonfishes their name) involved (see drawing below). Consistently, parallel swimming ends with abrupt turns away from each other.

Parallel swimming patterns of territorial blueline surgeonfish *(Acanthurus lineatus)*. (After Nursall, 1974.)

Chasing, or head-to-tail flight, on the other hand, is less ritualized in character and usually results when one of the fish becomes dominant while circling or from a simple intrusion by any fish. Sometimes chases begin without apparent warning, a surgeonfish rushing several yards in a straight path toward a transgressor, often a parrotfish, and perhaps continuing well beyond territorial boundaries. If the offending fish outdistances the defender, the chase ends, of course, but if it seeks shelter in the corals, it often provokes a distinctive harrying behavior on the part of the surgeon. A blueline chaser may attempt to nip the fish in its shelter or to enter its refuge; it may circle with head downward above the shelter in a conical pattern or it may engage in a lateral display at the entrance, flaunting its dorsal fin and flicking its tail toward the opening. Since the harried fish is apt to reappear when the surgeonfish moves away, the threatening procedure may recur. Indeed, Nursall recorded an extraordinarily persistent harassment of a damselfish *(Pomacentrus apicalis)* that was bullied by a blueline for fourteen days! It ended in the disappearance of the damselfish and the subsequent division of the spoils of its territory by two neighboring territorials of differing damselfish species, neither of which was paid heed by the victorious blueline.

Plankton-eating fairy basslets *(Gramma loreto)* are territorial gatherers, rather than farmers. They form small hierarchical communities in which the largest fish is dominant, never moving far from the shelter of vertical stands of coral. Led by the dominant basslet, each community defends its section of plankton-bearing current by chasing away certain rival planktivores.

SAFETY

All fishes are concerned for their safety, and all reef fishes make some use of territory for ensuring their safety; indeed, that is one important reason they *are* reef fishes, rather than free-ranging. The fact that some fishes dive into holes when frightened may not, however, strike us as a particularly important example of territoriality, since to a frightened fish, one hole may be as good as another, and the closer the better. But the choice of hiding places for many species is neither random nor dictated entirely by proximity.

The importance of having a specific and regularly defended hiding place is evident among fishes that most divers do not consider territorial at all. The blue chromis *(Chromis cyanea)*, a familiar sight on almost any Caribbean dive, is a kind of damselfish that, unlike threespots, is usually seen in huge aggregations made up not only of other blue chromises but of brown chromises *(Chromis multilineata)* and creole wrasses *(Clepticus parrai)* as well. This trio of species eats plankton and feeds in the open waters at varying depths a few feet off the reef, where currents make for richer nutrients. Although blue chromises appear to be frequent schoolers, each individual is quite specifically attached to a permanent hiding place in the reef, which it uses as a bedroom at night and as a refuge from predators whenever the need arises. The hiding place entrance is invariably of a size to exclude larger fishes and has more than one escape route. In contrast, the brown chromis, which also hides at night, is not site-attached and may or may not end up in a well-concealed haven, depending on the luck of the draw. Thus, the brown chromis is more frequently found by researchers in the stomach contents of predators than is the blue chromis. In a long-term study (three and one-half years) of the blue chromis on the reefs at Curaçao, Netherlands Antilles, Bart A. de Boer of the Caribbean Marine Biological Institute observed that male blue chromises maintained permanent territories adjacent to their hiding places, extending over the bottom a few feet and rising into the water column a yard or so. Nests were made within these areas, either in sand or in algae, usually as close to the hiding place as feasible. The total area of the territory, however, was found by de Boer to vary in relation to the distance over which neighboring males could be *seen.* The more vertical obstacles on the reef to obscure the vision of a neighbor, the more dense the population tended to be. Open, patchy reefs seemed to make the defending fish more uncomfortable and thus induced it to claim a larger space. Out of sight, out of mind.

For no fish is safety a more important consideration in defining a territory than for the clownfishes (the twenty-six or more species of *Amphiprion* in the family Pomacentridae). Discussed more fully in Chapter 9, on symbiosis, the clownfishes of the Red Sea, the Pacific, and the Indo-Pacific live in anemones whose tentacles will sting and even kill other fishes. The clownfish, however, is protected by mucus that coats its body and when threatened can take refuge in the (to it) protective tentacles. It would not have to do this were it a better swimmer, able to take evasive action or to retreat swiftly to nooks and holes in the reef. But it is a terrible swimmer (by fish standards), and hence it rarely ventures more than a short distance from its anemone home.

REPRODUCTION

Damselfishes acquire reproductive as well as food benefits from their farming territories, but for the bluehead wrasse *(Thalassoma bifasciatum)* territory is defended almost entirely for mating purposes. This small fish is a common resident of the Caribbean. As an adult, it may pass through two color phases. The yellow phase is the commonest. Sometimes these fish have a black stripe along their sides and sometimes a row of dark blotches that rapidly change from one color to another.

Many of the male yellows become blueheads in a second phase of their adult lives, thereby becoming known as terminal-phase male bluehead wrasses. These blueheads are larger than yellow-stage wrasses, and their heads are set off from their blue-green bodies by a pale band outlined on either side by a contrasting black bar. These terminal-phase blueheads are the only males that are territorial. Whereas yellow-phase males spawn with females in large, milling groups, terminal-phase blueheads mate singly with one individual at a time in territories specially set aside for the purpose. They spawn daily, usually between 11 A.M. and 2 P.M. at the down-current edge of the reef.

These territories are established because of the intense competition among male blueheads. Their behavior has been studied by several marine biologists. Terminal-phase blueheads set up temporary spawning sites along the outer rim of the reef, waiting for females, who attempt to mate with the largest males. Smaller yellow-phase males mill about just inshore, sometimes by the hundreds, creating a zone females must first pass through to reach the desirable blueheads. Here they chase and court. If not overstimulated by the sexual advances in these aggregations, a female will delay her spawning even though opportunities exist all about her in order to mate with a bluehead.

Once a territorial male entertains a mate the spawning rite consists of an upward rush of both fish, culminating in the release of eggs and milt about a yard above the coral or rocky bottom. A yellow-phase male may even then attempt to sneak in and deposit his own sperm or to induce the female to mate with him instead. The bluehead is usually successful in repelling such audacity, breaking off courtship for the while and vigorously defending his space with lateral displays and chases, fins stiffly erect. Bigger blueheads are estimated to spawn in this way more than forty times daily, as compared with an average of twice daily by the smaller territorials, whereas females spawn only once daily, figures that demonstrate the reproductive success of the dominant territorials.

THE MANY FUNCTIONS OF TERRITORY

Territory serves many purposes for some fishes. Even in the cases already mentioned of specific uses of territory, such as the farming threespots, the fishes also derive reproductive and safety advantages from their territories. But the efforts made by some fishes to develop the many benefits of a territory are especially remarkable. They deliberately improve their properties so as to maximize the value of that property for security, food, and reproduction.

The garibaldi damselfish *(Hypsypops rubicundus),* bright orange inhabitants of the coastal waters off southern California and Baja California, are some of the most enduringly territorial of all fishes. And their long life span (fish twelve years old have been reported) testifies to the benefits of successfully managing space. After the fish matures at age five to six, it will maintain a permanent territory that includes a shelter, a nesting site, and a grazing area in which it searches for the invertebrates that make up its diet.

The nest of the garibaldi is very special. It takes the male two years or more to cultivate the nest as he carefully nurtures a patch of small red algae. Once established, the patch is regularly trimmed every March to a height of from two to four centimeters in preparation for breeding. The garibaldi clears the nest of detritus and extraneous growth and fiercely defends it while eggs are present during the late spring to early fall spawning season. After the eggs have hatched the garibaldi allows himself a bit of relaxation, letting the nest overgrow, sometimes even permitting another species, the flatfish *Pleuronichthys coenosus,* to rest on it. The garibaldi remains, however, strict about his territorial boundaries, which expressly define an area of a few square yards. When breeding season rolls around again, the same nest is recultivated.

So much value does the nest site have that should the owner die or be removed in some way, the territorial successor will not choose a new nest but carefully cultivates the existing one. Nests pass from generation to generation.

Thomas A. Clarke, who has studied the garibaldis extensively, observes that their territories tend to be contiguous and that aggression between one garibaldi and another is unusual along their mutual borders. Neighboring garibaldis habitually graze peacefully near their common property lines as close as five to six inches to each other. They do practice, however, a ritualistic behavior that is probably designed to reinforce the concept of their spatial claims: jaw-locking.

Often, when two neighbors meet at a boundary, they face each other head on, beating their caudal fins rapidly, and about one-third of the time, Clarke estimates, end in coming together and physically locking their jaws for up to fifteen seconds. This is not accompanied by any particularly agitated behavior, and when concluded, the garibaldis slowly back away from each other and resume their ordinary routines. Perhaps they are also "dear enemies."

This calls to mind the ceremonial boundary behavior of California sea lions during their mating season. On the shores of channel islands bulls maintain contiguous territories and frequently rush barking toward one another, falling down on their chests with mouths open just short of encounter; they then shake their heads from side to side while weaving their necks back and forth at a rate slower than the head shaking. Finally they sit up high, turning their heads and staring sidewise at one another—all the while avoiding physical contact. Violent conflicts do occur, but these result from challenges by a direct, silent intrusion by the aggressor.

In another ritualized action similar to that of Cortez damselfish, garibaldis engage in a clustering activity, involving sometimes as many as eight nest-keeping males. Their clusters last several minutes and end with a return to respective territories. Aggressive acts are more commonly reserved for alien species, notably some bottom-grazing fishes, whereas a few predatory fishes are often tolerated and plankton feeders usually ignored. Regardless of species, however, males become very touchy during mating season.

The value of territory may change over the life cycle of a fish. The striped parrotfish *(Scarus iserti = S. croicensis)* is sequentially hermaphroditic; that is, over its life it changes from one sex to another. Individuals at birth may be of either sex, but as the females age they change sex, culminating in the large terminal male (or supermale) with a dramatic new coloration.

The social hierarchy of this species is complicated and not fully understood (except perhaps by striped parrotfish) but fascinating to contemplate. Striped parrotfish are the commonest of west Atlantic scarids. Like other parrotfishes, they are herbivores, using their rasping beaks—their teeth are fused—to bite off sediment and algae-covered calcareous material, which is then ground up in their unique internal jaws. The algae is separated out for digestion and the sediment is excreted as sand. Nancy S. Buckman and John C. Ogden of the Smithsonian Tropical Research Institute have made several behavioral studies of these parrotfish and have characterized three behavioral modes exhibited by them: stationary, foraging, and territorial. In the stationary mode are both striped-phase fish and supermales; day after day, they occupy the same areas, in which they feed but which they do not defend territorially. Foraging parrotfish form large schools, sometimes up to 500 individuals, together with smaller numbers of surgeonfish, blue tangs, spotted goatfish, barred hamlets, and others (just the sort of group the dusky damselfish considers bad news for its algae crop). These foraging parrotfish migrate daily from hidden shelters to large grazing pastures of perhaps 5,000 square meters in relatively shallow waters, departing mornings soon after sunrise along specific pathways and returning by evening.

In the territorial category are small groups of either striped-phase or terminal-phase males, which do not regularly join the foraging migrations but defend areas from ten to twelve meters square in which they graze and sometimes spawn and in which a distinct dominance hierarchy can be observed. Each territory is headed by a dominant female, dubbed a yellowfin because she extends her yellow pelvic (ventral) fins during aggressive displays (a fin color almost always lacking in nonterritorial striped parrotfish). The female may be aided in defense by a terminal-phase male. He, however, is less feisty than she, usually confining his chases to nonterritorial striped parrotfish passing through, and sometimes he swims off to join a foraging migration for the day, leaving the female to fend for herself. She, interestingly, tolerates the presence of one to three additional females, who are submissive to her and who rarely help at all in boundary defense. The yellowfin is mostly concerned with intraspecific defense, daily confronting other dominant yellowfins who hold neighboring territories and often engaging in mouth-to-mouth contacts with them. Buckman and Ogden found that these territorial yellowfins did not show consistent aggression toward any other species, even those competing for food or space. Within a territory the hierarchical associations remained stable for varying periods of time, but when a fish was experimentally or naturally removed, it was quickly replaced by a new one. The experimenters concluded that this territorial behavior may be related to the sex-reversal process, a process with social incentives described in Chapter 6.

Some fishes are aided in their attachments to territory by remarkable sensory abilities. Many blennies, small bottom-dwelling fishes, are tenaciously territorial. Sue Thompson experimented with the reef-dwelling mottled blenny *(Forsterygion varium)* off the coast of northeast New Zealand, removing individuals from their individually held territories, anesthetizing them, placing them in dark bags, and transporting them by boat to various sites 50, 100, 200, 700, and 2,000 yards distant from their place of capture. She found that none of the fish displaced by 2,000 yards were resighted at their homes, but the majority of both juvenile and adult mottled blennies returned from 200-yard distances and 85 percent of the males and 60 percent of the females were able to find their territories from 700 yards. Observing many blennies from the time of release, she noted that they immediately sought cover and remained sequestered for up to an hour, and then invariably moved in the homeward direction using a series of rapid darts from refuge to refuge. Depending on the displacement distance, the fish took from thirty minutes to six days to return to their dwellings. Left undisturbed, these blennies typically spend their lives within the confines of a few yards. Their extraordinary homing ability is thus all the more impressive.

TERRITORIAL FISHES

Angelfishes (some)	(Pomacanthidae)
Blennies (some)	(Blenniidae)
Clownfishes (Anemonefishes)	(Amphiprionidae)
Damselfishes (most)	(Pomacentridae)
Gobies	(Gobiidae)
Harlequin bass, *Serranus tigrinus* (Atlantic)	(Serranidae)
Lionfishes (some)	(Scorpaenidae)
Surgeonfishes (some)	(Acanthuridae)

EXPLAINING A PUZZLE

All reef-dwelling fishes (and many invertebrates as well) are attached to sites to some degree. They have their favorite hiding places, pathways, feeding grounds, or breeding spots. But the fishes that defend their territories the most vigorously and against the heaviest odds are either herbivores (plant eaters) or omnivores (eating both plants and small animal life) and usually brood their eggs within their territories. Insofar as we now understand the matter, the heroic actions of the damselfishes are to be explained chiefly by the fact that they are defending not only themselves but their food supply and their eggs as well. Removed from its algal lawn, a threespot will not survive unless it conquers another farm. Removed from its territory, the garibaldi's progeny become prey to egg-eaters. A grouper, barracuda, or other fish eater (piscivore) need only defend itself, since it ranges over the entire reef, and perhaps into the open ocean, in search of food. If you threaten it, you threaten only *it.* It may think of you as a rival in the search for food, but it knows, apparently, that the rivalry will take place over the whole reef and will not be determined by its ability to exercise sovereignty over some small part of the reef.

Not only do the herbivores and the piscivores have different attitudes toward territory, they also have different attitudes toward night and day. The damselfish works its farm during the day, and the piscivores chiefly hunt at dawn or dusk. A damselfish need not worry about another fish eating its algae during the night since other algae-eaters are also diurnal creatures that go to bed with the sun. At night, therefore, its first concern is safety, and it retreats into its hole. During the day, it need not worry too much about bigger fishes, since the most dangerous predators tend to hunt crepuscularly or nocturnally, when the damselfish is safe in its niche.

Beyond differences in diet, differences in the capacity for self-defense help to explain territoriality. A grouper or moray need not defend its particular hole to the death, for there are plenty of other holes to which it can move, and if the present occupants don't like it, there is little they can do about it. But for a clownfish, the security of its particular anemone is vital. Lacking speed and weaponry, it cannot survive outside the safety of the anemone's tentacles; the next anemone may be a dozen yards away (a vast distance for the clownfish) and occupied to boot, and so the protection of its present anemone is a life-and-death matter. Since the clownfish can add nothing to the defensive weapons of the anemone, all it can do is cower and cling.

Reproductive habits influence territorial demands. Fishes that mill about, mating indiscriminately and dispersing their eggs directly into the currents, form no lasting pair bonds and thus have no need of a safe niche in which the male can court and win his chosen female and watch over the fertilized egg clusters.

But all this still leaves much unexplained. How is it that an algae farmer can defend its turf against an algae farmer who lacks turf? How can a small fish who already occupies a hole successfully drive away a (somewhat) larger fish that wants the hole? How is it that home-ranging damselfishes are able to protect their pathways to grazing areas? The damselfishes and the clownfishes both have good reasons for defending their territories, but against an overpoweringly large adversary, such as a diver, the damselfish will charge the intruder and the clownfish will retreat.

It is possible that some of the successes achieved by those fishes that defend territories derive from familiarity, both with one another and with established dispositions and routes. Much of the defense of territory we observe is largely ritualistic, in that no wounds are inflicted. Scent marking of territorial boundaries by wolves, leopards, and many other mammals effectively establishes boundaries for others of their species. Generally, ceremonial communication is sufficient for California sea lions to maintain their spaces. Many territorial birds rely on song patterns and aerial displays for defense. For many species, blood is seldom spilled. "Possession is nine points of the law" is a rule that seems to govern, for whatever reason, the struggle for space in many parts of the animal world.

Part of the reason why ritualistic defenses, relying on display rather than injury, may work so much of the time is that territoriality and its defense are subject to economic considerations. Territorial "rights" permit species to economize on energy; without the recognition of such claims, life would be an endless struggle of all against all that would leave few survivors. But why do fish act in ways that are optimal from the point of view of the species as a whole?

The usual explanation is that no individual damselfish figures out for itself what is "rational" for all damselfishes and then acts accordingly. Rather, when an intruding damselfish breaks off, short of inflicting an injury, combat with a damselfish already occupying a territory, the former is being guided by an invisible hand, its instinct, that minimizes warfare in ways that permit the species to exist and reproduce itself. But how does a damselfish recognize the existence of a territory occupied by another fish and what instinct leads it to defer to the occupant after only a ritualistic attack? We cannot be certain, but we do know from experiments that fishes distinguish between conspecifics who do and do not have a territory. They recognize, so to speak, property rights.

For example, sticklebacks, a small freshwater fish frequently studied by scientists, will swim peacefully together in a swarm until one has found and established a territory. The belly of that fish then turns red; if another male stickleback approaches it, the territorially based fish will attack. The intruder typically backs off. To show how strong and precise this sense of territory can be, Niko Tinbergen placed two male sticklebacks that had established territories in separate glass tubes so that they could be moved about while still in their habitat. If male *a* was in its own territory and male *b* was brought near it, *a* would try to attack *b* through the walls of the tube, and *b* would try to flee. But if *b* was in its territory and *a* was brought near it, *b* would mount an attack and *a* would try to flee.

This sense of ownership is found throughout the animal world. H. Kummer placed two male baboons, previously unknown to each other, in an enclosure, with one of them, *a,* confined to a cage and the other, *b,* free to roam about. Then a female baboon was set loose in the enclosure. Male *b* quickly established his ownership over her. When male *a* was released from his cage, he acknowledged *b*'s claims and made no move to obtain access to the female. Two weeks later, Kummer repeated the same experiment, but now with male *a* free and male *b* confined. When a new female entered the enclosure, *a* claimed her and *b,* when released from the cage, did not contest *a*'s ownership. Baboons, like sticklebacks and damselfish, recognize property claims.

These experiments, and others like them, have suggested to some theoretical biologists, such as J. Maynard Smith, that there may be, in addition to instincts developed by evolution, some element of rational calculation and adaptive learning going on among individual animals, a calculation that reflects to some degree the differences between members in how vigorously they are prepared to fight. None of this should seem strange to us. Think how vigorously we behave when we feel we have a right to a threatened toy, place in line, or girlfriend or boyfriend, even when the person challenging us is larger and stronger. And recall how frequently people who could take these things from us retreat when we bristle. Now compare that behavior, and that of the bully, to how we and our rival act when we are racing to get a toy, place in line, or friend that no one has yet claimed. Unclaimed territory can bring us to shouts and blows, and now the bigger and stronger person is much more likely to succeed. We often suppose that such differences in behavior are only learned by humans having the power of speech and living in complex societies with elaborate rules and law-enforcement machinery. But we should pause and reflect on how similar such conduct is to a damselfish defending, successfully, its patch of algae against a bigger, stronger fish.

CHAPTER NINE

Symbiosis

$\mathcal{A}$nyone who believes that the underwater world is an arena of universal and ceaseless predation will be surprised when he comes upon his first cleaning station. There, atop a coral head, one might find a large grouper, motionless, its mouth open and its gills spread, with tiny gobies and wrasses swimming in and out of its fearsome jaw, sometimes continuing into the throat and out through the gill slits, busily removing tiny parasites that afflict the larger fish but provide tasty morsels for the smaller ones. With one swallow, the grouper would have a meal—or at least a snack—and yet the mouth never closes on the cleaners, which continue their work until the grouper, satisfied, swims slowly away and another fish takes its place in the station. Everywhere else, fishes watch piscivorous species warily, reacting to the slightest sign of an aggressive move, but here, at the cleaning station, all seems peaceful with the fishes being cleaned, or waiting to be cleaned, lined up much like automobiles at a car wash.

A cleaning station is but one example, albeit the most dramatic one, of symbiosis, which means "living together." Symbiotic relationships can be found throughout the animal kingdom but are especially common in the densely settled habitats of the tropical reef. Each member of such a relation is called a symbiont. When both partners benefit, as is the case with the groupers who have parasites removed and the wrasses and gobies for which the parasites are a meal, the symbiosis is called mutualism. If one partner must be in a symbiotic relationship in order to survive, it is an obligatory symbiont; if a partner gets some benefit from the relationship but could survive without it, it is a facultative symbiont. Commensals are symbionts that live together without harming each other, sometimes sharing food resources. Parasites are symbionts that are generally understood to take advantage of their hosts in a harmful or debilitating way.

PROTECTION

An example of protective symbiosis that is virtually unique and especially beautiful is that between the clownfishes (or anemonefishes), which belong to the genus *Amphiprion* of the damselfish family (Pomacentridae), and various anemones, principally of the genera *Stoichactis* and *Radianthus* (see Plate 42). Damselfishes are found worldwide in tropical and semitropical shallows, but the twenty-six recognized species of the genus *Amphiprion* live only in the Indo-Pacific; there are none on Atlantic reefs. The beautiful flowerlike anemones are carnivorous animals. Although zooplankton makes up part of the anemones' diet, their tentacles can also kill small fishes on contact and then convey the prey with impressive efficiency to their centrally located mouths.

But anemones do not kill the clownfishes and somehow the clownfishes know that they will not be harmed. Indeed, they make the anemones their homes, nestling down among the—to others— lethal tentacles, where they enjoy protection against possible predators. Until recently, scientists did not know what protected the clownfishes, and they still do not know what genetic signals or early experiences tell the clownfishes that they not only can find a safe habitat in the anemones' tentacles, but must if they are to survive in the marine environment. A clownfish is a poor swimmer with no defensive weapons save its immunity to the anemone's sting. Without its host, the fish most surely will be eaten.

Even more remarkable than the knowledge the fish has of its immunity is the knowledge it has that this immunity must be activated by a specific procedure. The anemone's toxin is delivered by stinging cells, called nematocysts, on its tentacles. The clownfish must acclimate itself to the nematocysts. This it does in a period of a few minutes to several hours in a series of undulating approaches by the fish to the tentacles. The fish repeatedly nibbles at the tentacles and presents its pelvic fins and tail briefly to the anemone, is stung, retreats, and reapproaches. Some sort of change in the mucus coating of the fish occurs during this process that renders it immune to the toxin of the anemone.

Over the years, Richard M. Mariscal has conducted extensive research in several oceans as well as in aquariums and surmises the change occurs in one of two ways. Either the fish, stimulated by contact with the anemone, alters its mucus coating by some internal physiological means or it changes its coating by acquiring some of the anemone's mucus. It has generally been thought that the latter is the case, that the clownfishes coat themselves with anemone mucus, thereby confusing the anemone nematocysts and preventing their discharge. However, recent experiments by W. R. Brooks and Mariscal suggest that the fishes are able to alter their own mucus coats in some way. Brooks and Mariscal simulated an anemone using pieces of rubber bands secured together. Anemonefish *(Amphiprion clarkii)* oriented to the surrogate anemones in the same manner as they do toward real ones. After being with the surrogate anemones these anemonefish took only one-seventh the time to acclimate to real anemones as did other *A. clarkii* that had not been with the simulated anemones, suggesting that the fish alter their own mucus coatings.

What is known is that if separation between the anemone and the clownfishes occurs for longer than about twenty-four hours, the fishes must go through the acclimation process again in order to enjoy immunity from the nematocysts. In laboratory experiments removal of small patches of mucus from the body of a fish results in the fish being stung in the uncoated area.

Once the clownfish establishes itself in its anemone host it derives the great benefit of protection. Most species of *Amphiprion* become fiercely territorial and remain permanently with their anemone partners, never straying more than a yard or so. When we have finned around a coral head and startled an anemonefish, we have seen frantic headlong dashes by the fish into the carpet of tentacles, accompanied by vigorous thrashing and nuzzling until the stimulated anemone enfolds its small partner almost entirely. Closer approach engenders intensified fluttering. In our marine tank we have watched at dusk our clownfish fluff up the folds of its anemone as if it were a hyperactive child in a down featherbed and, once secure, become pale and motionless for the night. Many times while cleaning the tank we have been repeatedly nipped by the clownfish when our hands violated the anemone's territorial boundaries.

Besides enjoying protection from its enemies the clownfish feeds on portions of the anemone's prey and waste material and may possibly receive resistance to various diseases. It has not been established that the sea anemone benefits from the clownfish's association, although in the course of defending their anemone territories from other fishes, clownfishes have been observed to drive off fishes (certain butterfly fishes and wrasses) that prey on anemones, and it is speculated that the clownfish aids the anemone by removing waste material from its surface, by occasionally depositing bits of food in it, and possibly by removing parasites from it. Since the anemonefish apparently has little chance of survival without an anemone home and, indeed, is never seen long without one, it is an obligatory symbiont; the anemone, while perhaps deriving benefits from the association, nevertheless can flourish without the fish and is consequently a facultative symbiont.

A few other species of Pomacentridae live in the protective tentacles of anemones in relationships similar to those of clownfishes, mostly as juveniles but also as adults. Like the clownfishes, they are able to acclimate themselves to the toxic tentacles. Sometimes they are found in a community arrangement, living in the same commodious anemone along with clownfish. These are some of the humbug damselfishes, such as *Dascyllus aruanus, D. trimaculatus,* and *D. albisella.* They are, however, facultative associates, not dependent on the anemones. Rather, they frequently make their homes in the protective branches of certain finger corals.

Occasionally, one finds fishes other than a clownfish or a humbug in or near anemones. They are not necessarily immune to the anemone's toxin. More than thirty species of Caribbean reef fishes have been found occasionally associated with anemones, primarily the anemone *Condylactis gigantea,* and the list of anemone associates in all oceans will undoubtedly grow as further field observations take place. Most of these fishes are juvenile facultative associates using the anemone for protection and must themselves carefully avoid being stung, but a few species of blennies (family Clinidae) are apparently able, like the clownfishes, to live as adults in contact with the anemone tentacles (see Plate 40). Cardinalfishes, which are nocturnal and thus do not ordinarily swim about during the day, will sometimes shelter in anemones, such as *Bartholomea annulata,* rather than in a coral hole and take refuge amidst its tentacles, being careful not to let the tentacles touch it. Some wrasses, gobies, and blennies do the same. It is a delicate maneuver, akin to a person hiding himself in a field of poison ivy. Everything is fine unless, by a careless move, an accident happens. And for fishes, as for people, accidents do happen. Patrick Colin and John B. Heiser have speculated that the occasional use by cardinalfishes of anemones for protection may be an evolutionary forerunner of a true symbiotic relationship involving the fishes acquiring immunity to the toxin. A diver who sees a cardinalfish in an anemone may possibly be witnessing a trial and error approach toward a lasting behavioral change.

Other underwater creatures also enter into symbiotic relationships with anemones for protection, including certain shrimps and crabs. Divers in the West Indies traversing sandy strips with scattered rocks and coral heads often come across the solitary ringed anemone, *Bartholomea annulata,* with one or more spotted cleaner shrimps *(Periclimenes yucatanicus)* or Pederson shrimps *(P. pedersoni).* If the diver disturbs the anemone, it retracts, taking its shrimps with it, but leaving them unharmed. These tiny, similar shrimps, neither species more than two or three inches in length, have transparent bodies patterned with longitudinal white lines set off by violet dots. Both species also live in the giant Caribbean anemone *(Condylactis gigantea),* though not together in the same one. They can be seen hanging on the side of a tentacle or sitting at its base, whipping their antennae about and advertising their readiness to clean parasites from passing fishes willing to approach close—but not too close—to the anemone (see Plate 41).

Arrow, or spider, crabs *(Stenorhynchus seticornus)* and small hermit crabs will also reside within an anemone's grasp in order to be protected from predators (see Plate 39). The difficulty with this arrangement, of course, is that being tied down to the area an anemone can guard sharply restricts the ability of the crabs to move about in search of food. Since they are scavengers, they must go where food is to be found. One way to do this is to move out at night, retreating to the anemone during the day. But a better way has been found by certain inventive crabs who have discovered how to take their anemones with them so that they will be protected wherever they go.

One kind of hermit crab *(Dardanus gemmatus)* scouts about until it finds a suitable anemone, usually of the genus *Calliactis.* By using its claws gently and rhythmically to stimulate the anemone's base, the crab induces the anemone to relax its grip on the rocky surface. The anemone is then lifted up onto the crab's shell, whereupon the crab moves off with a mobile guard securely attached to its home. Since the anemone is thereby exposed to a broader range of food by having this means of transport, we can assume it benefits as well from this symbiotic relationship.

The boxer crabs *Lybia tesselata* and *Polydectes cupulifera,* found in the Indian and Pacific oceans, respectively, waste no time on such subtleties as are involved in persuading an anemone to live on top of their shells. They simply pick up a small anemone in each claw and carry them about with them, using them for defensive purposes and as food catchers. The anemones make the crabs look as though they were wearing boxing gloves, hence their name.

Anemones are not the only source of protection on the reef. The familiar long-spine sea urchin *(Diadema antillarum)* is a protective host analogous to the anemone, its formidable weaponry providing refuge for a variety of marine creatures. On any given dive where *Diadema* are about, close inspection usually reveals a few sea urchins harboring newly hatched mysid shrimps wiggling convulsively among their needles. In East Indian waters *Diadema* shelters a species each of shrimpfish and clingfish *(Aeoliscus strigatus* and *Diademichthys deversor),* sometimes both at the same time. The latter have shapes adapted to their sanctuary, slender and elongated, and fit themselves among the urchin's spines head down. Indeed, the scientific name of the clingfish, *Diademichthys deversor,* derives from its prickly habitat and indicates it as an obligatory symbiont. In its evolutionary development it must have opted early on for safety over adventure. Somewhere along the way it also developed a taste for the tube feet of *Diadema,* among other things, for they have been found in stomach content analyses of the clingfish. Its symbiosis borders on the parasitical.

Even sponges, though they lack any weaponry, can provide protection for certain creatures. A sponge contains many hard, sharp spicules—bits of calcium—that are hard for most fishes to digest, and these make the inside of a sponge or under it a safe refuge for whatever can live there. Sponge crabs place living sponges onto the back of their shell and carry them about for life, achieving both concealment and protection. A diver may encounter these symbionts during night dives, when the crabs become active, creating an otherwise inexplicable sight: a walking sponge.

Small fishes, shrimps, crabs, and brittle stars live in association with sponges, not only for protection but also because sponges, being filter feeders, generate currents of water that bring food into the reach of the symbionts. The brittle stars are especially dependent on sponges (see Plate 54) because they are exceptionally vulnerable to predators, notably the larger wrasses. When we have extracted them from tube sponges to hold on our hands for closer inspection, as often as not a marauding Spanish hogfish has closed in for a quick hors d'oeuvre. Inside the sponges they can in safety rely on the planktonic nourishment pumped through by their hosts. R. V. Gotto, in his study of partnerships and associations, *Marine Animals,* notes that a single loggerhead sponge taken in the Tortugas in the West Indies yielded over 16,000 shrimps of the genus *Synalpheus.*

James C. Tyler and James E. Böhlke of the Academy of Natural Sciences of Philadelphia have noted at least thirty-nine species of fishes having some association with sponges. Some they characterize as obligate dwellers and some as facultative, while still others have been found to be fortuitous dwellers, chancing on the sponges' protective function, say for egg-brooding purposes, but not normally found inhabiting them. Of the obligate symbionts, consisting of at least a dozen species, chiefly gobies, some are morphologically specialized. The obligates probably spend all of their nonlarval lives within the sponges. Divers can look in massive sponges for roughtail gobies *(Evermannichthys metzelaari)* and smallmouth gobies *(Risor ruber).* Tyler and Böhlke found the record number of twenty-one roughtails in a single manjack loggerhead sponge about 20 inches in diameter.

Even shrimps—or more accurately, the homes of certain shrimps— can provide protection for other species. In the Red Sea, a small goby makes its home commensally with certain shrimps of the alpheid family. The shrimps excavate tunnels in the sand and, being nearly blind, welcome individual gobies in their tunnels. The shrimp depends on the goby to warn it of nearby threats. It does this by pushing the goby out of its hole ahead of it; if the goby sees an enemy, it communicates this by body language to the shrimp, which then retreats back down the hole, with the goby right behind it. In exchange for this watchdog service, the shrimp cleans parasites from the fish.

SYMBIOSIS WITH CORAL

Although coral provides protection for many creatures (indeed, as we saw in Chapter 1, without coral or some equivalent the fish life of the reef would be impossible), some of this protection is supplied in such special ways and involves such complicated exchanges with the coral polyps themselves that coral as a symbiont deserves separate treatment.

An example familiar to every diver is the tubeworms, the lovely flowerlike members of the serpulid family, which can be found on coral heads everywhere. At first glance, it looks as though the tubeworm has bored into the coral, but in fact it has simply deposited on the hard coral surface a tube that grows in length with the growth of the coral so as to avoid becoming encased by its host. From the tubes extend delicate, featherlike tendrils that filter the water and retract in a split second when disturbed (see Plates 55 and 56).

Several species of crabs inhabit specific coral niches, not simply as hideouts (mere shelter in a hole scarcely qualifies as symbiosis) but as homes with which they interact. The coral gall crab, *Hapalocarcinus marsupialis,* has developed a particularly specialized technique for achieving permanent protection. The female selects a site on growing coral and by her presence stimulates the coral to form a gall, or enclosure. The gall grows completely around her, leaving, however, tiny holes through which she can breathe and set up a circulating current for filtering food and through which the much smaller males can enter and mate with her. *H. marsupialis* is a Pacific inhabitant. More than two dozen other members of the hapalocarcinid family have been described, two of which are Atlantic varieties. The latter species live in open crevices in the coral, seemingly tailored to size, and with luck can occasionally be spotted, particularly at night.

Many species of shrimp live symbiotically with coral. Like their relatives, the crabs, some are facultative associates and some are obligatory to the point that over time they have modified their bodies to take best advantage of specific coral hosts. They may have adapted various of their appendages for holding on, their dorsal spines for digging into tissue or to act as a hook for jamming into crevices, or their mandibles for specialized feeding requirements.

Tiny holes in the coral are often occupied by diminutive blennies. The West Indian roughhead blennies *(Acanthemblemaria aspera)* live in solitary holes initially bored out by clams from the coral. Only the tops of their heads are visible as they wait securely for tiny amphipods and copepods to float by and become their dinner. A diver's smallest fingertip will easily cover up the habitat of one of these blennies, yet their exposure on large coral surfaces makes them relatively easy to find. Other small fishes, many of them juveniles, are facultative associates that use finely branched coral as refuges. The

Indo-Pacific whitetailed (banded) humbug *(Dascyllus aruanus),* the lyre-tail coralfish *(Anthias squamipinnus),* and the blue puller *(Chromis caeruleus)* are easily observed examples of such fishes.

Divers will not be able to see one of the most important and basic associates of coral, the symbiotic unicellular brown algae known as zooxanthellae. These are dinoflagellates of microscopic size that have a mutual relationship with various marine animals: sea anemones, tridacnids, coral, and even some protozoa; their photosynthetic abilities provide nourishment to their hosts. Although this partnership is not fully understood, it is generally thought that zooxanthellae also play a role in the calcification process of corals and in promoting the production of fatty materials necessary to the cell structure. In return, the algae, through the metabolic action of their host, receive elements needed for protein synthesis and other nutrients derived from the coral's diet of zooplankton.

The giant clams of the Indo-Pacific oceans, the tridacnids, are able to flourish because of their symbiotic association with zooxanthellae, and their evolutionary path includes an adaptation to accommodate the algae. C. M. Yonge traced this development in detail. It has occurred in all sizes of species of tridacnid clams, from *Tridacna crocea,* which reaches a maximum of about six inches in length (see Plate 54), through middle-size tridacnids, twelve to twenty inches in length, to the enormous *T. gigas,* which can grow to more than four feet and which have earned, mistakenly, a reputation for being "killer clams" able to trap divers between their huge shells. Tridacnids live in shallow waters on or near the upper reef surfaces in the sandy lee sides of reefs, where their symbiotic partners can receive the necessary sunlight for their photosynthetic activity. Such intense sunlight would, however, be destructive to the clam, except that over evolutionary time it has compensated by developing a protective pigmentation. Brilliant shades of blue to green or brown to yellow characterize their mantles,* making it possible for the clams continuously to face the sun on behalf of the needs of their resident zooxanthellae. Inside their shells the clams have, in contrast to other bivalves, achieved another evolutionary accomplishment. They have completely rotated

---

*Their intense colors make them easy to spot on Pacific reefs. Once, while diving in Truk lagoon, an atoll in the Pacific Caroline Islands, a Trukese dive guide noticed us admiring a striking deep blue *T. crocea.* He loosened it from its anchorage with his knife, then cut through the adductor muscle, severing it from the shell; next he removed his regulator from his mouth and swallowed the clam in one gulp. He grinned, replaced his regulator, and gallantly presented us with the still-hinged shell.

their anatomies in relation to the shell hinge, enlarging their siphonal muscles to compensate for their upside-down realignment. Yonge estimates this process took millions of years: a slow but irreversibly firm commitment to their symbiotic mutualism. The enlarged siphonal tissues are exposed to the sun's rays, and it is here that the zooxanthellae live and release organic nourishment into the tridacnid's bloodstream. Because the tropical waters around the reefs are poor in the minerals necessary to support the rich planktonic diet needed by the large tridacnids, without the zooxanthellae the clams probably could not reach the sizes that they do. At the end of their photosynthetic lives the algae are digested by their host. This does not happen to newly invading algae, however, which seem to be immune to consumption by an animal otherwise adapted to feeding on planktonic items.

CLEANING

Animals that groom other animals are a fascinating and highly diverse group of mutualists. Scavenging for nourishment, they clean their hosts of external parasites, diseased tissue, fungi, and bacteria. Cleaning relationships are found everywhere in both the terrestrial and marine worlds, and the list of animals involved, either primarily or occasionally, constantly grows. In our own saltwater aquarium two shrimps, the redbanded coral shrimp *(Stenopus hispidus)* and particularly the orange, red, and white peppermint or redbacked shrimp *(Hippolysmata grabhami)*, will clean us as well as fishes. They will perform a thorough, almost systematic combing of the surfaces of our hands for parasitical matter; apparently our ectoparasites are as tasty to them as those gleaned from the sides of fishes. Like a great many cleaners, they are not especially particular about their diet, and the redbanded shrimp cleans even its own exterior, pulling down its flamboyant antennae with its long, clawed appendages and scraping their lengths, transferring the results to its mouth. It also climbs about our featherduster tubeworm, cleaning its delicate cilia; the tubeworm, which normally retracts at the slightest disturbance, tolerates the shrimp. It must sense some benefit. In the ocean a patient diver with a hand extended toward cleaner shrimps sheltered in anemones will at times elicit a grooming response.

Cleaning symbiosis has resulted not only in strange-seeming partnerships but in the evolution of specialized body features. In some fishes, narrow, pointy noses have evolved along with delicately tooled teeth that function like tweezers. Many shrimps have long, conspicuous antennae and specialized claws for grasping, inspecting, and extracting.

Many cleaner fishes, always small in size and usually brightly colored, have distinctive swimming motions that seem to advertise their services. They undulate a foot or so above their chosen coral stations in plain view of prospective customers. The latter might ordinarily be their predators, but now they respond with their own ritualized posing to signify not only their readiness to be cleaned but a willingness to suspend any predatory behavior.

The poses struck by fishes waiting to be cleaned vary from species to species but usually involve a stationary hovering facing sidewise toward the cleaner. If there is an infected wound or a particularly severe infestation on one side, that will likely be the side presented. Some species pose with their heads downward. Triggerfishes almost stand on their heads (and some triggerfish have been observed to clean each other). Other fishes point their heads upward while posing, and one species of Hawaiian surgeonfish stands on its tail to signal cleaners. If the posing is successful, the cleaner will inspect its host and proceed to clean, although inspection does not always result in cleaning. The fish being cleaned often pales in color during the process and will elevate or erect its fins cooperatively and open its mouth and gill coverings wide to permit safe inner passage for the cleaners (see Plate 36). A diver can often look into the mouths of large groupers and out through their extended gill openings to the marine landscape beyond while cleaners work them over.

At busy stations, depending on the habitat, there may be many small cleaners congregated and scores, even hundreds, of fishes cleaned during the course of a day. Some individuals may return repeatedly and seem to spend as much time being cleaned as they do foraging for food. Despite an occasional brief chase, the placidity that seems to characterize such locations has always seemed more curious to us than the actual cleaning activity that is going on. This is not to say that accidents do not happen, but clearly the cleaning symbiosis must work satisfactorily most of the time for all concerned for it to be so common.

There is always somebody willing to spoil a good thing, of course. A trumpetfish sometimes smuggles its way into a cleaning station in order to take advantage of unwary customers. It does this—or tries to, since such attempts are often unsuccessful—by shadow stalking (that is, by swimming as close as possible to, say, a parrotfish or surgeonfish as it glides in for a cleaning, adopting the coloration of its chosen shield). At first glance, the trumpetfish seems to be engaged in a kind of mad and hopeless courtship, snuggling up to a fish with which it cannot mate and swimming so close alongside or on top as to be almost touching.

Most marine cleaners, as will already have been surmised, are small fishes or shrimps. Over four dozen species of fishes (at least) have been reported as tropical cleaners at one time or another, and cleaning has been noted in all waters of all oceans, so that the total range of species that clean can only be guessed at. The majority of tropical cleaners do not depend on parasite picking for survival, however, and some clean only when they are juveniles. They are primarily members of the wrasse, parrotfish, angelfish, butterflyfish, goby, damselfish, and remora families. Divers may be surprised to learn that the Caribbean juvenile Spanish hogfish is a frequent cleaner.

A few species clean almost all the time and apparently must do so in order to survive. These obligate cleaners include four kinds of wrasses, the best known of which is the common cleaner wrasse *Labroides dimidiatus* of the Indo-Pacific region (see Plate 37). These are little bluish fish with prominent black stripes and they are often encountered in pairs. Their stomach contents consist almost entirely of the crustacean ectoparasites of fishes. They prefer calm waters and have a distinctive, slow swimming motion, using their pectoral fins in a way that causes the rear portions of their bodies to rock up and down, a way of signaling their profession. *L. dimidiatus* cleans reef fishes from a broad variety of families, even sharks. In aquariums, they have repeatedly groomed sharks, which slowed their usual swimming speeds to accommodate the cleaners. In the ocean, these wrasses have been seen working over resting whitetip reef sharks.

Rougher waters, such as those around the Gilbert and Marshall islands, are a favorite habitat of *L. bicolor*, which have a vigorous, aggressive cleaning style and are willing to pursue prospects for several yards. One species, *L. phthirophagus*, is common to Hawaiian waters, while others are found in the southeast Pacific, where *L. dimidiatus*, *L. bicolor*, and *L. rubrolabiatus* often join together to service infested fishes and will also clean one another.

Of the twelve species of neon gobies in the tropical Atlantic, half are bold and avid cleaners, with all but one of the others being non-cleaning sponge commensals. These tiny, two- to three-inch, scaleless fishes have a bright horizontal body stripe and small suction discs on their undersides that enable them to perch motionless on large coral heads, awaiting customers. They quickly approach prospects and skate about the surface of these fishes, nibbling parasites while holding on with their suction discs. Their size makes it easy for them to penetrate mouth and gill cavities. We have seen them join shrimps in cleaning moray eels. The cleaning neon gobies are all similar in shape but vary in coloration; the stripes of some species are set off by yellowish backgrounds and of others by blue. Like cleaner shrimps, neon gobies will occasionally inspect a motionless diver's hand.

The Impact of Cleaning

The ecological significance of cleaning symbiosis in the sea is much debated. Field experiments involving the removal of known cleaners from a given area have produced differing results. An early experiment conducted in the Bahamas by Conrad Limbaugh, a marine biologist who has devoted years of study to the cleaning syndrome, indicated that withdrawing cleaners led, within a few days, to a drastically reduced fish population. Since the fish remaining were the territorial ones, it is possible that those that had departed had sought out cleaners in other locations. A similar experiment in Hawaiian waters led Marsh Youngbluth to dispute this depopulation theory. But the two oceans are different, as are the species of cleaners. Whereas Limbaugh removed all cleaning organisms known at the time, Youngbluth removed only the endemic cleaner wrasse *Labroides phthirophagus,* its effectiveness being the object of his curiosity. Both of these studies date from the 1960s but both are still cited in much of the current literature, indicating how much is still to be learned. Certainly there is general agreement that cleaning is an evolutionarily successful activity. The vast numbers of fishes that seek out cleaning and the body adaptations of the cleaners bear witness to that. It is entirely possible that population dispersal on the part of both cleaners and cleaned is affected.

Biological mimicry, an evolutionary achievement known in many plants and animals, has a classic example in the marine cleaning business. The cleaner wrasse *L. dimidiatus* has a mimic in the sabre-toothed blenny *(Plagiotremis azaleus = Aspidontus taeniatus),* described in detail by Wolfgang Wickler. The blenny imitates its model so well that it is nearly indistinguishable from it in both appearance and swimming habits. But if the blenny's seductive invitation for cleaning has been accepted in the mistaken belief that it is a wrasse, the blenny bites off and consumes pieces of the victim's fins. This con artist is usually able to deceive only juvenile fishes, indicating that some learning behavior takes place after a few well-placed nips occur. Since

L. dimidiatus flourishes throughout most Indo-Pacific reef waters, divers observing it may want to know that the blenny mimic differs from the wrasse in the position of its mouth: the wrasse has a terminal mouth, at the very end of its pointed head, whereas the blenny has a mouth situated just under its slightly more rounded snout.

A diver contemplating a busy cleaning station where several species of cleaners operate on a diversity of fishes can imagine a spectrum of convergent evolution taking place in one time frame. On the one hand are the highly specialized, morphologically adapted individuals that make their living picking parasites. On the other hand are fishes or shrimps that are—at present and perhaps forever—casual cleaners, either throughout their lives or while juveniles, and that enjoy a varied diet. One wonders whether much juvenile cleaning occurs as curious, imitative behavior of the obligate cleaners (we know, at least, that birds engage in imitative behavior), the way small children duplicate behavior of their peers, sometimes fleetingly, sometimes persistently. One can speculate that perhaps such copycat activity, somewhere in the distant past, started one of our present day subjects out on its evolutionary path toward obligate cleaning.

CHAPTER TEN

Sharks

Sharks have not been as fortunate as lions. Once, both creatures were regarded as vicious man-eaters to be killed if possible and avoided at all costs. Then, an orphan lion cub named Elsa was taken into the hearts of people all over the world as a consequence of the moving story of her intelligence and charm supplied by Joy Adamson in her book *Born Free.* As Cynthia Moss has observed in her splendid account of animal behavior in east Africa, *Portraits in the Wild,* the lion became the best-loved wild animal in America, with "Elsa clubs" springing up by the hundreds. Every tourist to the game parks of Kenya (ourselves included) wants above all else to see lions, the more the better.

There are no shark clubs, and few snorkelers or novice divers want to see even one of the creatures. The popular image of the shark is not of some cuddly orphan, but of "Jaws," a horrifying eating machine. And people who are not divers often suspect those who are of being a bit reckless, if not crazy, because they are, presumably, risking a shark attack. "Did you see any sharks?" and "What do you do when a shark sees you?" are among the commonest questions we encounter.

In fact, divers encounter the question much more often than they encounter a shark. Depending on where one dives, it may be years before one sees a shark. We began diving in the Caribbean and, save for a sedentary nurse shark, waited five years before seeing an actively swimming shark. But if one enters the water around such Pacific reefs as Ponape, sharks may be seen on almost every dive. Except in such places, most divers have to be content with a rare, brief, and distant glimpse of a shark or two. They will be lucky even to identify it.

A few divers and marine scientists have reacted so strongly against the popular stereotypes of sharks as to suggest that they are beautiful, peace-loving creatures amidst which a diver may move with almost complete safety. That is taking things a bit too far; it would be as if Elsa-lovers were to decide to jump out of their Land Rovers in Kenya and pet every adult lion they encountered. Lions are not man-eaters, but they prefer being left alone and have rather painful ways of enforcing that preference. Sharks are not man-eaters, either, nor are they unpredictable savages. There is little risk in diving on reefs where sharks are found, but there is substantial risk in approaching and "petting" (or poking, grabbing, or cornering) any shark. And in certain locations, where particular kinds of sharks are to be found, there may be a decided risk in swimming about on the surface.

But most important, sharks are not, like lions, a single species; there are, in fact, well over 300 species of sharks, grouped into eight orders, thirty families, and nearly a hundred genera. They include tiny sharks, such as *Squaliolus laticaudus,* which attain a mature length of only 6 to 10 inches, oddly shaped sharks such as the saw shark, the Pacific carpet sharks with their fringed mouths, the invertebrate-eating epaulette or blind shark of Australian waters, and the huge pelagic basking shark *(Cetorhinus maximus)* and whale shark *(Rhincodon typus)*, which swim about with mouths agape to strain tiny plankton from the water. The last is the largest known fish, attaining a length of 45 feet or more.

Although a rare diver may chance to meet a whale shark and may, in the Pacific, spot a carpet shark or even a saw shark, ordinarily there are only a few families of sharks likely to be encountered about the reefs: nurse sharks (family Ginglymostomatidae), mako or mackerel sharks (family Lamnidae), and hammerheads (family Sphyrnidae). But mostly the diver will see, if he sees any sharks at all, members of the family Carcharhinidae, commonly called the requiem sharks. Requiem sharks are the "typical" sharks; this family comprises more species than any other by far. Most are tropical or subtropical in range.

In the Caribbean the commonest requiem species that may be found in the vicinity of reefs are the lemon *(Negaprion brevirostris)*, tiger *(Galeocerdo cuvieri)*, spinner or large blacktip *(Carcharhinus brevipinna)*, blacktip *(Carcharhinus limbatus)*, and reef shark *(Carcharhinus perezi)*. The bull shark *(Carcharhinus leucas)* is more apt to be found in inshore coastal waters. (This species has a high tolerance for waters of varying salinity and often frequents the mouths of large rivers, such as the Mississippi, Zambezi, Amazon, Tigris, Euphrates, and Ganges, and it also flourishes far from the ocean in Lake Nicaragua.) Caribbean divers may also find one species of nurse shark, *Ginglymostoma cirratum*, several hammerhead species, and the shortfin mako *(Isurus oxyrinchus)*, a member of the mackerel shark family, or Lamnidae.

In the Indo-Pacific, there is more of everything, including shark species. Most of what we know of sharks is known about the most commonly encountered sharks found on central Pacific reefs: the gray reef shark *(Carcharhinus amblyrhynchos*, until recently also called *C. menisorrah)*, the blackfin (or blacktip) reef shark *(C. melanopterus)*, and the whitetip reef shark *(Triaenodon obesus)*.

There remains "Jaws"—the great white shark *(Carcharodon carcharias)*. A tropical diver is most unlikely to encounter one; indeed, to see and photograph great white sharks at all, it is usually necessary to seek them in remote places far from coral reefs and to lure them near by chumming the water, sometimes for days on end, with the blood and flesh of other fishes, as one of us did. But at times they are a menace to divers in, among other places, certain temperate coastal waters off California for reasons peculiar to that area.

SHARK BIOLOGY

Sharks differ from other fishes—the teleosts—in important ways. They, like skates and rays, are elasmobranchs. Although they are considered to be vertebrates, elasmobranchs are cartilaginous fishes; that is, they are not bony. Their skeletons and fin supports are made, not of bone, but of cartilage, a calcified substance, and their fins are rigid rather than hinged. Whereas other fishes have single gill slits on either side of their bodies, protected with a gill covering (the oper-culum), sharks, skates, and rays have from five to seven gill slits (five in requiems) with no coverings. Sharks have toothlike, or placoid, scales of coarse, abrasive material, capable of inflicting contact inju-ries.

Unlike most fishes, sharks have no gas bladders and thus they have had to solve their buoyancy problems in other ways. That problem is made a bit easier by the fact that a cartilaginous skeleton is not as dense as a bony one and that many sharks have huge livers filled with buoyant oil, which help to stabilize them while swimming. Moreover, more than thirty species of sharks do not even try to stay afloat, spending most of their time on or near the bottom, able to breathe by pumping water through their respiratory systems. Still, without gas bladders, sharks that are not bottom dwellers must swim almost con-tinuously to keep from sinking. Most streamlined sharks must swim continuously anyway, having no other way to force enough water through their gills to oxygenate their bodies and remove wastes, al-though many of these can pump water over their gills for a limited time—several hours—and may occasionally be found "resting" on the bottom.

Sharks have been around about 300 million years, far longer than man, and yet they have not diversified nearly as much as other fishes. Having such an ancient history has bestowed upon them the image of being "primitive," a word that in popular parlance connotes "in-sensitive" or "ill-adapted." But in this case, the word means the exact opposite; it is precisely because sharks are so splendidly adapted to their environment that they have so long a history and have under-gone so few adaptive changes. Sharks flourish in all the oceans, where they occupy the top of the marine food chain. By any standard, they are extremely successful fishes.

This success is due in great measure to their special biological quali-ties, especially their senses. Consider the problem a shark faces: It is a large fish needing to eat a great deal to sustain itself, yet it inhabits an ocean that is largely empty and in which visibility is often quite poor. Moreover, if it is a reef shark, it will live near coral formations offering all manner of hiding places to potential prey. To find, stalk, and attack another fish, a shark must have extraordinary sensory capacities. These senses provide long-range, medium-range, and close-range detection abilities.

A shark's long-range detection apparatus seems to consist largely of its acute sense of "hearing": a combination of sensitivity to sonic stimuli through its ears and to subsonic vibrations with its lateral line systems. Many fishermen have long known that sharks often seem to show up quickly when a speared or hooked fish struggles in the water. Some fishermen wishing to catch sharks have learned to duplicate the struggle sounds or vibrations to which sharks respond. Edward S. Hodgson has described the use of rattle lures by Pacific shark fishermen on different islands. Great care is taken to learn the "correct" rhythms for shaking the rattles in the surface waters to produce intermittent bursts of low-frequency sounds that sharks find worth investigating. What the fishermen knew all along has been corroborated by several scientists in the past decade. Their tests, conducted independently and in both oceans, leave no doubt about one way sharks use their hearing.

Researchers placed loudspeakers below the surface of the water from which various tones and rhythms were broadcast. They found that sharks are not attracted to pure tones, but to low-frequency sounds and vibrations that simulate the irregular, repetitive pulsing sounds and vibrations of fishes in stress. Although they might investigate regularly pulsed vibrations, they were far more curious about irregular ones. Sharks can detect such stimuli up to a distance of about 100 yards.

As sharks approach a loudspeaker, they may attack, bite, and even swallow it. All fishes, of course, have lateral line systems that detect vibrations and other piscivorous fishes have also been attracted to the same sorts of irregularly pulsed sounds. Working in the Bahamas, several investigators found that yellowtail snappers *(Ocyurus chrysurus)* and several species of groupers, including the Nassau grouper *(Epinephelus striatus)*, were responsive to sound stimulation. Groupers approached more cautiously than sharks, as is their hunting nature, but clearly zeroed in on the loudspeaker. Fishes, including sharks, are also stimulated by the feeding sounds of other fishes. Arthur Myrberg, one of the pioneers in this research, suggests that because sharks quickly check out such stress and feeding sounds, enough opportunities to capture prey thereby result to make routine investigation worthwhile. However, if the sounds are only those of a loudspeaker, frequently repeated tests over a short period of time will result in the sharks becoming habituated to the noises and ignoring them. Contrary to their mindless reputation, sharks can and do learn.

As the shark gets closer to the source of a sound, its medium-range detection system, the eyes, takes over. For many years, sharks were thought to have poor eyesight and to rely instead on olfactory cues and other senses for prey capture. They were believed, for example, to have only rods in their retinas. This would mean that shark eyes were adapted chiefly for nocturnal and twilight vision. We now know this to be wrong. Electron microscopy has revealed that most sharks have duplex retinas with both rods and cones and thus are capable of good vision in both daylight and at night; they may even have color vision.

Working with lemon sharks in the late 1950s, Eugenie Clark demonstrated that they could respond to visual targets and learn to obtain rewards by choosing the correct target. Since then, a number of conditioning experiments with various species by Samuel H. Gruber, Joel Cohen, and others have shown that several sharks have good brightness discrimination, perhaps almost as good as people have. Continuing studies have demonstrated their ability to adapt to darkness.

Sharks share with several other vertebrates a special visual structure called the "tapetum lucidum," a reflecting apparatus much like a mirror that lies behind the retina and helps to make the maximum use of such light as is available. The tapetum is responsible for what we call eyeshine in animals and is the reason the eyes of certain nocturnally active animals, such as cats, reflect in automobile headlights so spectacularly. Sharks are thought to have even better tapetal systems than cats, which among terrestrial vertebrates have the best-adapted vision for darkness. During the day, sharks' eyes are protected from too much brightness by a curtain of pigment granules that expand or contract over the surface of the tapetum as needed, providing them with the visual versatility they need to function as efficient predators in their habitat.

Aiding the eyes in detecting prey is the well-known sense of smell characteristic of sharks. As the animal swims, water flows through its nostrils and across its olfactory sacs, bearing with it any smells. To breathe, a shark must take water in through its mouth to its gills. In some sedentary sharks, water is pulled through their olfactory sacs and connecting grooves leading into the mouth by suction action resulting from respiration. Thus even sedentary sharks, which must actively pump water across their gills, continually receive olfactory cues. Experiments in the sea have shown that sharks not only show up from downstream directions where odors of bait reach them but can sense both injured and uninjured fish in a state of stress.

Once close to its prey, the shark moves in for the attack. In doing so, its nose can no longer provide a precise location for the struggling fish and its eyes, mounted on the sides of its head well above its underslung jaw, can no longer see where the prey is in relation to its mouth. For final guidance, as well as to detect fishes concealed under sand or in other hideaways, the shark can employ its remarkable ability to detect faint electrical signals generated by living creatures. In experiments, blue sharks attacked an underwater current as weak as eight microamperes. But this sensitive electroreception system may also confuse the shark. Large metal objects, such as steel-hulled boats, engines, and propellers, also have a galvanic field around them, and so, at the last second, a shark aiming for a piece of meat may be drawn to a piece of metal. This may explain why some sharks, lured to a fishing boat by the sound and smell of struggling or bleeding fishes, have been known to attack the boat itself or its propeller. This action, often described as an example of the shark's "crazed" or "ruthless" nature, may in fact only be action stimulated by a misleading electrical signal.

To process the information from its complex array of sensory organs, the shark must have a brain rather more complex than once supposed. Sharks are not the simple, mindless creatures they are sometimes made out to be. A variety of neurobiological studies have indicated that sharks possess ample brains with brain-body ratios that, according to R. Glenn Northcutt, fall within the range of birds and mammals. Moreover, the major areas of brain development have close similarities to those of birds and mammals. Earlier studies of sharks had viewed their brains as representing early, simple evolutionary stages rather than recognizing that different lines of evolution take place as required by particular adaptations to specific habitats.

The most obvious aspect of the shark's predatory skills has not been lost on its public: its feeding mechanisms. Teeth are the first thing most people call to mind when sharks are mentioned. And it cannot be denied that they are formidable. It is well known that sharks replace teeth routinely as the front ranks outlive their effectiveness. Their teeth are often broken or lost while biting large prey. Instead of taking the evolutionary tack of developing strong, disease-resistant, unshakably mounted teeth, sharks seem to do quite well with a rapid-replacement system. Sanford A. Moss marked the teeth of a group of young lemon sharks and followed them as they grew, finding a turnover of about one functional row of teeth *every week*. Other shark species have similar dental schedules. The advantage of such replacement, Moss points out, is that it allows for growth throughout life, as each tooth is a fraction larger than the tooth it supplants.

Sharks' teeth are not all the same. Varying with species, they are adapted to dealing with their prey preferences. The tiger shark, for example, sometimes dines on sea turtles and has sawlike teeth that can cut through their tough shells. Other sharks have teeth shaped for grasping and holding prey or for biting and grinding, often in combination. Many male sharks, as remarked in Chapter 6, have some specially curved teeth for grasping the female during copulation.

Sharks are among the few piscivores that attack prey larger than themselves. (Others include sargassum fish, some deep-sea gulper eels, and tiny flesh stealers such as the cleaning wrasse mimics that, while pretending to be parasite removers, nip fleshy morsels from their unsuspecting customers.) Being for the most part opportunistic, sharks often make do with smaller reef fishes taken whole or a mouthful of schooling squid or herring. But, at least for the white sharks and requiem sharks, it is possible when the opportunity presents itself to have a large, satisfying meal, for their jaws are capable of carving out large chunks from whales, sea lions, dolphins, and, occasionally, other sharks. They are able to do this owing to the way their jaws are constructed.

Because their mouths are not at the front of their heads, but underneath and often set well back, sharks have sometimes been thought to feed only while turned upside down. This is not the case at all. To eat, the whole jaw drops down and swings forward. The jaws, often reinforced with calcium deposits for extra strength, are combined with flexible joints that enable the shark to move its mouth along with movements of its body to shake, twist, or tear at its prey. The jaws have a powerful set of muscles, cartilages, and ligaments. This system permits the entire jaw complex to protrude down and forward and to be supported beneath the calcium-fortified cranium while feeding. Such a system, while allowing flexibility, braces the animal against the side-to-side forces it produces when it shakes its entire body in the effort to tear its meal loose from the body of its prey.

These forces are not to be taken lightly. In one of the studies conducted for the United States Navy in the 1960s, James M. Snodgrass and Perry W. Gilbert experimented with a shark-bite meter made of a soft aluminum core surrounded by stainless steel and several layers of strong filament tape, all made tasty for sharks with an outer wrapping of bonito, blue runner, or barracuda. Tiger, lemon, and dusky sharks were attracted to the meter. After they took the bait, microscopic measurements of tooth-mark indentations in the aluminum core were used to calibrate the impact of the bites. The highest force measured from a single tooth was calculated to be one of three metric *tons* per square centimeter. The experimenters rather anticlimactically concluded that "the shark does indeed possess great potentiality for damage." Indeed.

According to Moss, the diets of sharks can often be guessed at from the amount of jaw calcification present. Nurse sharks, which need strength for crushing and grinding their crustacean and molluscan prey, have heavier jaws than sharks that eat fishes. Their dietary preference works out well for them, since crustaceans and molluscs contain large amounts of calcium salts.

Except for some young sharks in captivity, we know little about their growth rate. Although we are aware of some sharks that have survived over twenty-five years, we have no idea of what their natural life spans are. We do not even know how much they need to eat or how often, although we do know that some sharks seem to be able to go for long periods without eating and some seem able to store food energy for a period of time. Studies on captive sharks show that they do not need anywhere near the enormous amounts of food once thought necessary. At Marineland in Florida a tiger shark went nearly one year before partaking of a large meal. In winter, basking sharks appear to shed their gill rakers, bony projections that help prevent food from being washed out through their gill openings, and go for months without eating. .

Sharks are, for obvious reasons, difficult to study. In addition to the need for caution in their presence, they swim fast and range far. Still, fascinating beginnings in behavior studies have been made.

SHARK BEHAVIOR

Sharks are not the solitary, indiscriminate "eating machines" they were once thought to be. Although they are not territorial, they have home ranges, exhibit social behavior, prefer some kinds of food to others, and ordinarily do not attack one another.

The sandbar shark *(Carcharhinus plumbeus = Eulamia milberti),* studied in the late 1950s by Stewart Springer, has definite seasonal ranges in its Atlantic habitat. Although large sandbar sharks may occasionally wander afar, they tend to keep to predictable home ranges in definable habitats. After a spring mating season in the vicinity of waters off Salerno, Florida, sandbars range in warm months north from Cape Canaveral to Long Island and Cape Cod, where females give birth in inshore nursery grounds. Males remain in cooler offshore waters and, except during mating season, live apart from the females. Cooler water temperatures apparently prompt adults of both sexes to move southward for the winter, some of them as far around the tip of Florida as Tampa, on the west coast in the warmer gulf waters. Young sandbars remain on their nursery grounds and do not join the migrations until they reach adult size; until then both sexes school together.

Springer introduced early evidence of the social organization of sharks. He later found a general tendency in many species of the Atlantic and gulf sharks he studied to segregate not only by sex (except, of course, during mating season) but by size. One theory for such separation is that it may protect newborn sharks from predation by mature ones. However, Springer found an exception in adult tiger sharks, which apparently live in mixed-sex groups.

Bonnetheads *(Syphyrna tiburo),* a species of hammerhead sharks, are gregarious animals usually found in groups. A behavioral study of sharks involving continuous direct observation (over 1,000 man-hours) was undertaken by Myrberg and Gruber, who observed a colony of ten of these fishes in the Miami Seaquarium. The constantly moving sharks soon exhibited a consistent daily schedule, their patrolling and other swimming patterns reflecting a social hierarchy in which dominance was based on size, and apparently somewhat on sex, with males often taking precedence—although the top shark in this group was an outsize female. Sharks deferred to larger members of their group by moving out of their way during encounters. Ritualistic aggressive behavior was directed at new sharks, usually during the first hour or so of their introduction. An established resident might rapidly overtake such an individual and then glide overtop it, during which it would hit the new shark between the first and second dorsal fins, causing it to accelerate forward. Hits were usually made by small males. Newcomers were not seen to hit established residents. The sharks never actively fought, even when competing for food. Instead, the sharks competed by maneuvering for position.

These sharks would frequently follow and imitate one another. One shark would follow another for four body lengths or longer, imitating all of the lead shark's movements. Again, size and sex seemed to influence who followed whom: bigger sharks of the opposite sex were more likely to be followed by either males or females, although not exclusively. The social significance of following is unclear, but it is a common practice, averaging once every twenty minutes in the group studied, and so it must be important to the sharks.

Many sharks display a daily and seasonal rhythm in their behavior, geared to the corresponding rhythms of their prey. Blue sharks *(Prionace glauca)* are a species found worldwide in temperate and semitropical waters, foraging near the surface waters. In California, seasonal shifts in prey populations influence whether blues stay in- or offshore. Terry Sciarrotta and Donald R. Nelson tagged and telemetrically tracked blue sharks. From March to early June they migrated at dusk from their daytime offshore habitats to shallow waters around Santa Catalina Island, possibly after large schools of squid available then. From late June to October, when squid populations near the island are low, they remained offshore where jacks and mackerel were abundant.

Periodic groupings of massive numbers of various shark species have been reported by fishermen and divers and from aerial and shipboard sightings. The social reasons for these groups are not understood, although it is thought they may be for mating purposes. Impressively large schools of scalloped hammerheads *(Sphyrna lewini)* occurring in the Sea of Cortez have recently been observed at close range by A. Peter Klimley and Nelson. The hammerheads congregated in schools at three separate locations during the summer months and permitted free divers to swim among them, seemingly oblivious to the presence of observers. Scuba divers made them wary, probably because of the noisy tank exhausts.

The groups averaged about twenty individuals, but one group was estimated to contain over 500 sharks. The sharks were of various sizes and both sexes, with females tending to predominate and to swim at the top of the schools. The sharks were not interested in bait, nor were they attracted to underwater sound stimuli. They were never seen taking prey (perhaps they fed at night). They engaged in several behavior patterns, which Klimley characterized as acrobatic, the most frequent of which involved tilting the body sideways, swimming rapidly while shaking their heads, thrusting out their midsections, and swimming in corkscrew patterns. Sometimes they bumped nearby sharks with their snouts. Occasionally male sharks flexed their claspers (the paired sexual organs). Some sharks, tracked by telemetry, sometimes left groups, particularly at dusk, and some rejoined, but for what purposes is not known.

Various functions have been suggested for such schooling among sharks, including reconnoitering before migrations, antipredator defense, and cooperation for hunting purposes. Klimley and Nelson found no evidence for any of this among hammerheads. Although direct evidence is lacking, the best guess seems to be that these sharks school for reproductive activity.

More may be known when all the results are in from one of the most comprehensive shark inquiries yet undertaken, a five-year study, sponsored by the National Science Foundation, of the lemon shark. One portion of the study involves tagging 2,500 young lemon sharks and releasing them back into the ocean. When some are recaptured, we shall know more about their range, growth rates, and life

Plate 34. Territorial damselfish *(Stegastes planifrons).* It will chase any intruder from its square yard or so of space. Bonaire, Netherlands Antilles.

Plate 35. This pikeblenny (genus *Chaenopis*) never strays far from its home in the sand. Cozumel.

Plate 36. Caribbean grouper in cleaning station, its mouth agape while small cleaner gobies groom inside its jaws. Bonaire, Netherlands Antilles.

Plate 37. A sweetlips (genus *Plectorhynchus*) whose snout is being plucked of parasites by a small cleaning wrasse *(Labroides dimidiatus).* Heron Island, Great Barrier Reef, Australia.

Plate 38. Spotted moray *(Gymnothorax moringa)* patiently posing while a tiny cleaner shrimp removes parasites from the side of its head. Bonaire, Netherlands Antilles.

Plate 39. The Caribbean arrow crab *(Stenorhynchus seticornus)*, immune to the toxic sting of the giant anemone *(Condylactis gigantea)*, is frequently found during daylight hours in the protection of the anemone's tentacles.

Plate 40. A tiny, symbiotic diamond blenny *(Malacoctenus boehlkei)* lives under the tentacles of the giant Caribbean anemone *(Condylactis gigantea),* deriving protection from its venomous tentacles. Grand Cayman.

Plate 41. When not grooming fish customers, this small cleaner shrimp *(Periclimenes yucatanicus)* lives in an anemone's tentacles. This one is in the giant Caribbean anemone *(Condylactis gigantea).* Bonaire, Netherlands Antilles.

Plate 42. A clownfish *(Amphiprion clarkii)* lives symbiotically with a Pacific carpet anemone, immune to the venomous sting of its tentacles. Ponape, Caroline Islands.

Plates 43 and 44. Great white shark *(Carcharodon carcharias)*. Dangerous Reef, South Australian coast.

Plate 45. Colony of sessile invertebrates established on dead coral base: lavender tube sponge, grey sponges, branched gorgonians, and fire coral (upper left). Grand Cayman.

Plate 46. An adult octopus exposed on the reef declines to take cover. It has most probably ceased feeding after breeding and will soon die. Palancar Reef, Cozumel.

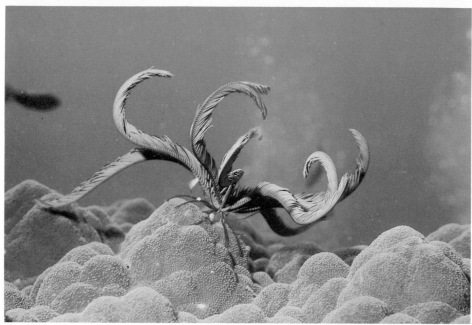

Plate 47. A crinoid elevated on its cirri, walking across coral surface. Apo Reef, Philippine Islands.

Plate 48. A variety of crinoids assembled atop a coral outcrop to feed in the current. Outer Batangas Harbor, Philippine Islands.

Plate 49. Nudibranch *(Notodoris metastigina)* on table coral. Ponape, Caroline Islands.

Plate 50. A garterlike ribbon of nudibranch eggs. Outer Batangas Harbor, Philippine Islands.

Plate 51. Caribbean bristleworm *(Hermodici carunculata),* a predator of soft coral, on gorgonian sea fan. Grand Turk, Turks and Caicos, Bahamas.

Plate 52. A holothurian (sea cucumber) that has eviscerated itself for defensive purposes. Its long intestinal strands will regenerate. Ponape, Caroline Islands.

Plate 53. A Caribbean brittlestar living commensally with a sponge. Grand Cayman.

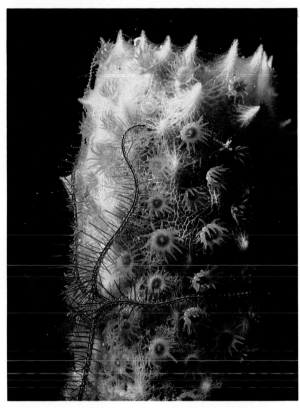

Plate 54. Pacific *Tridacna crocea,* a species of giant clam. Its bright blue fleshy mantle harbors symbiotic zooxanthellae algae. Ponape, Caroline Islands.

Plate 55. Christmas tree worms, serpulid polychaetes of the genus *Spirobranchia,* embedded in star coral. Two are unfurled to feed on plankton; the other has completely retracted into its calcareous, hookshaped shell. Roatan, Bay Islands, Honduras.

Plate 56. Filter-feeding featherduster worm, a sabellid polychaete, anchored in star coral. Truk Lagoon, Caroline Islands.

Plate 57. Purple tunicate, with crinoid arms at either side. Apo Reef, Philippine Islands.

Plate 58. Sea urchin with poison-bearing stalks among its spines. Outer Batangas Harbor, Philippine Islands.

Plate 59. Atlantic schooling glassy sweepers *(Pempheris schomburgki)* take refuge in caves and under ledges by day, school out at night to feed on plankton. Palancar Reef, Cozumel.

Plate 60. Squirrelfish *(Holocentrus rufus)* with large eyes adapted for nocturnal vision. British Virgin Islands.

Plate 61. Caribbean basketstar *(Astrophyton muricatum)* unfolded atop a gorgonian soft coral to feed on night plankton. British Virgin Islands.

Plate 62. Closeup of tentacles of a basketstar *(Astrophyton muricatum)*. Its mouth can be seen at the center. Grand Turk, Turks and Caicos, Bahamas.

Plate 63. A Caribbean surgeonfish, the blue tang *(Acanthurus coeruleus),* is attracted to the algae growing on a long-submerged mooring line. Bonaire, Netherlands Antilles.

span. Preliminary findings indicate that juveniles remain in fixed areas for several years and grow more slowly than captive sharks that have more reliable food sources. The lemons are born in inshore areas, increase their ranges with maturity, and move eventually to offshore waters and reef areas. Adult lemon sharks, tracked through transmitters, are thought to be somewhat site-oriented, probably for resting purposes, although their ranges are larger than those of juveniles. They have been found to be equally active day and night, but their peaks of activity are crepuscular. One interesting social note has been the discovery on several occasions of associations with several species of jacks, leading one of the researchers, Gruber, to hypothesize that the sharks may be using the sensory abilities of the jacks to help find prey. The conclusion of this multidisciplinary study may give us the most complete picture yet of the lifestyle of a common tropical shark.

Pacific Reef Sharks

The facts we know about shark behavior that are the most useful to divers probably are those that have been established about reef sharks in the Indo-Pacific region. Sharks that make reefs their home bases have been repeatedly studied during the past two decades in various locations by several prominent marine biologists. This research received a great impetus during World War II, when the United States Navy sought ways to protect servicemen who found themselves for one reason or another adrift in the Pacific. After the war, the Office of Naval Research (ONR) supported several projects, involving a great number of marine scientists and various institutions, designed to increase our biological and behavioral knowledge of sharks. Two decades of intensive study laid down a substantial base of knowledge. Although Navy funding is now greatly reduced, many researchers involved in the ONR studies are continuing their investigations, and in the next few years our understanding of shark behavior should literally multiply. At the same time many myths will undoubtedly dissolve.

At Eniwetok Atoll in the Marshall Islands a detailed ONR-supported study of the feeding behavior of the blackfin (blacktip), whitetip, and gray reef sharks was carried out by Edmund S. Hobson. John E. Randall has further improved our understanding of the whitetip. Nelson and Richard H. Johnson have devoted themselves relentlessly to shark behavior, tagging large numbers of sharks so that they could be followed by using a variety of sophisticated equipment. The discussion that follows of reef shark behavior draws heavily on these studies, especially those of Nelson and Johnson.

The three most commonly encountered reef sharks—blackfins, whitetips, and grays—share the same coral environment but have quite different temperaments and prefer different niches in the habitat. Blackfins *(Carcharhinus melanopterus)** hang around inner reef flats with sandy or rubble bottoms, usually preferring depths of under 50 feet; sometimes they are found in only 3 or 4 feet of water, being quite accustomed to turbid, low-visibility conditions. Here they live on a diet of reef fishes, eels, and crustaceans. Although sometimes found in small groups, they are mostly solitary in habit, being the shyest of the three species and cautious in approaching food. At Eniwetok it took a month of offering blackfins bait before they would unhesitatingly accept it. Once attracted to food, however, they would feed in excited numbers, their frenzy a seemingly mutual stimulation. Hobson speculated that their timid behavior, more pronounced in larger individuals, may be an adaptation to living in the shallows. Although blackfins, like several active shark species, can pump water over their gills for short periods when caught and restrained, normally they must remain in motion to breathe, and shallow waters permit less flexibility of maneuver and flight than do deeper waters. The behavior may not really be functional, however, for adult blackfins seem not to have enemies.

Whitetip sharks *(Triaenodon obesus)* have a placid if not sluggish reputation. They are as likely as not to be found sleeping or resting in protective coral, for they alone of the three major Pacific species can pump water through their gills without swimming for long periods each day. Like the blackfins, they also live in shallow reef areas, occasionally being found in even three feet of water, but instead of foraging over the flats for meals they generally frequent the coral heads, especially the areas around the seaward passages. They are mislabeled *obesus;* in fact, they have relatively slender forms well-adapted to hunting in the nooks and crannies of coral, where they pursue reef prey with considerable agility. Whitetips keep to definable home areas and sleep in home caves. Nelson and Johnson, in a long-term behavioral study at Rangiroa, French Polynesia, identified one whitetip that occupied the same home cave for at least eleven months. Although they seem to like the company of other whitetips

---

*These sharks are just as commonly called blacktips. We prefer the name blackfin, now also used by Nelson and Johnson, to avoid confusion with the oceanic blacktip, *C. limbatus.*

while at rest, several often sharing the same cave, when abroad they do not swim in social groups.

While they may occasionally feed during the day, whitetips are primarily active at night, as are the other reef sharks. Whitetips at Rangiroa were sometimes accompanied by juvenile yellow jacks in a cave. There they are thought to clean the sharks, as does the cleaner wrasse *(Labroides dimidiatus)*, which has also been seen working over whitetips when the latter were at rest.

The boldest and most active of the three major Pacific species is the gray reef shark *(Carcharhinus amblyrhynchos = C. menisorrah)*. It is usually found in stable packs of sometimes as many as fifty sharks that, during daylight hours, patrol the waters of the outer reef at depths of from 60 feet and below. Tracking devices at Rangiroa indicate that the packs pick up the pace of activity at night while ranging over the shallower reefs. Nelson and Johnson found that the grays in the Rangiroa reef area were grouped in at least five distinct packs, each oriented to its own area, with juveniles forming their own groups and keeping to shallower depths than adults. In one experiment a tagged gray was caught and transported by boat from its home area inside the Rangiroa lagoon to a site on the ocean reef. It returned to its home. Grays also display the imitative, follow-the-leader swimming pattern observed among bonnetheads.

Grays are decidedly bolder in behavior than the whitetip and blackfin sharks, quicker to satisfy their curiosity about proffered bait and potential prey, and readier to investigate divers. However, at Eniwetok, Hobson noted that if grays strayed into shallow water— an unaccustomed habitat for them—they were more wary of divers and often fled on encountering one. They appear to be dominant over other reef sharks in competition for food, although actual fighting does not take place. Whitetips were often observed to give way and turn aside when swimming toward grays, and they became more habituated to divers than did the grays.

Although these sharks have homesite attachments, there is little evidence that they, or any other sharks, are territorial. That is, they do not seem to defend their preferred spaces, although some observations suggest that sharks may behave more aggressively when near their homesites than when ranging afar. Not enough study of this possibility has taken place. What has been well documented for gray reef sharks, however, is that they behave with predictable aggression when directly approached by divers—when they apparently feel their "personal space" is threatened.

In the early 1970s Johnson and Nelson carried out a series of deliberate, rapid diver approaches to gray reef sharks at Eniwetok Atoll, carefully noting the reactions of the sharks and recording their movements on film. The sharks consistently responded with the same patterns of behavior, expressing a ritualized defensive threat. These threats, which have been called by some divers with extensive shark experience "preattack" behavior, were so graphic that after ten test trials Johnson and Nelson felt it prudent to stop the experiments, but not before they had corroborated the casual observations of gray reef sharks by scores of other divers, spearfishermen, and marine scientists from many Indo-Pacific locations.

The sharks did not bother divers in experiments during which the divers remained passive. Their aggression was released by provocation. They were found to display most aggressively if approached in such a way as to cut off their escape routes. They also reacted more intensely if charged head on rather than from behind or from an angle.

The display itself consists of the shark, either male or female, dropping its pectoral fins downward, arching or hunching its back, lifting its snout, and bending its body sideways (see drawing below). The more upset the shark is, the more exaggerated its swimming pattern becomes as it doubles back on its path in tight figure eights. The "preattack" or agonistic posture of the shark is much like that of a cornered dog and seems to signal much the same mood: "I feel threatened; I am on the verge of either fighting or fleeing; if you come closer, I will fight rather than flee."

Gray reef shark *(Carcharhinus amblyrhynchos)* in "preattack," or agonistic, posture.

Although the gray reef sharks exhibit the most conspicuous threat displays yet described, similar hunching and exaggerated motor patterns have been reported in other shark species. Bonnetheads, according to Myrberg and Gruber, dropped their pectorals and hunched their backs when they passed within two meters of an observer sitting in their pool, and one resident shark was observed hunching toward a newcomer. According to these scientists the hunching posture is known in at least five species of carcharhinid and sphyrnid sharks, always in circumstances similar to those described by Johnson and Nelson.

In his book *The Blue Reef,* marine biologist Walter Starck describes his experiences with these aggressive displays by grays. He reports deliberately charging a gray reef shark in the Eniwetok area in his two-person diver submarine. After making an agonistic display and watching the submarine continue to approach, the shark attacked and damaged it, all with dazzling speed.

Agonistic displays and subsequent aggressive attacks are not, so far as we know, the same as predation. The shark is not attempting to eat the intruder, but to drive it away. Although parts of the display behavior resemble movements made by sharks when attacking prey, it is thought by many shark researchers that threat displays are probably not related to feeding, although they may well be derived from them. George W. Barlow has pointed out that threat displays in other predatory animals commonly derive from the act of overpowering prey.

It was Barlow who suggested that the displays may represent a balance between fleeing and attacking. Johnson and Nelson feel that the stereotyped displays tend to occur more frequently in situations unfamiliar to the shark. Their exaggerated, ritualistic nature marks them as defensive in intent. Rapidly approaching divers are probably perceived by the shark as a potential threat. Most displays are followed by the sharks' withdrawals. We were treated to a mild display by a gray reef shark in about sixty feet of water on a drop-off wall outside Ponape lagoon in the Caroline Islands when we swam rapidly toward it in order to photograph it. Our retreat to the coral wall seemed to reassure the shark, which then went on its way.

SHARK ATTACKS

Because shark attacks always receive so much publicity and because so many myths attach to shark behavior, it seems appropriate to summarize here what *is* known to be characteristic of shark attacks. Sharks are not universal wanton killers that consider every encountered diver a meal. On the other hand, it is not true, as is sometimes asserted by seasoned divers, that sharks will never attack anyone except at the surface, although the latter is far nearer the truth than the former.

Many people who have studied sharks carefully feel that, although very occasionally a shark might attack a human with a meal in mind, feeding is probably rarely the aim of shark attacks. The displays in gray reef sharks (who are almost never involved in unprovoked attacks) and others seem rather to indicate that temperament, including curiosity, is involved in aggression. In a large percentage of shark attacks the shark bumps or bites once and disappears, as if making an investigation or serving a warning. If it were hungry, its efficiency as a feeder would surely enable it to prevail. And if invariably attracted to fresh blood, it would not leave the site of a bleeding victim. Experiments by Albert Tester in the early 1960s designed to test the response of sharks to human odors, though not entirely conclusive, showed that blackfins and gray reef sharks were excited by fresh human blood, but that blackfins were usually repelled by aged blood. (Several species of sharks had an aversion to human sweat, and more to that of some people than of others.) In other studies carried out by David Baldridge, rat blood was unattractive to sharks, which, however, quickly ate rats if they had been bathed in fish juices.

Most of what we know about shark attacks in general is based on information from the International Shark Attack File. With support from the Office of Naval Research, the Smithsonian Institution, beginning in the late 1950s, endeavored for two decades to collect worldwide as much data on shark attacks as possible. A detailed statistical analysis of all the shark attack cases known, 1,652 in number (the first known attack occurred in 1580), was made in the 1970s by H. David Baldridge, formerly of the ONR and then with the Mote Marine Laboratory in Sarasota, Florida. Enough information was available for 200 incidents to be studied in detail.

One of the difficulties with the data, as Baldridge points out, is that all reported incidents were counted as "attacks." An attack could be anything from a perceived threat by a menacing shark with no contact taking place, to a shark bumping a camera, to a fatality. Shark bites sustained by fishermen landing them in boats were included, as were bites that occurred in aquariums. Although various publications frequently assert that there are about 100 "attacks" worldwide every year, Baldridge emphasizes that since 1940, when two-thirds of the attacks documented have occurred, they have averaged twenty-eight a year. Mortality rates for these have decreased from 46 percent in 1940 to an estimated 16 percent in 1973, overall a 35 percent average. In sum, about five persons die per year, worldwide, from shark attacks, and these are rarely divers.

Shark attacks can occur in all waters—warm and cold, shallow and deep—but primarily they occur in warm surface waters, most probably because that is where the most people are. Well over 90 percent of the attacks are made by solitary animals, and 90 percent are at the surface or within five feet of it. Of 941 case histories for which enough information was available, it could be determined that about one-fourth of the attacks were directed at spearfishermen. (Among scuba divers experiencing a serious attack, the great majority were spearfishing.) Indeed, impressive percentages also involved people in the vicinity of spearfishing or other kinds of fishing.

Twenty or so serious attacks on scuba divers were reported by Baldridge between 1954 and 1972, or about one a year (worldwide). Of these, thirteen involved divers who were spearfishing or carrying captured lobsters. One involved a diver feeding a shark in the San Francisco aquarium. Four of the twenty cases involved a fatality. Nearly one-fourth of the diver victims had provoked their attackers by grabbing their tails or prodding or spearing them. Overall, injuries for divers were less severe in character than for shark attacks on other victims, perhaps because divers have more awareness of what surrounds them in the underwater environment.

There is one area where shark attacks on skin and scuba divers are apparently on the increase: the waters off the coasts of central and northern California and Oregon. Statistics gathered by the California Department of Fish and Game indicate increases in the frequency of attacks from Point Conception, just north of Santa Barbara, northward. Within this area the 100-mile section of ocean from Año Nuevo Island to Bodega Bay has a frequency of attack rate ten times as great as that of waters off the rest of the state. Point Conception demarcates the warm-temperate water zone off southern California from the cold-temperate zone, each of which has characteristic marine species. Shark attacks in the southern waters are comparatively rare (there has not been an unprovoked shark attack recorded there since 1959) and probably involve requiem and hammerhead species, whereas those in the colder waters are thought to be from great white sharks *(Carcharodon carcharias)*.

Daniel J. Miller and Ralph S. Collier have analyzed data from the Fish and Game Department and interviewed 87 percent of the forty-seven victims attacked between 1926 and 1979. They found the cold-water attacks to occur year-round but to peak from July through September. Nearly half of these unprovoked attacks were on skin divers, many in search of abalone. Unfortunately, Miller and Collier did not distinguish between scuba and free divers, although they do state that 80 percent of the incidents occurred at the surface. Interestingly, although the white sharks occur in Carmel Bay and along Cannery Row in Monterey Bay, which is the most heavily dived area off central and northern California, no attacks have taken place there. None has taken place, either, in the giant kelp beds. As mentioned above, most are concentrated in one particular stretch of water, occurring chiefly at Tomales Point and the Farallon Islands, areas north and west of San Francisco.

The reason may well be that those are the areas frequented by elephant seals, harbor seals, and California sea lions, favorite prey of white sharks. These prey have become more numerous in the past two decades. White sharks are also thought to be on the increase, perhaps as a consequence of the rise in their prey population. Divers clad in full black wet suits may have silhouettes that resemble the sharks' accustomed food.

THE GREAT WHITE

The infrequency of unprovoked shark attacks on divers in tropical regions makes sharing the seas with sharks safer than sharing the forest with bees and snakes. Some readers will accept that statement intellectually but still feel welling up from somewhere deep inside their consciousness a chilling, primordial anxiety, given form by their recollection of magazine and cinema portrayals of a monstrous jaw agape with horrible teeth. The great white.

It exists, but rarely in those tropical waters where divers and snorkelers like to visit. Although it can live in warm water, it is so large, and has so great a demand for food, that the thin biomass of the tropical seas cannot readily support such a carnivore. Reef fishes are small and elusive; no large shark could survive for long if it were confined to so impoverished an environment. The great white needs whales, seals, and sea lions (which are not easily caught), and these mammals live mostly in temperate or cold waters.

Even in its proper surroundings, the great white is not easily found. No one knows more about their locale and habits than Rodney Fox, an Australian who survived being bitten by one while he was competing in December, 1963, in a spearfishing contest off the South Australian coast near Adelaide. In the ensuing twenty years or so, Fox set out to learn as much as he could about his adversary by developing shark cages that could be floated in the water so that photographers and scientists might observe the big sharks in the animal's natural habitat. Virtually all the motion-picture footage and still photographs involving great whites that one has ever seen, including scenes for *Jaws, Blue Water, White Death,* and various *National Geographic* specials, has been taken off South Australia in cages designed by Fox and at sites located by him. Yet even in the seas where they are known to exist, where they are hunted by sport fishermen, and where Fox and other professional divers have been bitten, they are not easily found.

When Peter Gimbel was attempting to film great whites, he spent five fruitless months searching for them in the waters near the whaling station in Durban, South Africa. When one of us joined Fox and some friends on a shark expedition off Port Lincoln, Australia, we spent eight days constantly chumming the water by throwing whale oil, fresh blood, horse meat, and fish parts over the stern. On only three of those days did great whites appear and on one, the three sharks that did appear would not linger and seemed reluctant to approach the boat very closely, despite the feast we were supplying for them. For only a day and a half out of the eight were we able to enter the water with a great white about (see Plates 43 and 44).

We, of course, entered the water in the cages: metal frame structures covered with heavy-gauge wire mesh and supported in the water by two flotation tanks, one on each side of the top. To make photography easier, the mesh was cut away from a large area perhaps one foot in height and four feet in width on each side of the cage. The cages drifted in the current, tethered to the boat by one or two manila or nylon lines (steel cables are not used so that, if a shark becomes entangled, it can bite itself free). We hung horse meat and fish heads along the sides of the cages as well as off the stern of the boat, and deck hands would from time to time pour blood into the water.

One's first impression of a great white is, naturally, its size. We watched for the better part of a day one that was fourteen feet long and another that was somewhat shorter; the larger may have weighed a ton or more. These were small specimens by great white standards, but when they appeared out of the shallow, greenish water, they looked like gray buses going by. One's second impression is how slowly they move. They seem to swim no faster than a man, even when approaching and striking at a piece of bait. We estimated that the shark made one complete sweep of its caudal fin every second. There was no sudden rush, there were no quick turns until the bait had been seized, and then the animal would violently contort its body into a giant S shape, thrashing from side to side as it worked to cut the line holding the bait to its buoy or to the side of the cage. Those contortions were the most awesome display of brute power we had ever seen, but once the line was severed, the thrashing ended and the shark glided off at a slow, majestic pace.

The great white is countershaded, gray on top and white underneath. It can be distinguished from other sharks by three features: its gill openings run vertically almost the entire depth of the body (other species have shorter gill openings), the upper and lower lobes of its tail fin are roughly the same size and shape (most sharks have an asymmetrical tail fin), and as it swims along its teeth are visible, projecting down from its upper jaw. All the sharks we saw were male, evident from the large pairs of claspers on the undersides of their bodies. Fox, who has seen more great whites than any man alive, said that 90 percent or more of those that approach a boat and feed are male. No one seems to know why the females stay away. Certainly among lions, it is the female that does most of the hunting.

Scores of smallish fish ("Tommy ruffs") were about us, feeding on the chum. They took but small notice of the shark, keeping a few feet away from its jaws, and clearing the area when the thrashing started, but otherwise displaying no agitation. It was obvious that the shark presented little threat to them; they were much faster and more mobile than he. If he had to survive by eating reef fishes, he would be lucky to catch any.

This lack of mobility was evident as the shark neared the suspended bait. It would approach it straight on, swinging down and out its lower jaw and rolling back the black, protective, nictitating membrane over its eyes so that over the last few feet, the shark would be blind. When we tested its mobility by suspending meat from the end of a timber and then moving it about just as the shark closed, we saw that it often missed the food. It took a few tries before it could catch the bait.

Its lateral lines and electroreception system, as we have seen, give it sensory mechanisms that can take over for eyesight during the final approach, but these systems are easily fooled. Often, the shark would attack the steel flotation tanks on our cages rather than the bait suspended from them, perhaps because the metal disturbed the electromagnetic field through which the shark was groping. Once it bit the steel duckboard mounted on the stern of the boat, sending a shower of broken teeth spilling into the water. We received the distinct impression that a shark, once committed to an attack, cannot easily reassess the situation so as to change direction if the food moves or abandon the attack if the object turns out to be unappetizing. Once sharks attack, it is only after they taste what they have bitten that they decide whether it is food or not. Almost the entire left side of Fox's torso was bitten by a great white, but it did not stay to finish him off. Fox is not certain why. When a swimmer is attacked by a shark and other swimmers jump into the water to help him, the shark seems to ignore the opportunity for additional meals. Of course, even one bite by a great white can be fatal.

PRECAUTIONS

Scarcely any diver will ever see, or even be in the remote vicinity of, a great white. Probably no more than a few dozen divers have ever photographed one. No other shark presents anything like the hazards posed by it. This may explain why, when a great white is about, no other shark appears in the vicinity; even among sharks, the word is out that there is something a little special about these creatures.

Thus, the cautionary remarks we would offer to divers and snorkelers are few and easily followed. Avoid a few specific diving areas, such as certain parts of California's northern coast and the Farallon Islands, where sea mammals breed, and other rookeries, such as those of the sea lions off the South Australian coast.

For the rest of the diving areas—which is to say, for virtually all tropical and temperate ones—follow the obvious rules: Don't provoke sharks in any way and exercise prudence with regard to spearfishing. Baldridge advises a diver who confronts a shark to remain submerged if possible, where chances are best for keeping the shark in view and where one is not likely to be mistaken for a sea lion, and to back off, keeping one's movements calm. If surface swimming is necessary, it should be done with smooth, rhythmical strokes. In addition, never maneuver a shark into a position where it has no avenue of escape between you and another obstacle—another diver, a boat, a coral wall, or a sandbar.

Such advice will be rarely needed, however. When a diver does see a shark, it usually is in the distance, swimming away from him. Many who explore the coral reefs complain that they never have a chance to see a shark close up. At least in that regard, lions have won the competition for man's attention. In a Land Rover in Kenya, one can drive right up to a lion and remain parked four feet from him all day. Now, many divers wish that viewing sharks were as easy.

CHAPTER ELEVEN

Invertebrates

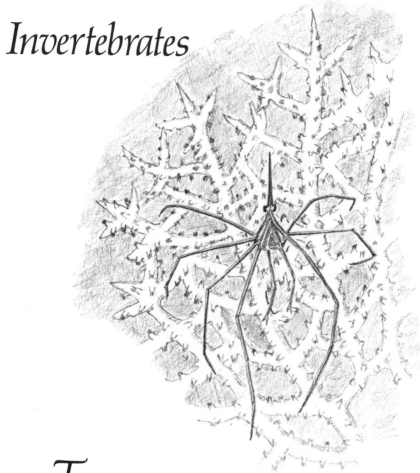

*T*his chapter could just as well be called "Almost Everything in the Sea Besides Fishes," for the umbrella term "invertebrates" is intended to embrace all animals not possessing backbones. That leaves lumped together approximately 95 percent of the over one million animal species. They have in common a sort of leftover status from the period when man's inquisitiveness about life on earth focused mainly on man himself and his terrestrial relations. Invertebrates are not united by any compelling characteristics. Rather, they are a more diverse group than one's wildest imaginings could ever produce. What does an octopus have in common with a honeybee, a worm, a sea lily, or a sponge? Well, none has a backbone.

The greatest variety of invertebrates live in the sea, and with good reason. The buoyant properties of salt water, together with the vast area of the sea bottom, are especially hospitable to animals lacking the support of an internal skeleton. It would be impossible in the space of this chapter to consider more than a tiny fraction of the marine invertebrates. Just one phylum alone, the echinoderms, a group that includes urchins, spiny sea stars, sea cucumbers, and feather stars, comprises over 1,000 known species inhabiting shallow tropical waters in the Indo-Pacific and 150 in the West Indies. Only ten of these species are common to both seas. But invertebrate life is so integral a part of the reef habitat, is so strange and beautiful, and displays so many curious forms of behavior that no discussion of fish life would be complete without some account of invertebrates.

To give some order to the discussion, we shall take up a few of the major forms of behavior of all animals—learning, defense, community life, reproduction—and indicate the nature of that behavior among several of the more commonly observed marine invertebrates.

LEARNING AND ADAPTING

All animals are born with a certain number of built-in behavior patterns, sometimes termed instincts. They are the inherited result of eons of trial and error on the part of their forebears and are passed on from one generation to the next because they enhance the animals' ability to survive. But environmental conditions change from time to time and vary at any given time from one region to the next. Thus most, if not all, animals, even the simplest, must have some ability to adapt to local conditions and many have, within the limits of their varied nervous systems, a surprising talent for learning. Among the creatures to be found on a tropical reef, it is certain invertebrates, not fishes, that display the greatest ability to learn.

Of all the invertebrates, octopuses are the most intelligent and, therefore, learn the most from experience and adapt their behavior accordingly. Although octopuses are referred to in the scientific vernacular as "lower animals," they seem in some ways to be smarter than a great many creatures with backbones. Yet for all their intelligence, these solitarily living animals have a brief life span. A female octopus matures and mates once. After mating, she ceases to eat and dies. Although the male may mate with more than one female, he, too, is destined for only one mating season before he dies. Our close-up photograph (see Plate 47) was taken of a mature octopus that remained motionless while we hovered about it; the creature was probably dying, otherwise it would never have allowed us to approach so near.

Unlike most fishes, the female octopus guards her eggs closely, continually aerating them with a current of water ejected from her siphon and stirring them up by the frequent fanning motion of her tentacles. Sometimes she will eat a few of her own eggs during the several weeks she guards them, but researchers have found evidence that she eats the infertile rather than the fertile ones. This careful maternal care is not reinforced by the subsequent pleasure of enjoying the company of her children, for as they hatch, she dies. A female octopus rarely attains an age in excess of fifteen months.

The intelligence of octopuses has been demonstrated experimentally. When kept in tanks, they will rush out from their lairs and attack anything smaller than themselves that moves. Martin Wells reports that octopuses could be trained to discriminate between moving objects of different shapes by giving them small electric shocks if they attacked the "wrong" shape and food if they attacked the right one. Only ten to twenty trials were necessary for the octopuses to recognize and act on the differences between the shapes, attack the correct ones, and claim their rewards. If blinded, octopuses could learn by touch.

Moreover, octopuses are capable, unlike many animals (and sometimes even man), of postponing immediate gratifications. Instead of eating prey on the spot or running home each time it makes a catch, most octopuses that are out hunting for crabs will collect several individuals, perhaps five or six, before returning home to feast.

Their hunting prowess is legendary. In 1873, the staff at the Brighton Aquarium in England noticed that every day there was one fewer lumpfish in a tank set up to display these fish. One morning, the staff discovered an octopus in the tank amidst the lumpfish. Although kept in a separate tank some distance away, the octopus had somehow learned that lumpfish were available nearby, left its tank, crawled across the intervening space, entered the fish tank, had a meal, and then (until caught in the act) slithered back to its own home. Later on, the staff learned that octopuses would leave their own tanks to forage for crabs and lobsters kept in other exhibits.

In the ocean, the octopus displays the same intelligence in searching for food. Several years ago the daily habits of one Pacific species, *Octopus cyanea*, were observed in detail by John L. Yarnall. He released eight octopuses into holding ponds built into a shallow reef in Hawaii's Kaneohe Bay and watched them from an observation platform so that his presence would not be noticed. In the sea, the octopus did indeed envelop crabs it saw moving in its path, but it also conducted rather systematic searches, inspecting likely places for prey and every one or two yards pouncing on a rock or small clump of algae, spreading its mantle over it in a weblike manner and feeling about underneath it with its arms, sometimes finding crabs, sometimes not.

When not eating, *Octopus cyanea* is often found in front of its home, a hole it digs under a coral head with a blast of water from its funnel. When it retires, it frequently piles up rocks at the entrance. Yarnall found that, although the solitary octopuses have a dominance hierarchy based on size, they do not defend hunting territories. When two octopuses meet, they advance toward each other with one arm held up and extended to the other in a display. On physical contact, or just before, one will retreat.

Alert divers can often spot the residence of an octopus because of its habit of eating crabs and molluscs at home in coral or rocky holes and tossing the shells out the front door. Snorkeling with our daughter and a friend in a shallow lagoon off Roatán, Honduras, we came across an octopus at home, its mantle about twelve inches across, sitting under a coral ledge having an early afternoon meal of queen conch. We dove down and tugged hard but unsuccessfully at the shell. The octopus disappeared into a hole, except for one long tentacle stuck into the conch—which wouldn't fit into the hole. It continued to hold on with impressive strength. We went our way and returned about ten minutes later to find the octopus again out on the ledge, still in firm possession of its conch. Apparently it had to dine outside its hole because its prey wouldn't fit through the door.

Next to octopuses, cuttlefishes are probably the most intelligent invertebrates. Like octopuses, they possess complex brains and superior vision. In the horizontal plane, the vision of cuttlefishes can extend a full 360 degrees. Nocturnal hunters of bottom-dwelling shrimps and crabs, the cuttlefishes use their eyes to locate prey and direct their attacks. Martin Wells has studied the biology and behavior of cephalopods, molluscs that include not only cuttlefishes but also squids, octopuses, and the chambered nautiluses, and has been able to distinguish between their learned and innate reactions. The minute a cuttlefish of the genus *Sepia* is hatched, it knows how and when to bury itself in the sand, blow out an inky camouflage, and run away from larger animals that approach it. Its visual system is instantly able to recognize one kind of prey: little swimming shrimps that are abundant where cuttlefishes lay their eggs. A young cuttlefish can orient itself toward the shrimps and execute a running attack, perfectly timing a seizure with its long arms. This infant skill does not improve with practice. On the other hand, young cuttlefishes must learn by trial and error about other kinds of food and how to catch it. Wells noticed that baby cuttlefishes are not attracted to crabs until they are two or three weeks of age, when, approaching the crabs from any old direction, they are often unsuccessful in the capture and even get pinched by the crabs in the process. But with practice, they learn the value of surprise and routinely approach crabs from the rear, just as grownup cuttlefishes do. Laboratory experiments have shown that cuttelfishes can recognize symbols (colored discs) associated with the availability or nonavailability of food.

Featherdusters, the beautiful filter-feeding tubeworms that look like small flowers dotting the reef (see Plate 56), are invertebrates about as unlike octopuses and cuttlefishes as one could imagine. Tiny-brained as they are, they nevertheless also have the capacity to adapt their behavior. Preyed on by, among other things, butterflyfishes, tubeworms protect themselves by rapidly retracting their feathery feeding arms into their tubes. They do not recognize their enemies, of course. They simply find it pays to withdraw in response either to shadows or to touch. Still, tubeworms can be habituated to these sensory stimuli. Subjected over and over to sudden changes in light intensity or to tapping on the sides of their aquariums, featherdusters quickly "learn" to ignore such changes. Touched repeatedly in the same way on its tentacles, the featherduster eventually stops retracting, although it habituates to touch less quickly than to light stimuli. In these laboratory experiments they even habituated to combinations of these stimuli, although it took longer. In the discussion of cleaning symbiosis in Chapter 9, we mentioned our tubeworm's tolerance of our peppermint or redbacked cleaning shrimp *(Hippolysmata grabhami)* in our aquarium. To our amazement, the worm readily allowed the shrimp to grope about its tentacled crown. Although we have not seen such behavior in the sea, it seems to make sense that the sedentary featherduster, and other polychaete filter feeders such as the spiral Christmas-tree worms, accustom themselves to unthreatening, familiar neighbors so that they can maximize the time they spend unfurled, feeding in the current.

Nocturnal-feeding basket stars spend the daylight hours tightly tucked into permanent coral homes that are conveniently situated near their nighttime feeding stations. Between twenty to eighty minutes after sunset, depending on the species and the region, they emerge and climb to an elevated position atop a coral head, a sea fan, or another pinnacled protrusion where the current-born plankton are unobstructed. Their sensory systems detect the direction of current flow before they anchor themselves and spread out their intricate arms, forming lacy baskets that sometimes reach a diameter of a yard or more (see Plates 61 and 62). They, too, seem to learn. The routes they follow to and from their daytime shelters and their favorite nocturnal summits are always the same. Elapsed-time movies of the basket star *Astrophyton muricatum* showed it night after night traversing the same paths and using the same "hand grips" on the reef surface.

DEFENSE STRATEGIES

Although invertebrates are born with instincts and are capable of learning, the observer must still wonder how so many of these small-sized, soft-bodied animals, prized in the diet of so many fishes or other invertebrates, survive on the reef. A wealth of sensory early warning systems, ruses, retreats, body armors, architectural constructions, and poisons are used. We have already seen that many invertebrates are nocturnal and hope to avoid detection in the darkness. Fishes that are nocturnal crustacean hunters generally migrate off the reef to eat; thus, nocturnal crustaceans that stay on the reef are relatively safe from fish predation. Many segmented worms (polychaetes) appear at this time.

Other invertebrates, like fishes, are cryptic—that is, they either blend in with their surroundings or live in hidden habitats. Many crabs inhabit branching corals, where they are safe from the reaches of most fishes and other predators. Several species of tiny shrimps match their chosen commensals, such as soft corals, anemones, algae nests, and sea stars, and thus are difficult to detect. Some shrimps, like reef fishes, are capable of changes in color intensity, although they do not change patterns. Baby octopuses, from birth on, have the ability to camouflage themselves by changing colors. A tiny octopus, on emerging from its egg into a saucer of water at an Australian zoological garden, instantly matched the color of the saucer. Some tiny shrimps take refuge among sea urchin spines, and several species cling to the arms of feather stars (crinoids). Some species of brittle stars burrow into the sandy bottom around coral patches, completely covering their discs and upper arms, leaving only the tips of their tentacles protruding to feed on detritus or on suspended particulate matter, sending with undulatory motions small columns of water down their bodies in order to breathe.

Hard-shelled gastropods, spiny lobsters, and stone crabs have developed structural defenses. Hermit crabs armor themselves by moving into abandoned shells. The female gall crab, which we met earlier in the chapter on symbiosis, uses coral architecture, settling on live coral and stimulating it to grow around her, sealing herself off against predation. Many feather stars, or crinoids, that feed in exposed habitats have large, stiff, spiky projections around their visceral discs. Even if their viscera are eaten by predators, they can regenerate lost parts in as little as three weeks. The longspine sea urchin *(Diadema)* has gained a formidable reputation among divers owing to its ability to point its spines in the direction of a shadow and inflict pain along with its punctures. Many shrimps and other commensals take shelter among its spines. But like everything else, it also has enemies. Two researchers have counted more than twenty species of fishes that attack *Diadema* sea urchins; spiny lobsters and helmet shells also prey on them. Triggerfishes blow jets of water under the urchins in order to turn them upside down so that the fish can get at the vulnerable underbody. No armor seems to guarantee safety.

Common defenses are poison and venom. A high proportion of the invertebrates that crawl about in exposed positions on the reef are toxic to fishes and to other would-be predators, or secrete various substances with a repulsive smell or taste. Gerald J. Bakus tested reef invertebrates of forty-two species from four phyla that live in exposed habitats on the Great Barrier Reef and found that 73 percent of them are toxic to fishes. By contrast, only 25 percent of the species that normally hide or are camouflaged are toxic. Sponges, soft corals, and sea cucumbers are particularly likely to be toxic if they are out in the open. Small bristleworms (or fireworms) seem unconcerned as they crawl about quite exposed (see Plate 51), and with good reason. They are both irritating to the touch and poisonous to eat. Some crinoids are poisonous as well. Of course, there are always a few predators that spoil the plan because they have developed immunity to an invertebrate's toxin. Some angelfishes, for example, eat toxic sponges other fishes avoid. Many snails consume sponges and sea cucumbers that are toxic to other animals.

An ingenious and economical solution to poison immunity has evolved among several nudibranch (or sea slug) species of the aeolid family. These beautiful snails without shells (nudibranch means "naked gill") crawl about exposed in the waters of all seas; they are especially numerous and diverse in tropical waters, where they are able to consume the stinging, venomous nematocysts of coral polyps, anemones, and tunicates or hydroids, sponges, and the like (see Plate

49).* Nematocysts, it will be recalled from the first chapter, are the chief defenses of the corals. On contact, they function like explosive charges. Somehow, nudibranchs consume nematocysts without setting off the explosives, storing the venom cells in special little sacs on their backs called "cerata." (It is the cerata that give so many nudibranchs their whimsical, ruffled appearance.) The stored nematocysts are thus recycled to become the toxic arsenal of the nudibranch, ready to repel its enemies.

Some nudibranchs manufacture their own toxins, which they secrete through their skins; others secrete distasteful substances. The tropical *Phyllidia* species secret toxins so powerful that a single nudibranch is capable of killing a whole bucketful of fish or crabs. Nudibranchs of the family Dorididae secrete sulfuric acid. A few nudibranchs are cryptic, deriving color pigments from the prey they live on, sometimes storing them in their cerata.

Decorator or spider crabs (family Majidae) camouflage themselves by attaching all sorts of material to their legs and bodies until they are scarcely recognizable as crabs. Some transplant living invertebrates to their carapaces: anemones, sponges, polychaete worms, and hydroids, supplemented with algae and debris. Whether by accident or design, many of their living decorations are toxic and thus contribute to the defensive array. These walking rummage sales will also scurry away from predators, display their pinching claws (chelae) if cornered, and even escape from nonswimming hunters by throwing themselves off promontories and floating spread-eagled to another level of the reef. As a last resort they will employ a strategy routinely used by sea stars: self-amputate a limb that has been seized by a predator (this ability is called "autonomy"). They will later regenerate the missing member.

Autonomy need not involve severe contact. Some threatened sea stars shed their limbs almost spontaneously, as if to say "King's X!" In laboratory experiments an electric shock has caused all five arms of a sea star to detach and walk away from the central body, which later grew five new tentacles. Some species of sea cucumbers (Holo-

*Each species is quite specialized in dietary preferences. Divers wishing to be kind to nudibranchs they have picked up for closer inspection should return them to whatever surface they were plucked from so that they can get on with their munching, for nudibranchs are slow travelers and few are free swimmers. Of course, such divers might want to side with the prey—a nudibranch can completely devour, over time, a soft coral colony.

thuriidae) practice what seems a more desperate form of autonomy. They eviscerate themselves, expelling from their posteriors not only their digestive tract and reproductive organs but parts of their respiratory systems as well (see Plate 52). Yet they can rapidly regenerate them. Perhaps the eviscerated anatomy attracts the predator, distracting it while the sea cucumber escapes. However, it is apparently more frequently a response to stagnant sea water. Other species of *Holothuria* practice a different, more aggressive expulsive strategy. They expel a mass of blind tubes, toxic in some species, stickily adhesive in others, and crawl away while the intruder—perhaps a small lobster or crab —is left poisoned or hopelessly entangled in the sticky discharge. Less badly frightened sea cucumbers have the ability to withdraw their detritus-feeding heads into their bodies.

Except for the jet-propelled squids and the slower-swimming cuttlefishes and octopuses (which can secrete ink screens to hide their retreats), invertebrates as a group are not noted for speedy locomotion. Still, it does not take phenomenal speed for a sea urchin, say, to stilt walk, on the short spines at the base of its shell, away from an even slower predatory sea star. Several invertebrates have evolved novel ways of locomotion. Some snails, such as turbans, use their feet to hurl themselves in a sort of cartwheel away from sea stars (see drawing on page 201). The common California black turban snail normally bumbles along at one inch a minute, but on contact with a predatory sea star it speeds up to four inches a minute. Depending on which side of its protruding foot is touched by a sea star, it makes a right-angle turn, twists the shell around, and "rushes" away.

Abalones (genus *Haliotis*) are able to raise their shells and whirl themselves violently from side to side. Some species can execute a leaping maneuver. Maori fishermen in New Zealand, mindful of this talent, have found a way to harvest abalones without having to pry them loose from the rocks. They touch them with a sea star known to prey on them and then grab the moving abalones before they again dig into the substrate. An abalone in distress because of sea star aggression even secretes a cloudy alarm substance, which sets off escape responses in nearby abalones. Sea urchins can also sense their sea star enemies chemically before contact is made and start to move away. So far, no divers have been injured in sea urchin stampedes.

Not all invertebrates are so marvelously sensitized to the predatory world. Although some bivalves clamp shut when danger is sensed and others, like the scallops, can manage propulsion by opening and closing their shells rapidly, some species seem unaware of attack. They

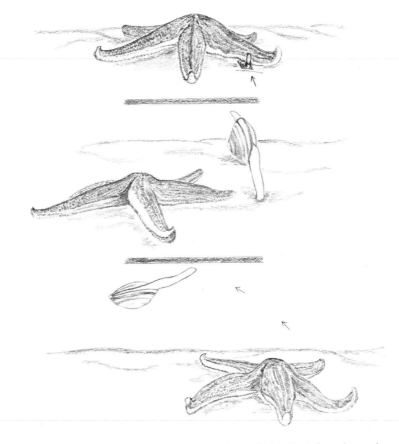

Top: Sea star (genus *Acmaea*) arm touches buried clam's siphon (arrow), a tube through which the clam pumps water in and out. Middle: Feeling the sea star's arm, the clam (genus *Spisula*) stretches out its foot and hurls itself upward. Bottom: The clam's momentum carries it up and over the predacious sea star. (After Feder, 1972.)

open up their shells and continue to siphon away at their own feeding tasks, insensitive to the devouring activities of their destroyers. Apparently their reproductive capacities are sufficient to ensure their genetic success, but who knows for how long.

SEDENTARY LIFE

Leaping abalones, tumbling clams, marching sea urchins—these and other examples should belie any notion that shellfishes and urchins live only sluggish, sedentary lives. But some invertebrates are entirely sedentary because they occupy that twilight zone between the plant and animal kingdoms (see Plate 46).

Sponges

On the reef, some of the most conspicuous and beautiful creatures are also among the most primitive. Sponges (phylum Porifera) were long thought to be plants. We now know they are animals (though just barely), but they have not, so far as we can tell, been the evolutionary progenitors of any higher animals. They seem to have persisted quite well just being sponges: sedentary layers of hollow, primarily independent cells with an outer, perforated covering. Planktonic nourishment is extracted from water continuously pumped by the flagellated cells through the tiny holes in the sponge's covering. A sponge must pump about a ton of water through its system to extract enough food to gain an ounce of body weight. Its lumpy mass is strengthened by needlelike structures, called spicules, made of various hardened substances. Spicules lend a skeletal strength that enables some sponges to reach huge sizes.

There are some 5,000 known species of sponges; all but about 150 are marine dwelling. They have been around a long time, having accomplished their species diversification early on, mostly in Cambrian times, and are said to have exceeded in Paleozoic times the combined biomass (the amount of living animals) of all the other bottom-living reef creatures. Sponges not only lend color, texture, and pattern to the reef but provide living accommodations for countless invertebrates and small fishes; brittle stars, for example, are commonly found in tube sponges. Their water-pumping systems make sponges an ideal environment for small planktivores. And they oblige some kinds of crab and worm inhabitants with lasting security, simply growing slowly around them. Not all are benign, however. Some, like the bright red or orange fire sponge *(Tedania ignis)* and the bulb-shaped brown touch-me-not sponge *(Neofibularia nolitangere)* of the Caribbean, are stinging to a diver's touch, and others, the boring sponges, encrust and destroy live coral.

Plantlike Animals

Many other sedentary invertebrates resemble plants. These include most of the polyp-form animals: the coelenterates (or cnidarians), especially the soft corals, colonies of corals without hard skeletons, and their anemone cousins, solitary-polyped animals with no skeletal framework. Like the stony, reef-building corals, all of these animals have stinging cells that enable them to stun and digest their microscopic prey. Rarely are these cells harmful to man, so that swimming through the great, waving fields of soft coral frequently encountered by divers ordinarily presents no hazard.

Something a bit more painful than a minor irritation can be acquired from one hydroid, the so-called fire coral *(Millepora)*. Touched, it inflicts a sharp pain akin to a bee sting. It takes many forms—upright, branching, encrusting—that make it easy for an unwary diver to mistake it for harmless true coral, which it resembles because of its calcareous skeleton. It has a smoother look, however, and lacks stony cups. It can easily be recognized by it characteristic buckskin color.

Particularly plantlike are the small, branched hydroids that look like tiny ferns or feathers. Many attain a length of only two to three inches, though some grow to six inches or more. They are found throughout reefs on dead patches of coral and on rocks, often in the company of sponges and tiny tunicate colonies, all of which compete for space so that they can attach themselves to bare patches of dead coral. Tunicates are smooth, translucent, tube-shaped creatures (see Plate 57) that look like invertebrates but aren't quite. Although they have no backbones, tunicate larvae possess a primitive support system made up of cartilage and thus are classified as a close relative of the vertebrates: as "urochordates."

Amidst the branches of gorgonian soft corals, such as sea fans, sea whips, and sea plumes, one can find many small invertebrates. Some, such as the common flamingo-tongue snail *(Cyphoma gibbosum)* and the rare fingerprint snail *(C. signatum),* are parasites that eat their gorgonian hosts (see Plate 12). One sea fan can often grow fast enough to stay ahead of the predation of the snail, but if two snails attack the same fan, it may be eaten faster than it can grow and die. Some invertebrates, like the arrow crab *(Stenorhynchus seticornus)* and various species of feather stars (crinoids), merely use the corals as useful perches for filter feeding. Gorgonians, which exist in all tropical seas, are for some reason more diversified in the Caribbean than anywhere else.

Sea anemones (Anthozoa) take their common name from the flower they resemble. Although lacking a brain and internal organs, the anemones are animals and more interesting ones from a behavioral point of view than their permanently attached coral relatives. They are common in shallow waters throughout the world but are more abundant in tropical waters, where they host many symbionts, especially, in the Indo-Pacific, the clownfishes *(Amphiprion)*. Anemones attach their bases to reefs and rocks and spread out their hunting tentacles, which convey captured food to a central mouth, the only opening in their body columns.

Anemones flourish under the same conditions as corals. Like corals and giant or tridacna clams, most harbor symbiotic algae, the zooxanthellae, which need light for their photosynthetic functions (see Chapter 9). Indeed, at least one anemone *(Phyllactis flosculifera)* on the Great Barrier Reef farms extra zooxanthellae in specially adapted areas of its body, storing them as a source of nutrients for itself in times when its carnivorous hunting isn't going well—a kind of private mariculture.

Smaller anemones can be found growing on the backs of some crabs and jellyfishes, and even on sea walnuts and comb jellies. These anemones, like other coelenterates, possess stinging cells (nematocysts) for capturing prey and defending themselves against predators. Some, as we have learned, can sting and consume fishes. While they are generally sedentary, they can and do change their positions when disturbed, loosening their grip on the bottom and propelling themselves with muscular contractions to new locations.

FINDING A NICHE ON THE REEF

Anemones must compete for space with corals that need the same bottom areas for starting new settlements. While some anemones capture fishes, sea stars, and molluscs, some feed on a diet of smaller, planktonic animals. In such competition for desirable spaces, anemones have the important advantage of movement, whereas corals, once settled, must see out their destinies where they are established.

These deceptively passive beauties, it turns out, are capable of aggressive behavior toward rivals as well as toward prey. There is evidence that they not only actively damage or overgrow corals but compete with anemones of other species, partitioning out living space among themselves. Fishelson described an aquarium encounter of a Mediterranean anemone with a *Stoichactis* anemone (the kind that are symbiont with clownfishes) in which the former seized some of the latter's tentacles, dragged them into its mouth, and digested them. The victim anemone contracted and was rescued but died shortly after when it was again attacked, this time by a raccoon butterflyfish *(Chaetodon lunula)*.

At the Smithsonian Tropical Research Institute on Isla Galeta off the Caribbean coast of Panama, Kenneth Sebens moved pairs of coral-attached anemones close to each other in laboratory aquariums. Some anemone species actively attacked others, causing tissue damage and the withdrawal of the injured anemone. Other anemones consistently moved away from apparently dominant species in what Sebens characterized as a nonaggressive spacing behavior. He observed that on the calm water reefs, the aggressive species in each of three habitat-specialized groups was always the most abundant.*

Anemones, then, are no different from most reef inhabitants in preferring specific habitats and some, like many animals, seem to be in their own way territorially defensive.

Crustacean Residential Preferences

Usually the social life of coral shrimps and crabs can be inferred from the habitats they select and even from their colors. Just as most of the fishes that stay close to the reef are poster-colored, so also are a large proportion of the crustaceans that live amidst the coral. Since they are of diminutive size and do not swim flamboyantly about, this is not immediately apparent. But in the past few years a number of censuses of coral have been carried out. Several involved encasing entire coral heads in plastic, uprooting them, and identifying and counting all the animal life therein.

Most of these counts have involved various species of shrub corals, such as branching, finger, or cauliflower corals. Crabs seem to form the bulk of their inhabitants, followed by shrimps and a few small fishes. On living coral, the crabs tend to be brightly colored, with their numbers being larger the greater the size of the coral heads. They mostly live, as do shrimps, in male-female pairs, and space themselves

---

*These are the common ringed, or corkscrew, anemones *(Bartholomea annulata),* a species that prefers sand pockets and that divers commonly see living symbiotically with tiny shrimps, notably the little translucent, violet-dotted Pederson cleaner shrimp, the similar *Periclimenes yucatanicus,* and the red snapping shrimp, *Alpheus armatus;* Florida false coral *(Ricordia florida),* an iridescent green or orange anemone that spreads its crowded polyps out in carpet fashion over massive corals; and *Heteractis lucida,* most often found on dead coral with a cemented base. Another favored symbiont of the Pederson and the *Periclimenes yucatanicus* shrimps, the common giant Caribbean anemone, *Condylactis gigantea,* with its long, thick, tan-colored tentacles, often tipped in purple, green, or pink, is one that appears to damage coral (see Plate 41). Although Sebens did not find that it attacked other anemones, both individuals of other species and the same species avoided established *C. gigantea.*

out in food-oriented territories. Thus situated, and barring misfortune (a snail with a very long proboscis, a crown-of-thorns sea star that kills their coral), they are set for life with shelter, food, and a handy mate for procreation. They are directly dependent on the coral. Most of the symbiotic crabs eat coral-secreted mucus. If the coral dies, the crabs must leave and attempt to colonize live coral hosts elsewhere. That is not easy because already established crustacean denizens will be anything but welcoming.

In contrast, the same species of coral when dead plays host to another kind of community, quite different but equally populous. Here, too, crabs abound, but instead of colorful, territorial symbiont pairs, drably colored scavengers move in, their gray hues blending with the background of dead coral. Most feed on detritus or algae.

Caribbean arrow crabs *(Stenorhynchus seticornis),* which look like a marine version of a granddaddy longlegs spider (see chapter head drawing and Plate 39), are nocturnal filter feeders. By day they hide. One arrow crab census off Grand Bahama Island found nearly two-thirds of them associated with anemones and crinoids for daytime protection. At night they find feeding perches atop nearby gorgonians, sponges, or other pinnacles where currents bring food to them, returning at dawn with infallible homing ability to their shelters. They seem to space themselves out in solitary territories rather than by pairs, starting out with homes in shallow waters but migrating to deeper reef niches as they grow larger.

The Caribbean stinging anemone *(Lebrunia danae),* like many anemones and other sedentary or sessile invertebrates, is a habitat for several decapod (ten-footed) crustaceans, such as the arrow crab. The anemone prefers to live in a crevice, into which it withdraws at night. Just as different anemone species prefer different reef environments, their symbiotic occupants prefer different parts of the anemones. A study of the stinging anemone by Gregg Stanton off Grand Bahama found that various small cleaner shrimps spent most of their time hovering just above the anemone's branched tips, entering their host when threatened. Another group of shrimps prefers to maintain continuous contact with the anemone fronds, at least during the day. *Mithrax* crabs and a few small fishes, including the blenny *Labrisomus haiatus,* prefer to dwell in the sheltered area underneath the anemone. Stanton counted ten different decapod and several fish species associated with the anemone, occurring in various combinations, but he never found more than three species together on the same host anemone, suggesting some sort of space limitations.

Feather Star Diversity

Crinoids, the feather stars, are perhaps the most plantlike appearing of all the invertebrates, both in texture and in form. An abundant assemblage on an Indo-Pacific reef looks like a horticultural heaven, with a spectacular array of curled, multicolored fronds waving gently in the currents (see Plate 49). But they are animals, cousins (among the echinoderms) to sea stars, brittle stars, sea cucumbers, and sea urchins, all with radially symmetrical bodies. Curiously, until less than twenty years ago, they were known mostly from fossil records and a limited number of observational treatises, and were thought by many scientists to be nearly extinct. Direct observations made possible with scuba equipment have brought them within reach of behavioral study.

Around their central discs, depending on the species, are arranged from five to more than 200 feeding arms, each with rows of small branches called pinnules. The pinnules have minute, mucus-coated tube feet that trap food particles and transfer them by way of grooves in the arms to the mouth. Ancestral forms, sea lilies, were fixed to the bottom; a few examples still exist on deep reefs below 300 feet. But the crinoids most divers encounter, though primarily sedentary, have gained the advantage of movement. They grip bottom surfaces with clawlike arms called cirri and can elevate their bodies on these short projections and crawl about (see Plate 48). A few species can swim, flapping their long arms up and down like a many-winged bird in slow motion.

The crinoids are host to a variety of commensals: small shrimps, crabs, brittle stars, annelid (segmented) worms, isopod and copepod crustaceans, and clingfishes, most of them color-adapted to their hosts. Some of these commensals prey on others, with the very small copepod crustaceans, no more than a few millimeters long, at the bottom of the predation chain. Crinoids have adapted to all kinds of environmental conditions. Some are nocturnal, resting with their arms coiled in spirals by day; some are diurnal; some feed both night and day. The pinnule patterns of some crinoids are adapted to feeding in strong currents whereas those of others are better suited to calm conditions (see drawing on page 208). The most commonly seen Caribbean species, the beaded crinoid *(Nemaster discoidea)*—tiny spots along each segment of the pinnules give it a beaded appearance—and the orange or gold crinoid *(N. rubiginosa),* avoid strong-current habitats and keep the bases of their bodies tucked well down in crevices, showing only loose, gracefully coiled arms. They probably feed day and night.

Two kinds of crinoid feeding poses showing "filter fan" adaptation to strong current by *Nemaster grandis* (left) and multidirectional orientation for calm water habitat by *N. discoidea* (right).

Although crinoids partition out their habitats with careful specialization, so far as we know there is no evidence of anemonelike aggressiveness. In fact, some strong-current feeders apparently join forces at times in a kind of cooperative fishing formation. The largest and most easily recognized Caribbean crinoid, the bushy black *N. grandis,* with white-tipped pinnules, perches in exposed "filter fan" positions in heavy currents. Often two or more individuals are perched side by side with interlocking arms, creating what D. L. Meyer, a crinoid authority, has termed a baffle effect. This probably increases the crinoids' chances of trapping food in swift water conditions. These crinoids are extremely sensitive to the direction of current flow, rotating their arms for maximum effectiveness when currents change direction. But in too strong a current they coil up their arms or retreat to more easily held footholds.

COMMUNITY ALLIANCES

The destruction of Indo-Pacific coral reefs caused by the infamous crown-of-thorns sea star *(Acanthaster planci)* has stimulated much research, one result of which has been the discovery of several small territorial coral dwellers that attack the outsize sea star when it threatens their habitat. The crown-of-thorns avoids contacting the coral nematocysts with its tube feet by walking on the tips of its thorny spines. It thus becomes the task of the coral's symbiotic allies to protect it. Like the Lilliputians after Gulliver, diminutive crustaceans strike out furiously. Probably alerted by chemical pheromones, the pistol shrimp *(Alpheus lottini)*, a shrub coral dweller, will emerge promptly from the coral branches when a crown-of-thorns begins an assault, touch the arm of the sea star with its claw, and then snap away vigorously. It also pinches the spines in the feeding groove of the sea star arms. Its fellow symbiont, a crab named *Trapezia ferruginea*, snips the invader's tube feet and spines with its claws and jerks the arms back and forth.

Combined efforts, not surprisingly, are more successful in turning back the enemy than individual ones, but each has some effect. As a result, it often seems easier to the crown-of-thorns to choose another variety of coral than to persist against the irritating attacks of the crustaceans. In laboratory experiments conducted at the Smithsonian Tropical Research Institute, sea stars given unpopulated, live shrub corals to eat were able to mount them in two minutes. Switched to a diet of corals populated with defensive crustaceans, successful mountings by the crown-of-thorns (which in the laboratory setting had no alternative food) took almost two hours to achieve. Overall, in the field and in the laboratory, shrub coral crustaceans were effective in preventing crown-of-thorns attacks about one-third of the time. From his studies of coral off the western coast of Panama, Peter W. Glynn has suggested that a reef attacked by the crown-of-thorns will in time become dominated by branching corals because that is the kind that harbors those crabs that attack the predatory sea stars.

An even more complex communal life than that which exists between coral polyps and symbiotic crabs exists among three dissimilar animals that often live together in small Indo-Pacific communities of cauliflower, or shrub, coral *(Pocillopora damicornis)*. Each is capable of bullying, attacking, and even eating the other. Instead, the members of this trio maintain a sort of truce, communicating periodically among themselves in ritualized ways that apparently serve to reaffirm their residential status. But all reject newcomers, both of their own species and those of their neighbors. Adult wartyheaded, or redheaded, gobies *(Paragobiodon echinocephala)*, another species of goby *(P. lacunicola)*, sedentary snapping pistol shrimps *(Alpheus lottini),* and two species of trapezid crabs benefit from sharing a sort of communal defense against potential intruders. At Heron Island on Australia's Great Barrier Reef, B. R. Lassig recently completed a study of these neighboring individuals and described the intricate balance of power these creatures preserve among themselves.

Among the established residents of one of the groups, relationships were governed by elaborate rituals. The gobies, on encountering shrimps and crabs, regularly assumed a display posture involving the rapid shivering of their bodies. The shrimps grabbed at juvenile gobies but left adult residents alone, often resting their antennae against the bodies of *P. lacunicola,* perhaps to make sure of their identities. Crabs displayed back at shivering gobies with aggressive postures, claws held apart and agape, grabbing at them intermittently, which caused the fish to dart forward a bit while continuing to display. But no injury was done.

Nonresident fishes, however, were actively pursued by the crabs and sometimes caught and eaten. In fact, immigrants of all species were unwelcome to all members of the community triangle. Lassig described a downright free-for-all that resulted from the introduction of four wartyheaded gobies into a colony of a pair of resident fish of that species and several crabs. The crabs went wild and pursued *all* the fish for about twenty minutes, at which point the resident gobies turned on the crabs and started bumping them about from the rear, restoring order. The intruders were expelled, and the ritualistic displays resumed among the old community members.

Such complicated interactions among fishes and invertebrates are not immediately apparent to the casual observer on the reef, but they probably are far more commonplace than we might think. The crowded "urban" conditions of the reef habitat affect the social lives not only of fishes but of all the reef's living creatures and have resulted in a proliferation of strange associations and competitive adaptations the likes of which we have scarcely begun to comprehend.*

---

*More is known about mutual defenses between symbiotic pairs. The best-known examples of these, of course, are the protections exchanged between various anemones and clownfishes. Another example is that of the Caribbean red snapping shrimp *(Alpheus armatus),* a relative of the sea-star-attacking pistol shrimp and one of the several shrimp symbionts of the ringed anemone *(Bartholomea annulata).* The red snapping shrimp is ever vigilant against the predatory approaches of the anemone-eating fireworm, *Hermodice carunculata,* rushing out and snapping its claws (chelae) until the worm retreats.

REPRODUCTION

The Indo-Pacific painted or clown shrimp *(Hymenocera picta)* lives in stable male-female pairs in coral niches. These small crustaceans—adults are about two inches long—belong to a group of sea-star-eating shrimps, to which they are attracted by chemical cues. (The painted shrimp sometimes eats the crown-of-thorns, but this is not its favorite species.) Although large sea stars may be assaulted by both members of a shrimp pair, the shrimps hunt individually. Sometimes they return to their homes with smaller bits of food, but they only share these when they have satisfied themselves and lost interest in the leftovers. Their pair bond is thought to function not for cooperative hunting purposes but primarily for reproductive success. These coral shrimps are not speedy travelers. They can make swimming motions but cannot sustain momentum for long. Living in stable pairs reduces the time spent searching for a mate and increases the time available for hunting sea stars.

Besides, a male shrimp searching for a mate would have to be lucky to come across a female at just the right time in her molting cycle. Their mating rituals and egg-brooding habits are typical of a wide range of crustaceans. As they grow, these crustaceans shed their skeletal coverings, just as snakes shed their skins. With each molting, which occurs about every eighteen to twenty days, a sexually mature female releases pheromones signifying to the male that she is ready to spawn her eggs (about 1,000 of them), which she broods underneath her abdomen. After a courtship period of about thirty minutes the shrimp pair copulates. Until the larvae hatch about eighteen days later, the female aerates her egg clutch, fanning them with her minute abdominal legs, and keeps them clean with her front claws, or chelae. Uta Seibt and Wolfgang Wickler studied painted shrimps for three years in aquariums and on east African reefs. They reported an interesting thing about the pair bond: The male will mate with other females should they be in his proximity during their attractive molting periods, but he always returns to his permanent partner, whom he also defends against the advances of rival males. In laboratory experiments fights over receptive females (those at the molting stage) were severe, sometimes resulting in claw amputations. Nonreceptive females could be more easily defended, with ritual, tournamentlike claw waving.

Male-female pairs of coral-associated shrimps and crabs, such as those of the painted shrimp, are probably common because these crustaceans tend to be permanently attached to specific homesites, either for protection or food or both, a condition reinforced by their limited mobility.

Some invertebrates are not sexually differentiated. Sea anemones that have sexual identities discharge sperm and eggs into the water, where fertilization takes place, or incubate them in a gastric pouch. Some female anemones have been reported to lean toward males at times of spawning, or even move closer to them to better the chances of fertilization. Other sea anemones are hermaphroditic and reproduce by dividing, developing two mouths before splitting apart to form two individuals, breaking away parts of the foot, which regenerate into new anemones, or producing and releasing small lobes from the disc.

Nudibranchs are all hermaphroditic, their reproductive organs producing both sperm and eggs. However, like many hermaphroditic animals, almost without exception they copulate with other nudibranchs of their species—a genetic safety habit—cross-fertilizing each other's eggs. Their eggs are often spectacularly colored, arranged in a gelatinous ribbon coil much like a woman's garter (see Plate 50) or in long strings.

Shortly after sunset is a favored spawning time not only of many fishes but of some invertebrates as well, probably for the same strategic reason: to elude planktivores. Although the reproductive anatomy of many invertebrates is known from laboratory dissection, their spawning behavior is not well understood, and for many species it has been observed, if at all, only in the artificial environments of aquariums. Precious few marine invertebrates (or fishes, for that matter) adapt well enough to aquarium conditions to spawn. If they do, their offspring rarely survive to maturity.

Brittle stars have been seen, as the observers termed it, *in flagrante delicto* just after dark on a reef off Palau in the Caroline Islands of the Pacific. The first reported observation of brittle stars and sea cucumbers spawning in nature was published by Gordon Hendler and David L. Meyer in 1982. Normally reclusive both day and night, clusters of the brittle star *Ophiarthrum pictum* emerged from concealment and climbed to exposed positions atop corals. Once established, groups of from two to five animals stood on "tiptoe," elevating their central discs, which they expanded and contracted. This activity, which lasted about three-quarters of an hour, released clouds of gametes (sperm and eggs) into the current (see drawing on page 213) and ended with the return of the brittle stars to the safety of their crevices. Other species of brittle stars, observed in laboratory spawnings, have different habits: some elevate an arm or two and thrash it about, perhaps to aid in the dispersal of the gametes, but the nocturnal timing seems to be a common feature.

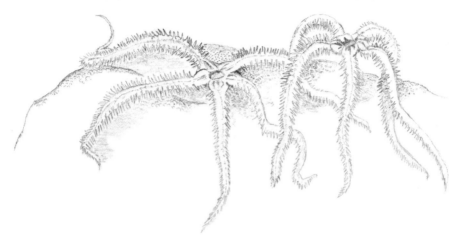

Pacific brittle stars *(Ophiarthrum pictum)* spawning at dusk. The one at left is crawling in "normal" posture. The individual at right is elevated on its spidery legs to release gametes from its disc into the currents. (Drawn from photograph in Hendler and Meyer, 1982.)

In 1977 three sea cucumbers were spotted and photographed by Hendler and Meyer at midnight atop a coral head, lifting up their heads—which contain the genital apparatus as well as the feeding tentacles of these animals—and issuing forth gametes for thirty minutes.

Feather stars, or crinoids, were first observed spawning in nature by Fishelson in the Red Sea near Elat. He witnessed the crepuscular emergence of the nocturnal crinoid *Lamprometra klunzingeri,* which lives in colonies of up to sixty animals in one square yard of space. Male and female crinoids assembled close together on a coral block and anchored themselves along a notch in the coral, their arms fully extended. The tiny branched feathery appendages (pinnules) that characterize crinoids include some adapted for reproductive purposes (as one arm of male octopuses and cuttlefishes is adapted to serve as a reproductive organ). These pinnules, noted Fishelson, were swollen with gametes. As if by prior arrangement one crinoid, later determined to be a male, began intensely waving its arms and was immediately imitated by a simultaneous frenzy of mass arm-whipping undulations. A cloud of greenish-colored gametes enshrouded the vicinity, then was borne off by the current. This procreative ritual was brief, lasting only twenty-five seconds. Chancing on it was a rare stroke of fortune. Another such piece of luck occurred in Palau waters when Hendler and Meyer photographed a female crinoid of the species *Capillaster multiradiatus* releasing eggs that mingled with what apparently were mucus strands of sperm.

IN CONCLUSION

Attempting in one chapter or even one book to summarize what is known about marine invertebrates is a hopeless task, not simply because there are so many creatures but because, unlike fishes, the invertebrate classification lumps together such a varied spectrum of species. Some have symbiotic relationships and a few, as we have seen, are participants in community life. But most are a diverse group with only the lack of a backbone to unite them under one label. Experienced scuba divers will have seen many invertebrates; the casual snorkeler, attracted to brightly colored fishes and unable to explore for long below the surface, may notice only a few: the corals themselves, perhaps a stray conch crawling along the sandy bottom, the spiny sea urchins, or a sea star. There are many good reasons to progress from snorkeling to scuba diving; a chance to explore the extraordinary variety of invertebrates is one of the best.

CHAPTER TWELVE

Day, Night, and In Between

The water over the reef is opaque and quiet. Only the movements of a few nocturnal fishes catch the eye. Here and there a squirrelfish hovers above its coral home and a few companionable bigeyes appear together in the midwater distance. More squirrelfishes arrive from their night feeding regions, seeking their familiar daytime hiding places. Schools of bigeyes increase in number and, as the first angled rays penetrate the water, promising a sunrise, they mill about, then descend into their caves and holes as if by common accord. Small cardinalfishes, some with stomachs full of night plankton and others with meals of shrimps and small invertebrates to digest, go to bed. The sun is not yet up.

A brief stillness follows the disappearance of the night fishes. The reef seems again deserted. A small squadron of tiny nocturnal flash-light fishes makes its final foray for plankton. As the light expands, a few butterflyfishes emerge, moving slowly, their pale night colorations gradually brightening. Here and there a pair of moorish idols glides along. Hunchback couples drift about, getting their bearings. A pufferfish, still sleeping, is visible against a coral shelf. Early rising territorial damselfishes begin defending their small domains. Planktivores emerge from the protective coral, warm up their swimming muscles, and look about for their schooling confederates.

The pyramid butterflyfishes *(Hemitaurichthys polylepis)* mill about in small groups at the edge of the coral drop-off, not yet ready to venture out into the open planktonic currents. Unicorn fishes appear. No one, apparently, wants to risk the perils of open water until enough company is present. Smaller schoolers—blue pullers *(Chromis caeruleus)* and lyretail coralfishes *(Anthias squamipinnis)*—begin fluttering while still nestled in their branching finger-coral shelters, each colony slowly levitating as a group to form territorial swarms above their homes. A triggerfish here and there swims above its nest.

A parrotfish casts off its diaphanous "mucus envelope" nightgown, which snags on a coral outcrop and flickers above the sand in the current. Late-rising surgeonfishes appear. Small groups merge to form larger ones, which mingle with the ranks of plankton feeders milling at the edge. On a small outer coral ledge, a hawkfish takes up its sedentary, carnivorous watch. Nearby, anxious-looking clownfish poke their noses out from an anemone's tentacles. With sunlight now streaming onto the reef, the awakening becomes too rapid to follow. As clouds of planktivores move off over the drop-off and other reef inhabitants begin their day, the bright-light sensations of color and pattern familiar to the daytime snorkeler or diver appear.

A few fishes begin their day waiting in line. At a cleaning station apparently familiar to reef residents, several customers—a bicolored angelfish, a brown sailfin tang, small parrots—have gathered even before the cleaning wrasses open shop. Eventually, enough bright light assured, the slender wrasses slide out of their coral holes and stretch, taking their time before commencing their cleaning duties. Once the wrasses are up and about, the reef day has officially begun. At just this moment, a trumpetfish torpedoes in, seizing a small chromis *(Chromis caeruleus)* for breakfast. While the trumpetfish is still gulping, a cleaner wrasse *(Labroides dimidiatus)* busily cleans parasites from the rear portion of the trumpetfish's body: two meals are had at once.

This was dawn as we experienced it below the waters around Apo Reef in the Philippines. Similar progressions, orderly and predictable, occur in the changeover from nocturnal to daytime activities on reefs everywhere. As with all animal communities, densely packed reef populations follow systematic patterns. In following these patterns, fishes strike a balance as best they can between getting enough to eat and avoiding being eaten. They know when and where, without expending undue energy searching, to find opportunities to propagate their kind. For each species, life is easier if they can count on their neighbors to follow predictable schedules.

Dawn and dusk are among the most rewarding times to watch the reef. Unfortunately, most snorkelers and divers tend to enter the water at midmorning or midafternoon, when there is much to see but little change is occurring. But at whatever time a diver enters the water, it is helpful to know how behavior changes during the daily cycle of reef life.

It was not until the early 1960s that an ambitious effort to study reef fishes at night was made. Between 1962 and 1966 at Alligator Reef in the Florida Keys, Walter A. Starck II and William P. Davis made over 100 night dives, dividing the reef into zones that they swam following a compass. E. S. Hobson later spent more than 1,000 hours surveying a large reef area in the sea of Cortez, as well as completing comparable studies off Kona, Hawaii, watching fishes in the early morning period as well as in the evening and at night. As part of the Tektite program in the Virgin Islands, Bruce B. Collette and Frank H. Talbot paid particular attention to the dawn changeover. Since these pioneering descriptions many recent studies have detailed the round-the-clock habits of particular species.

Waking up is apparently triggered for most fishes by light intensity, rather than by internal clocks. S. B. and A. J. Domm, who recently catalogued the sequence of appearance and disappearance of fishes at dawn and dusk near Hook Island on Australia's Great Barrier Reef, found that for most fishes, the light intensity was lower at dawn when they appeared than it was in the evening when they retired. The Domms suggested that this differential sensitivity to light intensities may stem from physical differences in how the fish eye adapts from light to dark as opposed to the transition from dark to light, with the result that at dawn the fish's eye is more light sensitive.

Individual fishes wake up fairly quickly and almost simultaneously with others of their species—often as little as five minutes is enough for all the members of one species in a given reef area to awaken. The time for the entire reef to awaken is much longer. In their Tektite observations, Collette and Talbot calculated that the morning awakening on the St. Croix reef took an hour and five minutes, ending with the conspicuous appearance of the yellow, juvenile, bluehead wrasses *(Thalassoma bifasciatum)*. In Kona, Hawaii, Hobson noted that morning reveille began about thirteen minutes before sunrise, well after nocturnal fishes had sought cover, and ended sometime after sunrise. The morning arousals of the eighteen species the Domms watched spanned nearly thirty minutes. The Domms, however, observed the reef from inside an underwater observatory and thus may not have had the habitats of some species within their field of vision. At any rate, most wake-up periods are well within the limits of a one-tank dive or an easy early morning snorkeling trip.

THE DAYLIGHT HOURS

The majority of reef fish species are diurnal, that is, active only in daylight. These include the poster-colored fishes: the butterflyfishes, angelfishes, parrotfishes, surgeonfishes, and wrasses. Most damselfishes are also diurnal, as are triggerfishes and gobies. Some fishes, such as the goatfishes (family Mullidae) and basses (groupers and hamlets of the family Serranidae), are divided between species active during daylight and those that are nocturnal. And, as we shall discuss later, many species are opportunistic, feeding when the possibility is at hand, resting when convenient; probably, however, they are most active during crepuscular hours. (For a partial listing of the times of activity of various fishes, see the chart on page 219).

Some fishes first attend on arising to grooming, visiting their neighborhood parasite cleaners. Depending on the species and sometimes the season, early morning is also a time for a few species to spawn. But for most daytime fishes the morning hours are largely devoted to feeding. Solitary daytime hunters haunt favorite lairs. The territorial damsels feed within their home areas. Butterflyfishes and angelfishes range over wider, but to them familiar, spaces.

Not enjoying the advantages of territorial security, some gregarious species, discussed in earlier chapters, group together in feeding guilds —surgeons, opportunistic wrasses, goatfishes, parrotfishes, and others —and follow traditional routes in their habitats. Assembling in the morning, the core groups are gone all day. Although their composition is always somewhat in flux, essentially the same groups return home together along the same paths in the late afternoon. Groups may occasionally divide to go around coral obstacles. Small subgroups may peel off momentarily to inspect some promising curiosity. Intense feeding may sometimes attract temporary camp followers. These are

SOME FISHES THAT ARE
DIURNALLY ACTIVE

Angelfishes	(Pomacanthidae)
Blennies	(Blenniidae)
Butterflyfishes	(Chaetodontidae)
Clownfishes	(Amphiprionidae)
(or anemonefishes)	
Damselfishes	(Pomacentridae)
Fairy basslets	(Grammidae)
Garden eels	(Congridae)
Goatfishes (some)	(Mullidae)
Gobies	(Gobiidae)
Hamlets	(Serranidae
Hawkfishes	(Cirrhitidae)
Parrotfishes	(Scaridae)
Pufferfishes	(Tetradontidae)
Surgeonfishes	(Acanthuridae)
Tilefishes	(Branchiostegidae)
Triggerfishes	(Balistidae)
Trunkfishes	(Ostraciontidae)
(or Boxfishes)	
Trumpetfishes*	(Aulostomidae)
Wrasses	(Labridae)

*Also active crepuscularly.

often various species of the larger wrasses, which seem to respond first to any possible picnic opportunities. Fishelson has called them "pioneers in food detection." However, the bulk of the migrations remains defined. These associations give their participants protection from predation, heighten the chances of finding food, and aid in overcoming the territorial objections of property holders along the way. For some, the itinerary may include midday courtship sessions.

Various species often join together in these daily migrations. Striped parrots *(Scarus iserti = S. croicensis)* combine regularly with surgeonfishes, blue tangs, spotted goatfishes, and the barred hamlet. The latter two species are carnivorous: goatfishes snuffle invertebrates out of the sand and hamlets, more solitary in nature, prey on small fishes as well as invertebrates. But neither poses a threat to the larger schoolers, and they probably tag along for other motives. Similar migrations, some of one species and some with mixtures, have been described for the rainbow parrotfish *(S. guacamaia),* the midnight or purple parrotfish *(S. coelestinus),* the margate *(Haemulon album),* and many species of surgeonfishes worldwide.

A few of these species remain active in other pursuits after morning feeding, such as the bluehead wrasse *(Thalassoma bifasciatum),* described in Chapter 8. Blueheads, it will be remembered, participate in frenetic pair and group spawning sessions at midday on the down-current edges of reefs. Noontime is also used for spawning by the abundant eastern Pacific rainbow wrasse *(T. lucasanum,* also called the Cortez rainbow wrasse). The rainbows' reproductive fervor attracts the scissortail damsel *(Chromis atrilobata),* a small planktivore that eats wrasse eggs. Hobson described swarms of scissortails hanging about spawning rainbows, timing their egg-stealing rushes expertly with the wrasses' surface-oriented dashes. Premature attacks caused the wrasses to abort their spawning runs. Since dawn and dusk are the favored times for reef spawning, wrasses, which rise late and retire early, may find noon the best of the remaining daylight hours for spawning, even though much of their activity only provides a meal for the scissortail damsel. Wrasses distrust all muted light conditions. Cloud cover affects their activity; they often disappear when the skies cloud over, or rise even later than normal in the morning if the skies are gray. Some species handle any daytime stress with a quick "nap," diving into the sand until threats disappear.

Cleaner fishes also seem to remain busy throughout the daylight hours. Even nocturnal fishes are serviced in their beds during the day. We have seen small black-and-white wrasses of unidentified species cleaning Pacific squirrelfishes deep in coral caves. For many fishes, however, midday is a lazy interlude until the intensity of feeding picks up again around midafternoon.

THE TWILIGHT TRANSITION

About an hour before sunset the plankton feeders up in the water column signal the approach of evening. With the coming of waning light they appear uneasy. Still feeding, they gradually sink lower and lower toward the reef and its waiting shelter, crowding closer to one another as they descend. Although the sun may still seem bright at the beginning of the descent, the angles of its rays as they strike the water create an underwater spectrum favorable to predators hunting from below, sharpening silhouettes. It is a critical period for survival on the reef, which explains why observers invariably perceive a heightened sense of nervous activity at this time, not related to feeding.

Schooling migrators are by now back in the vicinity of their individual homes. Camp followers have dispersed. Hobson has observed that, as sunset nears, the distance of each fish from the reef surface is usually related to its size, the smallest species taking cover first. Larger fishes, such as surgeons and parrots, often mill about in groups before taking cover. Fishes generally seem more irritable at this time. Brief chases and displays are routine. Some of this takes place near sleeping holes and is obviously aimed at defending these sites. Some simply reflects a case of bad nerves.

During a brief interval around sunset, some species take time to spawn. Several species of angelfishes, butterflyfishes, lyretail coralfishes, and others apparently accept a greater risk of predation on themselves in exchange for the reduced risk of predation on their planktonic progeny.

Dusk finds all diurnal species scurrying to their beds, sites that are often used over and over. As discussed in Chapter 8, some fishes live out their lives in one defended space, and so, of course, sleep there. Thus, many damselfishes find bedtime a simple routine, and many territorial damsels are among the last to retire. Small blennies, gobies, and hawkfishes quietly slip into their holes. (Indeed, some blennies and gobies may never leave them.) Others, such as some butterflies and wrasses, are only briefly territorial about their nocturnal shelters, chasing away competitors for their favorite nooks, which usually are just large enough to fit their shapes and sizes.

Watching bedtime in Kona waters, Hobson noted a nervous saddleback wrasse *(Thalassoma duperreyi)* that repeatedly swam about him as he lay against a coral head. Finally, Hobson moved and the wrasse immediately darted into a hole that he had been blocking. Noticing similar behavior by a wrasse on a subsequent evening, he deliberately kept his position until twelve minutes past sunset, well after other saddlebacks had secreted themselves. The wrasse became increasingly agitated but did not seek alternate cover. Instead, it waited until Hobson took pity and moved aside, then hurried into its niche.

Fishes that are not permanently territorial can adapt to alternative sleeping sites. Although we do not know why they change, we can speculate. Perhaps a more secure-seeming bedroom has become available or perhaps a nearby one has recently been taken over by an unpleasant neighbor.

Some fishes protect themselves in various ways while sleeping. Triggerfishes squeeze their compressed bodies into rocky crevices or holes and lock themselves in for the night by erecting their triggers—their hinged, strong dorsal spines—so that they cannot be extracted. Some parrotfishes secrete transparent mucus envelopes about their bodies at night, thought to block olfactory cues from predators, perhaps eels (see drawing on page 223). Howard Winn first described the process. The mucus sheath starts as a fold at the fish's mouth and extends backward to surround the body completely. Covering the fish's open mouth is a small flap with a hole in its center that moves in and out as the fish breathes; after the water flows over the fish's gills it passes out from another opening near the tail fin. Parrotfishes seem to be among the soundest sleepers on the reef, sometimes lending themselves to gentle handling without awakening. Such deep sleepers obviously would benefit from a protective wrapping. Several observers have noted that within a given species, smaller-sized individuals are the most likely to form the mucus cocoons. Adults, often seen napping without them, are perhaps large enough to elude most coral hunters. Exactly how parrots arrive at decisions to sleep in mucus envelopes is not fully understood. C. L. Smith and James C. Tyler reported observing a male queen parrotfish *(Scarus vetula)* during the Tektite program that sometimes formed a cocoon and sometimes did not. Hobson reported an envelope worn by a large female parrotfish in the Sea of Cortez with a wound in its side and speculated that adult parrots may only form the coverings when feeling vulnerable.

Although parrotfishes have been the most often observed in their transparent nightwear, a few other species form mucus cocoons, at least at times. In the Sea of Cortez, juvenile Mexican hogfishes *(Bodianus diplotaenia),* but not adults, form mucus envelopes, and other wrasse species have also been reported to do so. Since wrasses are so secretive, they are very hard to find at night, and like parrotfishes, they are deep sleepers. Some species bury themselves in sand or gravel, having snouts adapted to rapid burrowing. They also use this talent to escape from danger during the day, turning their bodies at right angles to the sand and, in headstand position, quickly burying themselves. In our seawater aquarium we have regularly watched a wrasse retire, first swimming in jerky circles about its favorite burial ground, then disappearing in a cloudy flash of sand. Sometimes it buries itself imper-

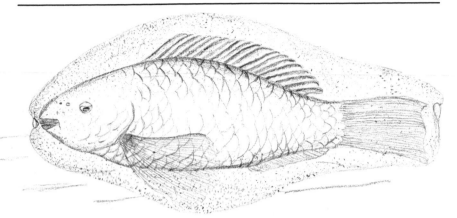

Parrotfish in nocturnal mucus envelope.

fectly, and thus we know that it turns at an angle under the surface so that its body is parallel to the substrate. It remains close enough to the surface for its gills to function. Occasionally its lidless eye is exposed; when this is the case, watching it awaken reveals the change from a motionless, seemingly sightless staring eye to one that rotates, checking out the morning scene before arising.

Just as dawn has a brief period when nearly all the reef inhabitants seem absent, so also does twilight. Within ten minutes after sunset, most daylight fishes are hidden from sight. Few fishes stir and those that do seem to do so quietly. Perhaps this crepuscular period, when some light is still available for silhouetting targets, is the most dangerous of all. Or one could hypothesize that it represents a sort of truce, evolved over the ages, helping to keep order between diurnal and nocturnal animals in what otherwise might be a rush-hour traffic jam. Probably, however, no one except the predator feels comfortable being abroad under alien light conditions. At Alligator Reef, Starck and Davis noted that fishes sometimes were startled by the divers' underwater lights and that the strongest flight reactions to lights took place in the period when some natural light was still available. Hobson found that this evening interlude began ten to fifteen minutes after sunset in Kona, Hawaii. During this time larger surgeons, moorish idols, butterflyfish pairs—already dimming their colors—and a few damselfishes were still about, but close to their shelters. As they gradually disappeared, small cardinalfishes, in an unvarying species sequence, began to emerge from their caves, staying close to the bottom. Next to appear, also in an orderly progression, were the noisy squirrelfishes, their staccato calls having reached a peak of twilight intensity.

In Caribbean waters this period would also see the quickening of activity among the many species of grunts (family Pomadasyidae), which rest in mixed schools by day in coral valleys and canyons. John C. Ogden and P. R. Ehrlich, W. N. McFarland, and J. N. Lythgoe, who have studied their migratory habits there (see Chapter 7), report the departures of the grunts from the reef to be dependably regular, with slight variations caused by the effect of any cloud cover on the light level. Measurements show that the light intensity is always the same, both for evening departures and morning returns. Larger fishes move off the reef first, following their habitual paths, streaming out close to the bottom, coalescing with other schools as they near the reef edge —their "staging area." There may be several false starts necessitating reassembling, but finally they move rapidly away from the reef to forage for nocturnal invertebrates crawling about in sea grass beds. Their false starts are thought to result from the time needed for the rods and cones in their eyes to adapt to night vision. Similar ambivalence occurs prior to the reverse migration in the morning.

At night the grunts' colors change: instead of wearing their bright, daytime stripes they change, in the five minutes following sunset and before sunrise, to faded stripes and blotchy spots that disguise them for their nocturnal activities. Significantly, the change occurs after they depart the reef or just before they regain it. On the way to the grass beds they stay close to the bottom, minimizing the shadows cast and the chance of predation from below. Once they have reached their destinations they split up, eating the night away in solitude.

Somewhat similar habits are practiced by the sweepers (family Pempheridae). Smaller and shyer than the grunts and with more reclusive daytime resting areas—they are often found under ledges and in deep coral cavities (see Plate 59)—their migrations are not so apparent to unpracticed eyes. Copper sweepers *(Pempheris schomburgki)*, as described by W. B. Gladfelter, are partial to the deep cavities under shallow elkhorn coral *(Acropora palmata)*. The coppers begin stirring before the sun goes down, appearing at the openings of their diurnal hideaways, but not emerging until fifteen to twenty minutes after sunset, when they form milling aggregations and practice what Gladfelter termed "flashing" behavior. Individual coppers turned slowly on their iridescent sides, creating flashing reflections from the waning skylight. A signal, perhaps, for others to join them? Similar behavior has been noted in schools of grunts assembling for evening migrations. Copper groups seem to be formed on the basis of size, with smaller fishes forming the most numerous groups, from 200 to 400 hundred individuals. Gradually becoming more restless—they are hungry, after all—the coppers, with the smallest fishes leading the biggest, migrate out to forage on night plankton in the dark open waters, perhaps somewhere above the feeding grunts.

Crepuscular Fishes

Several fishes do not fit comfortably into diurnal and nocturnal categories. They primarily make their living during the dawn and dusk transitional periods, although, as emphasized above, they have no objection to eating at other times, should a timely meal appear at hand, and are often seen active during the day. They are piscivorous predators that take advantage of the (to them) favorable crepuscular light and the predictable appearance in certain places of numerous vulnerable fishes. Barracudas and many groupers and jacks fit this

---

SOME FISHES THAT ARE PRIMARILY CREPUSCULAR*

Barracudas	(Sphyraenidae)
Eels (some)	(Muraenidae)
Groupers	(Serranidae)
Graysbys	(Serranidae)
Jacks	(Carangidae)
Lionfishes	(Scorpaenidae)
Lizardfishes	(Synodontidae)
Sharks	(Carcharhinidae, Lamnidae, Sphyrnidae, and others)

*These fishes are mostly piscivorous, opportunistic feeders and hunt at other times as well.

---

description. Starck and Davis often saw large yellow jacks *(Caranx bartholomaei)* preying on schools of grunts. One or more jacks rushed into tightly packed groups to scatter them and then pursued individual fishes. The predominant targets for crepuscular predators, such as these jacks, seem to be those species that rest in daytime schools and move off-reef in the evening to feed. Lizardfishes will station themselves in the paths of grunt schools vacating reef locations and prey on the juveniles. Ten minutes or so after sunset is a favorite time for trumpetfish and graysbys to prey on emerging copper sweepers. On Indo-Pacific reefs lionfishes also become more active during this time, hunting for small fishes. Hobson noted that attacks by large predators on schooling prey in the Sea of Cortez become increasingly frequent at sunset and peak about twenty minutes after. By this time the light starts failing and they cease to hunt.

Interestingly, this same period in Kona, Hawaii, is much quieter. Attacks on nocturnal schoolers are less evident. This regional variation in predation probably occurs because, as Hobson suggests, Hawaiian waters lack both many of the major predatory fishes that harass fishes elsewhere, particularly the larger species, as well as many of the large schools of prey fishes. Still, the general pattern of crepuscular hunting seems to hold true for most reefs.

Divers entering the water immediately after the sun goes down will see many aspects of fish activity similar to those described above. Within an hour after sunset the nocturnal business of the reef will be in full swing.

THE REEF AT NIGHT

The chief difference between daytime and nighttime migrations of schooling fishes is their destinations. The schools of fishes that feed during the day, such as those made up of surgeonfishes or mixed-species groups of parrotfishes and others, follow pathways that lie within the reef or directly along its periphery, never risking open water, where piscivores might lie in wait, except occasionally to hurry small distances between patch reefs. Small planktivores that feed in the water column (the open water away from the reef where plankton is abundant) usually stay within reach of the coral, although some, such as the blue chromis *(Chromis cyanea),* rise considerably up and out from the reef. But the nighttime migrations are made up of fishes that move out and away from the reef's protection, either to feed on sand or grassy flats or on plankton in the darkness of the open water column. Some schools break up into small groups and forage a short distance from the reef. Others move as far away as a mile or so. Predation on these active, exposed reef fishes is not nearly so great a threat at night as in the daylight or transition hours, although some of the smaller bottom-feeding fishes sometimes fall prey to, say, a lurking nocturnal scorpionfish.

The majority of nocturnal fishes are carnivores out for a meal of invertebrates, as contrasted to the more herbivorous nature of most daytime reef fishes. The available food is also different at night. Just as there is a nocturnal population of fishes, there are nocturnal varieties of invertebrates. Even the plankton changes. Small shrimps and other invertebrates that live in the sandy bottom by day migrate upward at night to feed on microplankton, thereby becoming sitting ducks for the night fishes. Other crustaceans, together with polychaete worms, starfishes, molluscs, and a host of other invertebrates, emerge from hiding places to scour the sea floor for food. The tiny ones are eaten by various species of squirrelfishes (Holocentridae) and cardinalfishes (Apogonidae) and the larger ones furnish meals for larger predators, such as stingrays.

Squirrelfishes and cardinalfishes are well adapted for the night shift. Their pinkish-red color renders them nearly invisible in the darkness and their huge eyes give them excellent night vision. Cardinalfish species vary from region to region but always cover a spectrum of diet specialties in a variety of habitats. In Hawaiian waters, for example, a study of six species showed that each forages in a different location: some high in the water, some in midwater, some where water is calm, some where currents are strong, some near large objects such as coral heads or gorgonians, and some close to the bottom. Comparable diversity was found in a study of eleven species on a Madagascar reef. E. H. Chave, who observed cardinalfishes in Hawaii, found the various species to have similar behavior, sleeping and courting in holes and caves by day and coexisting peacefully with one another, their specialized diets apparently reducing the level of competition.

Cardinalfishes around the world exhibit many variations in their daytime shelter preferences and in their associations with other marine animals. Some hide in sponges or in the spines of sea urchins or live in the company of basket stars or conchs. On a night dive off Bonaire we once watched a feeding basket star with a cardinalfish positioned upcurrent close to it, snapping up planktonic items, with the arms of the basket star forming a rear guard. We trained our light too long on the photosensitive arms of the basket star, stimulating its arms to retract and causing the commensal cardinalfish to flutter anxiously about its coils. A check a few minutes later showed both basket star and cardinalfish again preying on the plankton. Cardinalfishes that live in coral crevices and caves risk daytime predation from hunters that share their habitat, particularly morays.

Squirrelfishes, bigger in size than the cardinals, are easier to find by day. Some species hide in coral nooks, where they are often visible, and others seem to be more social, resting in daytime groups in coral valleys or over holes, much like grunts. The abundant Caribbean longjaw and blackbar squirrelfishes *(Holocentrus ascensionis* and *Myripristis jacobus)* are two such social species. Whereas cardinalfishes predominantly feed in the water column at night, the majority of squirrelfish species are benthic, or bottom, feeders. Since many species do not forage very far away from their daytime coral haunts, they can often be seen on night dives.

Many species of snapper (family Lutjanidae) are primarily nocturnal, resting in large aggregations by day, when they may occasionally feed, but dispersing from reef areas at night to eat crustaceans and smaller nocturnal fishes. A Caribbean example is the gray snapper *(Lutjanus griseus),* which often makes a meal of small grunts. Another fish seen at night in Caribbean waters is the ubiquitous yellowtail snapper *(Ocyurus chrysurus),* a boldly curious, opportunistic feeder that seems to be evident around the clock (see Plate 15).

Drumfishes, or croakers (family Sciaenidae), are active nighttime predators, their voracious habits belied by their reclusive daytime behavior. Named for their ability to produce impressive resonant sounds with the aid of their gas bladders, drums are nearly all found about inshore reefs or sandy areas where they have access to estuarine waters for breeding. Island reefs that are any distance from continents rarely have any drumfishes, the exception being the western Atlantic genus, *Equetus,* which has evolved several species common to reefs. Unlike other members of the Sciaenidae, and, for that matter, most nocturnal fishes, the *Equetus* drums are spectacularly patterned fishes of stark black and white combinations, which invite comparison with the diurnal, poster-colored fishes. These are the highhat, or striped drum *(E. acuminatus),* the spotted drum *(E. punctatus),* and the spotted jacknife fish *(E. lanceolatus)* that Caribbean night divers often see near their diurnal holes in groups of two or three or by themselves. (Their patterns vary somewhat from reef to reef and their taxonomy is in flux.) The reef croaker *(Odontoscion dentex)* is of a related genus. John E. Randall found that the largest, the spotted drum *(Equetus punctatus),* eat primarily crabs, while shrimps make up the bulk of the diet of the other species, although all eat a variety of invertebrates, both hard- and soft-bodied.

Soapfishes (family Grammistidae, sometimes classified with the grouper, or Serranidae, family) are thought to be active nocturnally, but probably are opportunistic, like their grouper cousins. They are sometimes seen about at night, but their stealthy hunting technique of sudden dashes from coral cover—where they lie about looking ill when they are anything but—makes their behavior hard to document. Box-, trunk-, or cowfishes (family Ostraciidae) are active at night as well as during the day. Starck and Davis reported seeing over 100 adult scrawled cowfishes distributed over a two-mile area one night in the Alligator Reef lagoon. This species is known to prefer sandy habitats to the more structured reef areas. Many scorpionfishes are adapted to nighttime predation.

SOME FISHES THAT ARE NOCTURNALLY ACTIVE

Bigeyes	(Priacanthidae)
Cardinalfishes	(Apogonidae)
Drums	(Sciaenidae)
Eels	(Muraenidae)
Goatfishes (some)	(Mullidae)
Grunts	(Pomadasyidae)
Jewfish	(Serranidae)
Sharks (some)	(Several families)
Snappers (many)	(Lutjanidae)
Soapfishes	(Grammistidae)
Squirrelfishes	(Holocentridae)
Sweepers	(Pempheridae)
Stingrays	(Dasyatidae and Urolophidae)

Eels are at home in the nocturnal world, and morays are often encountered free-swimming then. They, too, are also active, if more secretively, during the day. A recent study of morays (family Muraenidae) off St. Thomas in the Virgin Islands, involving nearly 200 observations of five species, indicates they may not be the continuously voracious predators that their reputation suggests. They were found to move about at times among groups of fishes with no aggressive actions. They also seemed to coexist with other eels, occasionally interchanging holes, and once a pair was noticed in the same lair. We have witnessed, however, a spotted moray swallowing a brown moray at midday.

Most nocturnal predation is wreaked upon invertebrates, which comprise a seemingly endless and varied supply of food for reef fishes as well as for other invertebrates. The night diver will rarely notice this extensive carnivorous predation, perhaps because we tend to think of predation on a larger and, to us, more dramatic scale. Usually, a night dive leaves only memories of sleeping daytime fishes interspersed among a spectacular array of invertebrate life not encountered by day. Slender butterflyfishes and surgeonfishes motionless in crevices, sleeping parrotfishes too large to find concealing caves, even mesmerized barracudas lend an impression of a drowsy, inactive world. We have been bumped into by a sleeping trumpetfish rocking quietly in the surge, alternately knocked gently against a coral wall and our bodies. We have cradled somnolent sharpnosed puffers in our hands. Starck and Davis mention a sleeping barracuda so startled by their night light that it spun around and darted into the reef face at full speed, striking its snout with fatal force.

Bright moonlight apparently affects fish behavior. In the Sea of Cortez, Hobson sometimes found daytime species active at such times, especially those species that frequent sandy areas where light reflected from the sandy bottom produces maximum illumination. The finescale triggerfish *(Balistes polylepis)* excavates invertebrates from the sand while hovering in headstand position and blowing jets of water downward. Dark nights find it locked in bed, but if there is enough moonlight, it goes out to look for midnight snacks. The leopard or gulf grouper *(Mycteroperca jordani)* hunts on bright nights, and the yellowtail surgeonfish *(Prionurus punctatus)* was observed to graze in social groups on algae by the light of the moon. Butterflyfishes were sometimes seen active at night, but an examination of their stomach contents produced no evidence of feeding. Perhaps, like some people, they have difficulty settling down without sufficient darkness.

Many more corals feed at night than during the day. If the season is right, a diver can lure with his light swarms of light-sensitive plankton into the extended coral polyps and watch the latter begin the digestive process externally (see Plate 8). In midwater, light directed into the darkness often picks up the myriad shapes of small, tentacled comb jellies and minute, almost microscopic plankton: tiny, self-propelled organisms pulsating along. They seem to have endless swimming techniques: inch-worm motions, corkscrew twists, Roman-candle-like forward bursts. When the light is turned off in midwater, one sees small bioluminescent animals shining with chemically generated light, especially if one agitates the water with an arm stroke.

On coral heads, basket stars unfold (see Plates 61 and 62), and nocturnal crinoids, having crawled out from their daytime crevices, feed by extending their arms into the current. Sea urchins emerge from their holes and march about the reef borders, grazing on algae and creating bare pathways as they go. Brittle stars and any of a number of small shrimps and crabs are on view. Bristleworms, or fireworms, are out swallowing coral polyps, leaving naked patches on staghorn corals, or munching on anemones. This is the time to look for active octopuses, lobsters, giant crabs, large and small polychaete and annelid worms, and, extruding from small coral burrows, the long, thin tentacles of terebellid polychaetes—six, seven, eight inches long—that immediately retract in response to light. Hermit crabs are everywhere, clanking about noisily in their borrowed shells as they scavenge for detritus. Many of them are best viewed at night in the narrow beam of the diver's light, when all the distracting movements and surroundings of the coral setting are excluded from one's vision.

About an hour before dawn a reversal of the evening changeover commences. Schools of foragers reassemble from the sandy and rock bottom surrounding the reef and prepare to make their mass transit back to daytime resting valleys and crevices. Planktonic foragers, some in groups and some as individuals, scurry back to bed in coral recesses as the night sleepers awaken.

REEF ECOLOGY

The daily cycle reveals the extraordinary complexity of the community shared by reef inhabitants. The abundance of marine life made possible by the hospitality of coral nooks, caves, and internal interstices is further amplified by the day-night turnover of their use. Except for permanently territorial fishes, sleeping shelters are shared by nocturnal and diurnal occupants. The reef is like a hot-pillow motel that rents out its rooms to some customers during the day and to others at night. Symbiotic relationships augment the space-sharing phenomenon. Animals not competitive for resources find advantages in cohabitation. An extreme example is the use by various species of tiny pearlfishes (family Carapidae) of the internal cavities of sea cucumbers, from whose insides they emerge in darkness to forage in the protective vicinity of their hosts. Of course, we cannot be certain that the sea cucumber actively cooperates in this relationship, if, indeed, it is even aware of it.

The day-night spectacle underscores not only the importance of space sharing for the stability of reef life, but of the way food resources are exploited. Species that use the reef for daylight protection probably would not occur in such abundance if they were restricted to food available on the immediate reef and had not adapted to diets available in its outlying vicinity. Only tropical rain forest environments are comparable to reefs in the intensity of their use.

Glossary

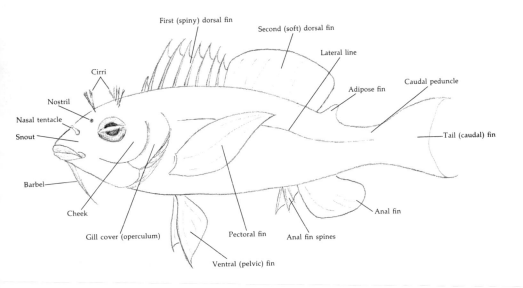

First (spiny) dorsal fin
Second (soft) dorsal fin
Lateral line
Cirri
Caudal peduncle
Adipose fin
Nostril
Nasal tentacle
Snout
Tail (caudal) fin
Barbel
Cheek
Anal fin
Gill cover (operculum)
Pectoral fin
Anal fin spines
Ventral (pelvic) fin

Parts of a fish.

adaptation   A term used in evolutionary biology to denote a physical structure, a behavior, or a physiological function that contributes to the ability of a species to survive and procreate; the term also refers to the evolutionary development of these traits.

agonistic   Combative; competitive.

alcyonacea   An order of soft corals of the subclass Octocorallia (or Alcyonaria) having no continuous skeletons.

algae   Primitive, mostly aquatic plants that lack true stems, roots, and leaves.

amphipods Small, mostly marine members of a diverse order of crustaceans; they are usually laterally compressed like shrimps; beach fleas, for example, are amphipods.

autonomy The self-amputation or casting off of a portion of the body.

benthic Bottom dwelling.

biomass The total mass of living matter within a given area of environment.

calyx In corals, the skeletal cup in which the polyp is fixed; in crinoids, the cuplike calcareous plates that surround the oval body from which the arms rise.

carapace The hard, bony outer covering of animals such as crustaceans and turtles.

caudal fin Tail fin.

cephalic fins Fins that project from the head.

cerata In nudibranchs, the tentaclelike projections on the backs.

chromatophore A cell containing or producing a pigment; a color cell that in some animals produces color changes.

cilia Tiny hairlike projections from cells; they are often capable of motion.

cirri Slender, jointed appendages; in crinoids they spring from the base of the animal and are used for grasping the surface and for walking.

clustering A periodic behavior pattern of territorial fishes characterized by milling about and sometimes including ritualistic displays and chasing.

coelenterates A phylum of radially symmetrical animals that includes the hydra, jellyfishes, sea anemones, and corals.

commensal An organism that lives with another in an association that harms neither; literally, one who eats at the same table with another.

conspecifics Members of the same species.

copepods A class of crustaceans, mostly marine and generally small in size; some are parasitic and may be seen attached to fishes, others are planktonic or benthic and a source of prey for many fishes.

crepuscular Active at dawn and/or dusk.

demersal Living at or near the bottom of the sea.

diurnal Active in daylight hours.

dorsal fin Fin that extends longitudinally along the upper surface or back.

echinoderms Members of the phylum Echinodermata, which includes sea stars, sea urchins, and crinoids.

ecosystem A given unit of living organisms together with their physical environment.

ethology The scientific study of animal behavior.

facultative symbiont An associate that does not depend on its partner for survival.

filamentous algae Algae that grow in a threadlike series of cells.

fusiform Spindle-shaped; tapered at both ends.

gametes Eggs or sperm.

gas bladder An internal gas-filled bag in many fishes that expands and contracts to function as an aid in buoyancy control (also called swim bladder or air bladder).

gill rakers Bony projections that protect the arch of the gill and strain food.

gorgonian One of the order Gorgonacea of the subclass Octocorallia (or Alcyonaria); plantlike soft corals that include sea fans and sea whips.

gravid Ripe with eggs or pregnant with young.

lateral line A series of sensory pores that extends in most fishes from the back of the head to the caudal fin.

mantle   In molluscs, the membrane between the body and the shell; it sometimes extends outward to envelop or cloak the shell.

milt   Fish sperm.

morphological coloration   The characteristic, identifying coloration of a fish.

nematocyst   Specialized, threadlike stinging cells that contain toxic substances, used by many coelenterates to capture prey.

nictitating membrane   An inner eyelid occurring in some vertebrates, also in sharks, particularly the carcharhinids; in sharks, these membranes are dense and opaque and protect the eye from thrashing prey.

nudibranch   A sea snail without a shell; means literally "naked gills."

obligatory symbiont   An associate that depends on its partner for survival.

ocellus   A marking that resembles an eye; an "eyespot" or "false eye."

pectoral fins   Paired, lateral fins set forward, often just back of the gill opening.

pelagic   Living in open ocean waters as opposed to reef or coastal areas.

pharyngeal jaws   In fishes, various apparatus in the throat region that are specialized for grinding, crushing, or milling food.

pheromones   Chemical secretions of an animal that function to enable it to communicate with other animals of the same species.

photosynthesis   The process by which the energy in light is used by chlorophyll-containing plants to create energy-rich organic compounds.

phylum   In taxonomy, a group of related, similar classes.

phytoplankton   That portion of the plankton consisting of plants, primarily algae.

pinnules   Featherlike appendages.

piscivorous Fish eating.

plankton Small, free-floating organisms including both plants and animals.

planulae Free-swimming larvae of coelenterates.

polychaetes A class of marine annelid worms that are characterized by paired, lateral, bristlelike appendages (parapodia); they may be free-moving, like the bristleworm shown in Plate 52, or sessile, like the featherduster worm in Plate 57.

polyp A coelenterate, such as a coral or sea anemone, with a cylindrically shaped body, having an oral opening usually surrounded with tentacles; it can be solitary or colonial.

protandrous hermaphrodites Animals that change sex from male to female.

protogynous hermaphrodites Animals that change sex from female to male.

requiem sharks The common name for sharks of the family Carcharhinidae.

scleractinians The stony corals that produce calcium carbonate skeletons.

sequential hermaphrodites Animals that make a permanent change from one sex to another, as opposed to simultaneous hermaphrodites, which are capable of functioning either as males or as females.

sessile Attached.

simultaneous (or synchronous) hermaphrodites Animals that function as both males and females.

spawning In aquatic animals, producing offspring in numbers.

spicules Needlelike structures made of silicate or calcium carbonate that support the soft tissues of some invertebrates, such as sponges and soft corals.

stridulation Friction-produced sound in fishes such as that from grinding teeth, erecting fin spines, or beating pectoral fins against gas bladders.

substrate   The bottom surfaces of the sea to which sessile organisms attach.

superfemale, supermale   (also terminal female or male) A behavioral term applied to those sequentially hermaphroditic fishes that have permanently changed sex.

teleosts   Fishes with rayed fins and bony skeletons.

terminal female, terminal male   See *superfemale, supermale.*

trophic level   The position of a species in the food chain that indicates what it eats and what consumes it.

tunicates   Small sac-shaped marine animals attached to a substrate, enclosed in leathery, often transparent tunics secreted by the animals, that siphon water in and out for respiration and feeding purposes (see Plate 58); they are members of the subphylum Urochordata, an evolutionary bridge between invertebrates and the vertebrates of the phylum Chordata; so classified because they have an abbreviated notochord: a stiff, inner support for their bodies.

zooplankton   That portion of the plankton consisting of tiny, free-floating animals.

zooxanthellae   Symbiotic, photosynthetic algae that live in the tissues of corals, sea anemones, tridacnid clams, and other organisms.

A Note on the Color Plates

All photographs were taken on Kodachrome 64 slide film. Those on plates 43 and 44 were taken from a distance of 4 inches using a Nikonos III camera fitted with a 28mm lens and a 2-to-1 extension tube; illumination was by a Subsea 50 strobe light. Those on plates 8, 9, 12, 22, 55, and 62 were taken with a Nikon F2 camera fitted with a 24mm lens and mounted in an Ikelite housing with dome port; no artifical illumination. That on Plate 31 was taken with a Nikonos III camera fitted with a 15mm lens and an Oceanic 2003 strobe light. All other photographs were taken using a Nikon F2 camera, equipped with a motor drive and a 55mm macro lens, mounted in an Oceanic Products underwater housing; illumination was by an Oceanic 2001 strobe light.

With the exception of Plate 31, all photographs are by the authors.

References

(Complete entries for these references can be found in the Bibliography, page 248.)

Preface

3   French grunt study: G. Helfman and E. T. Schultz, 1984.

Chapter 1: Coral Reefs

8   Zooxanthellae role: T. F. Goreau, N. I. Goreau, and T. J. Goreau, 1979.

10–11   Reef evolution: N. D. Newell, 1972.

11   Tectonic effects on reefs: J. W. Valentine and E. M. Moores, 1974.

12   Pacific evolutionary center: J. S. Levinton, 1982.

14   East Pacific barrier: J. C. Briggs, 1961; G. J. Vermeij, 1972 and 1978.

15–16   Atlantic-Pacific contrasts and reef structure: B. Goldman and F. H. Talbot, 1976; H. S. Ladd, 1977; J. D. Milliman, 1973; N. D. Newell, 1972; J. A. Steers and D. R. Stoddart, 1976.

20   Coral feeding: J. B. Lewis and W. S. Price, 1975; J. B. Lewis, 1977.

22–23   Fish predation on corals: P. W. Glynn, 1973; L. Kaufman, 1977.

23–24   Lang studies: J. C. Lang, 1971 and 1973.

24   Sweeper tentacle study: C. A. Richardson, P. Dustan, and J. C. Lang, 1979.
Sheppard study: C. R. C. Sheppard, 1982.

25   Shade corals: Z. D. Dinesen, 1983.

26   Transport of organic matter into reef: R. N. Bray and A. C. Miller, 1981.

27   Odum study: H. T. Odum and E. P. Odum, 1955.
Algal productivity: S. H. Brawley and W. H. Adey, 1977.

27–29   Storm studies: R. Endean, 1976; R. C. Highsmith, A. C. Riggs, and C. M. D'Antonio, 1980; N. Knowlton, J. C. Lang, M. C. Rooney, and P. Clifford, 1981; R. G. Pearson, 1981; J. W. Porter, J. D. Woodley, G. J. Smith, J. E. Neigel, J. F. Battey, and D. G. Dallmeyer, 1981; C. R. C. Sheppard, 1982.

29 Crown-of-thorns damage: R. Endean and W. Stablum, 1973; R. G. Pearson, 1981; C. R. C. Sheppard, 1982.

30 Pollution: L. Fishelson, 1973; Y. Loya, 1976.

30–31 Artificial reefs: M. C. Molles, Jr., 1978; J. C. Odgen and J. P. Ebersole, 1981.

32–33 Chaos theory: P. F. Sale, 1978a and 1978b; P. F. Sale and R. Dybdahl, 1975 and 1978; F. H. Talbot and B. C. Russell, 1978.
Order theory: J. A. Bohnsack, 1983; W. B. Gladfelter, J. C. Ogden, and E. H. Gladfelter, 1980; C. L. Smith, 1977 and 1978; C. L. Smith and J. C. Tyler, 1973 and 1975.

33 Gulf of Elat study: N. Gundermann and D. Popper, 1975.

Chapter 2: Swimming

34 Energy cost in motion: K. Schmidt-Nielsen, 1972.

36 Effect of mucus on drag reduction: N. B. Marshall, 1965.
Gray's Paradox: C. C. Lindsey, 1978.
Lindsey quote: Ibid., 8.

38 Motion of sharks and rays: M. H. A. Keenleyside, 1971, chapter 1; K. S. Thomson and D. E. Simanek, 1977.

38–39 Fin function: R. McN. Alexander, 1967; J. R. Nursall, 1979.

39 Breder citation: C. M. Breder, 1926.

42 Marshall quote: N. B. Marshall, 1965, 26.
Swimming musculature: A. R. Blight, 1977.

Chapter 3: Eating

44 Feeding biology: R. McN. Alexander, 1967.

45 Liem research: K. F. Liem, 1980a and 1980b.

45–46 Butterflyfish feeding: E. S. Reese, 1977.

46–47 Fish diets: (Except for Smith and Tyler, which is a behavioral report, cited studies are based on stomach content analyses.) R. W. Hiatt and D. W. Strasburg, 1960; E. S. Hobson, 1974; J. E. Randall, 1967; C. L. Smith and J. C. Tyler, 1972.

48 Hunting behavior of jacks: G. W. Potts, 1980.

50 Hunting by shadow stalking: L. Kaufman, 1976; R. F. G. Ormond, 1980.

51 Böhlke and Chaplin quote: J. E. Böhlke and C. C. G. Chaplin, 1968, 714.
Lionfish hunting: L. Fishelson, 1975b.

52 Sea of Cortez jewfish: D. A. Thomson, L. T. Findley, and A. N. Kerstitch, 1979.

53 Planktonic feeders: W. P. Davis and R. S. Birdsong, 1973.

Chapter 4: Senses

62   Moulton quote: J. M. Moulton, 1964, 435.
       Sound production in fishes: M. L. Fine, H. E. Winn, and B. L. Olla,
       1977; J. M. Moulton, 1964; W. N. Tavolga, 1971.
63   Fish hearing: R. McN. Alexander, 1967; J. H. S. Blaxter, 1980; W.
       N. Tavolga, 1971.
       Lateral line: S. Dijkgraaf, 1963; W. N. Tavolga, 1971.
64   Behavioral responses to sound: J. M. Moulton, 1958; A. A. Myr-
       berg, Jr., 1981; Myrberg and J. Y. Spires, 1972.
       Frillfin goby behavior: W. N. Tavolga, 1958.
65   Squirrelfish behavior: H. E. Winn, J. A. Marshall, and B. A. Hazlett,
       1964.
66   Electroreception in sharks: A. J. Kalmijn, 1978 and 1982; P. R.
       Ryan, 1981–82.
67   Atema quotes: J. Atema, 1980, 15, 18.
67–68 Sense of smell in fishes: J. E. Bardach and J. H. Todd, 1970; J. E.
       Bardach and T. Villars, 1974.
68–70 Bullhead catfish senses: J. H. Todd, 1971.
71   Atema quote: J. Atema, op. cit., 18.
       Vision in water: J. S. Levine, 1980; J. N. Lythgoe, 1968.
       F. W. Munz and W. N. McFarland, 1977.
74   Visual cues in predator recognition: I. Karplus and D. Algom, 1981;
       I. Karplus, M. Goren, and D. Algom, 1982.
       Sun navigation: H. E. Winn, M. Salmon, and N. Roberts,
       1964.

Chapter 5: Color

76   Flounder changes: N. B. Marshall, 1965.
77   Poster coloration: H. J. Brockmann, 1973; P. R. Ehrlich, F. H.
       Talbot, B. C. Russell, and G. R. V. Anderson, 1977; K. Z. Lorenz,
       1963.
80   Juvenile butterflyfish coloration: H. W. Fricke, 1973a.
       Garibaldi coloration: T. A. Clarke, 1970.
       Blue tang coloration: R. E. Thresher, 1980b.
81   Wrasse coloration: M. J. Roede, 1972.
82   Trumpetfish coloration: B. B. Collette and F. H. Talbot, 1972.
83   Parrotfish coloration: G. W. Barlow, 1976.
83–84 Graysby coloration: Collette and Talbot, 1972.
84–85 Surgeonfish coloration: G. W. Barlow, 1974a. J. R. Nursall, 1974b.
85   Damselfish eye coloration: O. A. E. Rasa, 1969.
       Freshwater fish coloration: Barlow, 1974a.
86   Goatfish camouflage: J. P. Hailman, 1982.
       Pigeon recognition of fishes: R. J. Herrnstein and P. A. de Villiers,
       1980.
87   Butterflyfish coloration: Ehrlich et al., 1977.

87–88 Function of eyespots: C. D. Kelley and T. F. Hourigan, 1983; I. Karplus and D. Algom, 1981.

89–90 Function of eyelines: R. E. Thresher, 1977b; G. W. Barlow, 1972.

91 Color and lateral displays: D. Coates, 1980b.

Chapter 6: Reproduction

94 Spawning rush behavior: R. E. Johannes, 1978.
Gyre spawning: Ibid.; P. S. Lobel, 1978.

95–96 Lunar spawning: Ibid.; Johannes, 1978; P. H. Pressley, 1980.

97 Grouper spawning: C. L. Smith, 1972.

97–99 Sergeant major spawning: L. Fishelson, 1970a.

99 Wrasse spawning: R. R. Warner, D. R. Robertson, and E. G. Leigh, Jr., 1975; Warner and Robertson, 1978.

99–100 Parrotfish spawning: J. Randall and H. A. Randall, 1963.

100–101 Angelfish spawning: Lobel, 1978; S. Neudecker and Lobel, 1982.

101 Lionfish spawning: L. Fishelson, 1975b.

102 Anemonefish spawning: R. M. Ross, 1978.

103–104 Damselfish nesting: H. Albrecht, 1969; M. H. A. Keenleyside, 1972; A. A. Myrberg, Jr., D. D. Brahy, and A. R. Emery, 1967.

104–105 Triggerfish nesting: H. W. Fricke, 1980; P. S. Lobel and R. E. Johannes, 1980.

105–106 Goby nesting: R. C. L. Hudson, 1977.

108–109 Harlequin bass hermaphroditism: E. Clark, 1959.

109 Advantage of simultaneous hermaphroditism: P. H. Pressley, 1981.

109–110 Wrasse hermaphroditism: D. R. Robertson, 1972.

110 Anemonefish hermaphroditism: H. W. Fricke, 1979; R. M. Ross, 1978.

110–112 Lyretail coralfish hermaphroditism: L. Fishelson, 1975a and 1970c; D. Popper and L. Fishelson, 1973; D. Y. Shapiro, 1977 and 1981.

112–114 Advantages of sequential hermaphroditism: J. H. Choat and D. R. Robertson, 1975; K. F. Liem, 1968; C. L. Smith, 1967 and 1975; R. R. Warner, 1975.

114 Frogfish parental care: T. W. Pietsch and D. B. Grobecker, 1980.

114–115 Humbug parental care: D. R. Robertson, 1973.

115–116 Shark mating: R. H. Johnson and D. R. Nelson, 1978; A. P. Klimley, 1980.

116 Stingray mating: R. M. McCourt and A. N. Kerstitch, 1980.

116–117 Octopus mating: J. Z. Young, 1962; M. J. Wells and J. Wells, 1972.

118 Cuttlefish mating: E. S. Reese, 1964.

Chapter 7: Social Life

121 Fricke citation: H. W. Fricke, 1980.

121–122 Schooling studies: B. L. Partridge, 1982; E. Shaw, 1970.

123 Silversides experiment: M. M. Williams and E. Shaw, 1971.

124   Schooling mechanics: Partridge, 1982; E. Shaw, 1962.

124–125   Speed and schooling: V. V. Belyayev and G. V. Zuyev, 1969; J. J. Magnuson, 1978; Partridge, 1982.

126   Safety from predators: J. W. Burgess and E. Shaw, 1979; D. H. Cushing and F. R. Harden Jones, 1968; M. H. A. Keenleyside, 1955; S. R. St.J. Neill and J. M. Cullen, 1974.
    Hamilton citation: W. D. Hamilton, 1971.

127   Jacks and anchovies: P. F. Major, 1978.
    Grouper predation: E. S. Hobson, 1968.
    Lionfish predation: L. Fishelson, 1975b.
    Schooling mackerels: T. A. Clarke, A. O. Flechsig, and R. W. Grigg, 1967.
    Resting schools: P. R. Ehrlich and A. H. Ehrlich, 1973.

128   Blue tang schools: W. S. Alevizon, 1976.
    Pacific sweeper schools: L. Fishelson, D. Popper, and N. Gunderman, 1971.
    Snapper schools: G. W. Potts, 1970.

129   Plankton feeding schools: A. C. Hartline, P. H. Hartline, A. M. Szmant, and A. O. Flechsig, 1972.

130   Surgeonfish schools: G. W. Barlow, 1974c; D. R. Robertson, H. P. A. Sweatman, E. A. Fletcher, and M. G. Cleland, 1976.

131   Parrotfish schooling: J. C. Ogden and N. S. Buckman, 1973.

132   Lyretail coralfish social life: L. Fishelson, 1975a and 1970c; D. Popper and L. Fishelson, 1973; D. Y. Shapiro, 1977 and 1981.

133   Clown wrasse social life: R. E. Thresher, 1979.
    Cleaner wrasse social life: G. W. Potts, 1973; D. R. Robertson, 1972.
    Humbug social life: H. W. Fricke, 1975.

133–134   Surgeonfish social life: D. R. Robertson, N. V. C. Polunin, and K. Leighton, 1979.

134   White-bellied sergeant major social life: L. Fishelson, D. Popper, and A. Avidor, 1974.

134–135   Butterflyfish pairs: H. W. Fricke, 1973a; E. S. Reese, 1975.

Chapter 8: Territoriality

138   Dusky damsel citation: J. C. Ogden and N. S. Buckman, 1973.

140 ff.   Threespot damselfish: S. H. Brawley and W. H. Adey, 1977; M. Itzkowitz, 1978; D. R. Robertson, S. G. Hoffman, and J. M. Sheldon, 1981; R. E. Thresher, 1976a and 1977a; A. H. Williams, 1978 and 1979.

143–144   Cortez damselfish: R. E. Thresher, 1980a.

144   *Abudefduf zonatus* clustering: M. H. A. Keenleyside, 1972.

144–146   Blueline surgeonfish: J. R. Nursall, 1974b.

146   Fairy basslets: S. Freeman and W. Alevizon, 1983.

146–147   Blue chromises: B. A. de Boer, 1978.

147 Anemonefishes: W. R. Brooks and R. N. Mariscal, 1983a and 1983b; D. Davenport and K. S. Norris, 1958; L. Fishelson, 1963; R. N. Mariscal, 1970, 1971, and 1972; J. T. Moyer and C. E. Sawyers, 1973.

148 Bluehead wrasses: R. R. Warner, D. R. Robertson, and E. G. Leigh, Jr., 1975; Warner and S. G. Hoffman, 1980.

149 Garibaldis: T. A. Clarke, 1970.

150–151 Parrotfishes: J. C. Ogden and N. S. Buckman, 1973.

151 Homing in blennies: S. Thompson, 1983.

154 Sticklebacks: N. Tinbergen, 1970.

154–155 Baboons: H. Kummer, 1971; J. M. Smith, 1976.

155 Smith theories: J. M. Smith, 1974 and 1976; Smith and G. R. Price, 1973.

Chapter 9: Symbiosis

157–159 Anemonefish symbiosis: See references for anemonefishes in Chapter 8.

159–160 Other fish symbionts of anemones: P. L. Colin and J. B. Heiser, 1973; R. T. Hanlon and L. Kaufman, 1976; Hanlon, R. F. Hixon, and D. G. Smith, 1983.

160–161 Anemone-crustacean symbiosis: D. M. Levine and O. J. Blanchard, Jr., 1980; C. Limbaugh, H. Pederson, and F. A. Chace, Jr., 1961; C. Mahnken, 1972.

161 Boxer crabs: R. V. Gotto, 1969.
Clingfishes: Ibid.; A. R. Teytaud, 1971.

161–162 Sponge associations: J. C. Tyler and J. E. Böhlke, 1972.

162 Shrimp-goby associations: I. Karplus, R. Szlep, and M. Tsurnamal, 1972 and 1974.

163 Coral symbionts: W. K. Patton, 1973.
Shrimp-coral symbiosis: A. J. Bruce, 1976.
Roughhead blenny in coral: J. E. Böhlke and C. C. G. Chaplin, 1968.

164–165 Zooxanthellae and giant clams: C. M. Yonge, 1975.

166 Cleaning poses: G. S. Losey, Jr., 1971.
Cleaning stations: D. L. Gorlick, P. D. Atkins, and G. S. Losey, Jr., 1978.

167 Shark cleaning: R. S. Keyes, 1982.

168–169 Cleaner wrasses: G. W. Potts, 1973; M. J. Youngbluth, 1968.
Cleaning ecology: Youngbluth, 1968; Gorlick, Atkins, and Losey, 1978; C. Limbaugh, 1961; E. S. Hobson, 1969a.
Sabretoothed blenny mimic: W. Wickler, 1968; E. S. Hobson, 1969b; J. E. Randall and H. A. Randall, 1960.

Chapter 10: Sharks

174 Shark fishing with rattles: E. S. Hodgson, 1970.
Attraction to sound: A. A. Myrberg, Jr., 1978; D. R. Nelson, R. H. Johnson, and L. G. Waldrop, 1969.

174-175   Shark vision: J. L. Cohen, 1981–82; S. H. Gruber, 1977; Gruber and
           J. L. Cohen, 1981–82; A. L. Tester and S. Kato, 1966.
           Lemon shark vision: E. Clark, 1960.
175   Olfactory experiments: A. L. Tester, 1963; E. S. Hobson, 1963.
176   Blue shark hunting sense: P. R. Ryan, 1981–82.
           Northcutt citation: R. G. Northcutt, 1977.
           Sharks' teeth: S. A. Moss, 1977 and 1981–82.
177   Shark-bite meter: J. M. Snodgrass and P. W. Gilbert, 1967.
178   Sandbar behavior: S. Springer, 1960.
179   Bonnethead behavior: A. A. Myrberg, Jr., and S. H. Gruber, 1974.
179-180   Blue shark behavior: T. C. Sciarrotta and D. R. Nelson, 1977; T. C.
           Tricas, 1979.
180   Hammerhead behavior: A. P. Klimley, 1981–82; Klimley and D. R.
           Nelson, 1981.
180-181   Lemon shark behavior: S. H. Gruber, 1981–81.
181ff.   Reef sharks' behavior: G. W. Barlow, 1974b; E. S. Hobson, 1963;
           R. H. Johnson and D. R. Nelson, 1973; Nelson and Johnson, 1980;
           J. E. Randall, 1977.
185   Starck citation: W. A. Starck, 1979.
186   Tester study: A. L. Tester, 1963.
186-187   Baldridge study: H. D. Baldridge, 1974.
187-188   California shark attacks: D. I. Miller and R. S. Collier, 1980.

Chapter 11: Invertebrates

194   Female octopus eating eggs: W. F. Van Heukelem, 1973.
           Octopus conditioning: M. J. Wells, 1968.
           Delayed gratification: M. Wells, 1978; J. L. Yarnall, 1969.
           Hunting prowess: S. Spotte, 1973; Yarnall, 1969.
195   Cuttlefish learning: Wells, 1968.
196   Featherduster learning: Ibid.
196-197   Basket star learning: G. Hendler, 1982.
197   Octopus color change: A. S. LeSouef and J. K. Allen, 1937.
198   Feather star regeneration: D. B. Macurda, Jr., and D. L. Meyer,
           1983.
           Sea urchin defenses: A. M. Clark, 1976.
198-199   Toxic defenses: G. J. Bakus, 1981.
199   Phyllidia toxin: L. G. Harris, 1975.
           Spider crab defenses: M. K. Wicksten, 1980.
           Starfish autonomy: Spotte, 1973.
200   Sea cucumber evisceration: G. J. Bakus, 1973.
           Mollusc defenses: H. M. Feder, 1972.
202   Sponge evolution: P. R. Bergquist, 1978.
204   Anemone farming of zooxanthellae: R. D. Steele and N. I. Goreau,
           1977.
           Anemone aggression in aquarium: L. Fishelson, 1965.
205   Smithsonian research: K. P. Sebens, 1976.

205–206   Crab color and habitat: S. L. Coles, 1980.
   206   Arrow crab census: G. Schriever, 1977.
           Anemone commensals: G. Stanton, 1977.
   208   Crinoid feeding behavior: D. L. Meyer, 1973.
   209   Crustacean defense against crown-of-thorns: P. W. Glynn, 1976.
209–210   Communal cooperation: B. R. Lassig, 1977a.
   210   Shrimp-anemone mutual defense (footnote): W. L. Smith, 1977.
   211   Shrimp pair stability: U. Seibt and W. Wickler, 1979.
   212   Anemone courtship: U. E. Friese, 1972.
212–213   Brittle star and sea cucumber reproduction: G. Hendler and D. L. Meyer, 1982.
   213   Feather star reproduction: L. Fishelson, 1968.
           Hendler and Meyer, 1982.

Chapter 12: Day, Night, and In Between

217–218   Diel behavior studies: B. B. Collette and F. H. Talbot, 1972; S. B. Domm and A. J. Domm, 1973; E. S. Hobson, 1965 and 1972; W. A. Starck and W. P. Davis, 1966.
218–219   Wrasse feeding habits: L. Fishelson, 1977.
219–220   Fish migrations: J. C. Ogden and N. S. Buckman, 1973; H. E. Winn, M. Salmon, and N. Roberts, 1964.
   222   Parrotfish envelopes: H. E. Winn, 1955; C. L. Smith and J. C. Tyler, 1972.
   224   Grunt migrations: J. C. Ogden and P. R. Ehrlich, 1977; W. N. McFarland, J. C. Ogden, and J. N. Lythgoe, 1979.
           Sweeper migrations: W. B. Gladfelter, 1979; L. Fishelson, D. Popper, and N. Gundermann, 1971.
   227   Cardinalfish specialization: E. H. Chave, 1978.
   228   Spotted drum diet: J. E. Randall, 1967.
   229   St. Thomas eel study: R. W. Abrams, M. D. Abrams, and M. W. Schein, 1983.

Bibliography

Abrams, R. W., M. D. Abrams, and M. W. Schein. 1983. Diurnal observations on the behavioral ecology of *Gymnothorax moringa* (Cuvier) and *Muraena miliaris* (Kaup) on a Caribbean coral reef. *Coral Reefs* 1:185–192.

Adey, W. H., P. J. Adey, R. Burke, and L. Kaufman. 1977. The holocene reef systems of Eastern Martinique, French West Indies. *Atoll Res. Bull.* 218, May, 1977 (Smithsonian Institution).

Albrecht, H. 1969. Behaviour of four species of Atlantic damselfishes from Colombia, South America *(Abudefduf saxatiles, A. taurus, Chromis multilineata, C. cyanea;* Pisces, Pomacentridae). *Z. Tierpsychol.* 26:662–676.

Alevizon, W. S. 1976. Mixed schooling and its possible significance in a tropical western Atlantic parrotfish and surgeonfish. *Copeia* 1976:796–798.

Alexander, R. McN. 1967. *Functional Design in Fishes.* London: Hutchinson.

Ali, M. A., ed. 1980. *Environmental Physiology of Fishes.* New York: Plenum.

Allen, G. R. 1977, 1979. *Butterfly and Angelfishes of the World.* 2 vols. New York: Wiley.

Anderson, G. R. V., A. H. Ehrlich, P. R. Ehrlich, J. D. Roughgarden, B. C. Russell, and F. H. Talbot. 1981. The community structure of coral reef fishes. *Am. Nat.* 117:476–495.

Atema, J. 1980. Smelling and tasting underwater. *Oceanus* 23(3):5–18.

Atz, J. W. 1965. Hermaphroditic fish. *Science* 150:789–797.

Bakus, G. J. 1981. Chemical defense mechanisms on the Great Barrier Reef, Australia. *Science* 211:497–499.

——. 1973. Tropical holothurians. In *Biology and Geology of Coral Reefs,* O. A. Jones and R. Endean, eds., vol. 2. New York: Academic.

Baldridge, H. D. 1974. *Shark Attack.* Anderson, S.C.: Droke House/Hallux.

Bardach, J. E. 1961. Transport of calcareous fragments by reef fishes. *Science* 133:98–99.

——, and J. H. Todd. 1970. Chemical communication in fish. In *Advances in Chemoreception,* J. W. Johnston, D. G. Moulton, and Amos Turk, eds., vol. 1, 205–240. New York: Appleton.

——, and T. Villars. 1974. The chemical sense of fishes. In *Chemoreception by Marine Organisms,* P. T. Grant and A. M. Mackie, eds., 49–104. New York: Academic.

Barlow, G. W. 1972. The attitude of fish eye-lines in relation to body shape and to stripes and bars. *Copeia* 1972:4–12.

———. 1974a. Contrasts in social behavior between Central American cichlid fishes and coral-reef surgeon fishes. *Am. Zool.* 14(1):9–34.

———. 1974b. Derivation of threat display in the gray reef shark. *Mar. Behav. Physiol.* 3:71–81.

———. 1974c. Extraspecific imposition of social grouping among surgeonfishes (Pisces: Acanthuridae). *J. Zool., Lond.* 174:333–340.

———. 1975. On the sociobiology of some hermaphroditic serranid fishes, the hamlets, in Puerto Rico. *Mar. Biol.* 33:295–300.

———. 1976. On the sociobiology of four Puerto Rican parrotfishes (Scaridae). *Mar. Biol.* 33:281–293.

Belyayev, V. V., and G. V. Zuyev. 1969. Hydrodynamic hypothesis of school formation in fishes. *Problems of Ichthyology* 9:578–584.

Bergquist, P. R. 1978. *Sponges.* London: Hutchinson.

Blaxter, J. H. S. 1980. Fish hearing. *Oceanus* 23(3):27–33.

Blight, A. R. 1977. The muscular control of vertebrate swimming movements. *Biol. Rev.* 52:181–218.

de Boer, B. A. 1978. Factors influencing the distribution of the damselfish *Chromis cyanea* (POEY), Pomacentridae, on a reef at Curaçao, Netherlands Antilles. *Bull. Mar. Sci.* 28:550–565.

Böhlke, J. E., and C. C. G. Chaplin. 1968. *Fishes of the Bahamas.* Wynnewood, Pa.: Livingston.

Bohnsack, J. A. 1983. Species turnover and the order versus chaos controversy concerning reef fish community structure. *Coral Reefs* 1:223–228.

Brawley, S. H., and W. H. Adey. 1977. Territorial behavior of threespot damselfish *(Eupomacentrus planifrons)* increases reef algal biomass and productivity. *Env. Biol. Fish.* 2:45–51.

Bray, R. N., and A. C. Miller. 1981. The fish connection: a trophic link between planktonic and rocky reef communities. *Science* 214:204–205.

Breder, C. M. 1926. The locomotion of fishes. *Zoologica* (New York), 4:159–297.

Briggs, J. C. 1961. The East Pacific barrier and the distribution of marine shore fishes. *Evolution* 15:545–554.

Brock, R. E., C. Lewis, and R. C. Wass. 1979. Stability and structure of a fish community on a coral patch reef in Hawaii. *Mar. Biol.* 54:281–292.

Brockmann, H. J. 1973. The function of poster-coloration in the beaugregory, *Eupomacentrus leucostictus* (Pomacentridae, Pisces). *Z. Tierpsychol.* 33:13–34.

Brooks, W. R., and R. N. Mariscal. 1983a. Acclimation behavior of the anemone fish *Amphiprion clarkii* (Bennett) towards two species of sea anemones. Research paper.

———. 1983b. The acclimation of anemone fishes to sea anemones: protection by changes in the mucous coat of the fish. Research paper.

Bruce, A. J. 1975. Shrimps that live with echinoderms. *Sea Frontiers* 21:42–53.

———. 1976. Shrimps and prawns of coral reefs, with special reference to commensalism. In *Biology and Geology of Coral Reefs,* O. A. Jones and R. Endean, eds., vol. 3, 37–94. New York: Academic.

Bruce, R. W. 1980. Protogynous hermaphroditism in two marine angelfishes. *Copeia* 1980(2):353–355.

Buckman, N. S., and J. C. Ogden. 1973. Territorial behavior of the striped parrotfish *Scarus croicensis* Bloch (Scaridae). *Ecol.* 54:1377–1382.

Budelmann, B. 1980. Equilibrium and orientation. *Oceanus* 23(3):34–43.

Burgess, J. W., and Shaw, E. 1979. Development and ecology of fish schooling.
Oceanus 22(2):11–17.

Carcasson, R. H. 1977. *A Field Guide to the Coral Reef Fishes of the Indian and West Pacific
Oceans.* London: Collins.

Charnov, E. L., J. M. Smith, and J. J. Bull. 1976. Why be an hermaphrodite? *Nature*
263:125–126.

Chave, E. H. 1978. General ecology of six species of Hawaiian cardinalfishes. *Pac.
Sci.* 32:245–270.

Cheng, T. C., ed. 1971. *Aspects of the Biology of Symbiosis.* Baltimore: University Park,
1971.

Choat, J. H., and D. R. Robertson. 1975. Protogynous hermaphroditism in fishes
of the family Scaridae. In *Intersexuality in the Animal Kingdom,* 263–283. Heidelberg: Springer-Verlag.

Clark, A. M. 1976. Echinoderms of coral reefs. *Biology and Geology of Coral Reefs,* O.
A. Jones and R. Endean, eds., vol. 3, 95–125. New York: Academic.

Clark, E. 1959. Functional hermaphroditism and self-fertilization in a serranid
fish. *Science* 129:215–216.

————. 1960. Instrumental conditioning in lemon sharks. *Science* 130:217–
218.

————. 1965. Mating in groupers. *Nat. Hist.* 74:22–25.

Clarke, T. A. 1970. Territorial behavior and population dynamics of a pomacentrid fish, the garibaldi, *Hypsypops rubicunda. Ecol. Monogr.* 40(2):189–212.

————, A. O. Flechsig, and R. W. Grigg. 1967. Ecological studies during Project
Sea Lab II. *Science* 157:1381–1389.

Coates, D. 1980a. Anti-predator defense via interspecific communication in humbug damselfish, *Dascyllus aruanus* (Pisces, Pomacentridae). *Z. Tierpsychol.* 52:-
355–364.

————. 1980b. The discrimination of and reactions towards predatory and nonpredatory species of fish by humbug damselfish *Dascyllus aruanus* (Pisces, Pomacentridae). *Z. Tierpsychol.* 52:347–354.

————. 1982. Some observations on the sexuality of humbug damselfish, *Dascyllus
aruanus* (Pisces, Pomacentridae) in the field. *Z. Tierpsychol.* 59:7–18.

Cody, M. L. 1974. *Competition and the Structure of Bird Communities.* Princeton University Press.

Cohen, J. L. 1981–82. Vision in sharks. *Oceanus* 24(4):17–22.

Coles, S. L. 1980. Species diversity of decapods associated with living and dead
reef coral *Pocillopora meandrina. Mar. Ecol. Prog. Ser.* 2:281–291.

Colin, P. L. 1973. Associations of two species of cardinalfishes (Apogonidae:
Pisces) with sea anemones in the West Indies. *Bull. Mar. Sci.* 23:521–523.

————, and J. B. Heiser. 1973. Associations of two species of cardinalfishes
(Apogonidae: Pisces) with sea anemones in the West Indies. *Bull. Mar. Sci.*
23:521–523.

Collette, B. B., and S. A. Earle, eds. 1972. *Results of the Tektite Program: Ecology of Coral
Reef Fishes.* Natural Hist. Mus. Los Angeles County Science Bulletin, no. 14.

Collette, B. B., and F. H. Talbot. 1972. Activity patterns of coral reef fishes with emphasis on nocturnal-diurnal changeover. In Collette and Earle, op. cit., 98–109.

Compagno, L. J. V. 1981–82. Legend versus reality: the jaws image and shark diversity. *Oceanus* 24(4):5–16.

Connell, J. H. 1973. Population ecology of reef-building corals. In *Biology and Geology of Coral Reefs*, O. A. Jones and R. Endean, eds., vol. 2, 205–245. New York: Academic.

———. 1976. Competitive interactions and the species diversity of corals. In *Coelenterate Ecology and Behavior*, 51–58. G. O. Mackie, ed. New York: Plenum.

———. 1978. Diversity in tropical rain forests and coral reefs. *Science* 199:1302–1310.

Cott, H. B. 1940. *Adaptive coloration in animals.* London: Methuen.

Cushing, D. Y., and F. R. Harden Jones. 1968. Why do fish school? *Nature* 218:918–920.

Dale, G. 1978. Money in the bank: a model for coral reef fish coexistence. *Env. Biol. Fishes* 3(1):103–108.

Dartnall, H. J. A. 1975. *Vision in Fishes.* New York: Plenum.

Davenport, D., and K. S. Norris. 1958. Observations on the symbiosis of the sea anemone Stoichactis and the pomacentrid fish, *Amphiprion percula. Biol. Bull.* 115:397–410.

Davis, W. P., and R. S. Birdsong. 1973. Coral reef fishes which forage in the water column. *Helgol. wiss. Meeresunter.* 24:292–306.

Dewey, John F. 1972. Plate tectonics. *Scientific American* 226(5):56–68.

Dijkgraaf, S. 1963. The functioning and significance of the lateral-line organs. *Biol. Rev.* 38:51–105.

Dinesen, Z. D. 1983. Shade-dwelling corals of the Great Barrier Reef. *Mar. Ecol. Prog. Ser.* 10:173–185.

Ditlev, Hans. 1980. *A Field-guide to the Reef-building Corals of the Indo-Pacific.* Klampenborg: Scandinavian Science.

Doherty, P. J. 1982. Some effects of density on the juveniles of two species of tropical, territorial damselfish. *J. Exp. Mar. Biol. Ecol.* 65:249–261.

———. 1983. Diel, lunar and seasonal rhythms in the reproduction of two tropical damselfishes: *Pomacentrus flavicauda* and *P. wardi. Mar. Biol.* 75:215–224.

Domm, S. B., and A. J. Domm. 1973. The sequence of appearance at dawn and disappearance at dusk of some coral reef fishes. *Pac. Sci.* 27(2):128–135.

Dubin, R. E. 1981. Pair spawning in the princess parrotfish, *Scarus taeniopterus. Copeia* 1981:475–476.

———. 1982. Behavioral interactions between Caribbean reef fish and eels (Muraenidae and Ophichthidae). *Copeia* 1982:229–232.

Ebersole, J. P. 1977. The adaptive significance of interspecific territoriality in the reef fish *Eupomacentrus leucostictus. Ecology* 58:914–920.

Ehrlich, P. R. 1975. The population biology of coral reef fishes. *Ann. Rev. Ecol. Systems* 6:211–248.

———, and A. H. Ehrlich. 1973. Coevolution: heterotypic schooling in Caribbean reef fishes. *The Am. Nat.* 107:153.

———, F. H. Talbot, B. C. Russell, and G. R. V. Anderson. 1977. The behaviour of chaetodontid fishes with special reference to Lorenz's poster colouration hypothesis. *J. Zool. Lond.* 183:213–228.

Eibl-Eibesfeldt, I. 1970. *Ethology: The Biology of Behavior.* New York: Holt.

Emery, A. R. 1973. Comparative ecology and functional osteology of fourteen species of damselfish (Pisces: Pomacentridae) at Alligator Reef, Florida Keys. *Bull. Mar. Sci.* 23:649–770.

———. 1978. The basis of fish community structure: marine and freshwater comparisons. *Env. Biol. Fish.* 3:33–47.

Endean, R. 1976. Destruction and recovery of coral reef communities. In Jones and Endean, *op. cit.,* 3, 215–254.

———. 1977. *Acanthaster planci* infestations of reefs of the Great Barrier Reef. *Proc. Third Intl. Coral Reef Symp.,* 185–191.

———, and W. Stablum. 1973. A study of some aspects of the crown-of-thorns starfish *(Acanthaster planci)* infestations of Australia's Great Barrier Reef. *Atoll Res. Bull.* 167:1–62.

Estes, R. D., and J. Goddard. 1967. Prey selection and hunting behavior of the African wild dog. *J. Wildlife Management* 31:52–70.

Feder, H. M. 1966. Cleaning symbiosis in the Marine environment. In *Symbiosis,* S. M. Henry, ed., vol. 1, 327–380. New York: Academic.

———. 1972. Escape responses in marine invertebrates. In *Scientific American, Life in the Sea,* 163–170. San Francisco: Freeman, 1982.

Fine, M. L., H. E. Winn, and B. L. Olla. 1977. Communication in fishes. In *How Animals Communicate,* T. A. Sebeok, ed., 472–518. Terre Haute: Indiana University Press.

Fischer, E. A. 1980. The relationship between mating system and simultaneous hermaphroditism in the coral reef fish, *Hypoplectrus nigricans* (Serranidae). *Animal Behavior* 28:620–633.

L. Fishelson. 1963. Observations on the biology and behaviour of Red Sea coral fishes. *Bull. Sea Fisheries Res. Station Haifa* 37:11–26.

———. 1965. Observations and experiments on the Red Sea anemones and their symbiotic fish *Amphiprion bicinctus. Bull. Sea Fisheries Res. Station Haifa* 39:1–14.

———. 1968. Gamete shedding behaviour of the featherstar *Lamprometra klunzingeri* in its natural habitat. *Nature* (Lond.) 219:1063.

———. 1970a. Behaviour and ecology of a population of *Abudefduf saxitalis* (Pomacentridae, Teleostei) at Eilat (Red Sea). *Animal Behaviour* 18:225–237.

———. 1970b. Littoral fauna of the Red Sea: the population of non-scleractinian anthozoans of shallow waters of the Red Sea (Eilat). *Mar. Biol.* 6:106–116.

———. 1970c. Protogynous sex reversal in the fish *Anthias squamipinnis* (Teleostei, Anthiidae) regulated by the presence or absence of a male fish. *Nature* 277:90.

———. 1973. Ecological and biological phenomena influencing coral-species composition on the reef tables at Eilat (Gulf of Aqaba, Red Sea). *Mar. Biol.* 19:183–196.

———. 1974. Ecology of the northern Red Sea crinoids and their epi-and endozoic faunas. *Mar. Biol.* 26:183–92.

———. 1975a. Ecology and physiology of sex reversal in *Anthias squamipinnis* (Peters), (Teleostei: Anthiidae). In *Intersexuality in the Animal Kingdom,* R. Reinboth, ed., 284–294. Heidelberg: Springer-Verlag.

———. 1975b. Ethology and reproduction of pteroid fishes found in the Gulf of Aqaba (Red Sea), especially *Dendrochirus brachypterus* (Cuvier, Pteroidae, Teleostei). *Pubbl. Sta. Zool. Napoli* 39(suppl.):635–656.

————. 1977. Sociobiology of feeding behavior of coral fish along the coral reef of the Gulf of Eilat (= Gulf of Aqaba), Red Sea. *Israel J. of Zoology* 26:114–134.

————, D. Popper, and A. Avidor. 1974. Biosociology and ecology of pomacentrid fishes around the Sinai Peninsula (northern Red Sea). *J. Fish Biol.* 6:119–133.

————, D. Popper, and N. Gunderman. 1971. Diurnal cyclic behaviour of *Pempheris oualensis* Cuv. and Val. (Pempheridae, Teleostei). *J. Natur. Hist.* 5:503–506.

Fox, D. L. 1978. *Animal Biochromes and Structural Colors.* Berkeley: University of California Press.

Freeman, S., and W. Alevizon. 1983. Aspects of territorial behavior and habitat distribution of the fairy basslet *Gramma loreto. Copeia* 1983(3):829–833.

Fricke, H. W. 1973a. Behaviour as part of ecological adaptation—in situ studies in the coral reef. *Helgol. Wiss. Meeresunter.* 24:120–44.

————. 1973b. Individual partner recognition in fish—field studies on *Amphiprion bicinctus. Naturwissenschaften* 4:204–205.

————. 1975. Evolution of social systems through site attachment in fish. *Z. Tierpsychol.* 39:206–210.

————. 1979. Mating system, resource defense and sex change in the anemonefish *Amphiprion akallopisos. Z. Tierpsychol.* 50:313–326.

————. 1980. Mating systems, maternal and biparental care in triggerfish (Balistidae). *Z. Tierpsychol.* 53:105–122.

————. 1983. Social control of sex: field experiments with the anemonefish *Amphiprion bicinctus. Z. Tierpsychol.* 61:71–77.

————, and S. Fricke. 1977. Monogamy and sex change by aggressive dominance in coral reef fish. *Nature* 266:830–832.

Fricke, H. W., and S. Holzberg. 1974. Social units and hermaphroditism in a pomacentrid fish. *Naturwissenschaften,* 61:367–388.

Friese, U. E. 1972. *Sea Anemones.* Hong Kong: T. F. H.

Gladfelter, W. B. 1979. Twilight migrations and foraging activities of the copper sweeper *Pempheris schomburgki* (Teleostei: Pemheridae). *Mar. Biol.* 50:109–119.

————, J. C. Ogden, and E. H. Gladfelter. 1980. Similarity and diversity among coral reef fish communities: a comparison between tropical western Atlantic (Virgin Islands) and tropical central Pacific (Marshall Islands) patch reefs. *Ecology* 61:1156–1168.

Glynn, P. W. 1973. Aspects of the ecology of coral reefs in the western Atlantic region. In Jones and Endean, op. cit., vol. 2, 271–324.

————. 1976. Some physical and biological determinants of coral community structure in the eastern Pacific. *Ecol. Monogr.* 46:431–456.

————. 1980. Defense by symbiotic crustacea of host corals elicited by chemical cues from predator. *Oecologia* 47:287–290.

Glynn, P. W., G. W. Wellington, and C. Birkeland. 1979. Coral reef growth in the Galapagos: limitations by sea urchins. *Science* 203:47–49.

Goldman, B., and F. H. Talbot. 1976. Aspects of the ecology of coral reefs. In Jones and Endean, op. cit., vol. 3, 125–154.

Goreau, T. F., N. I. Goreau, and T. J. Goreau. 1979. Corals and coral reefs. *Scientific American* 241:124–136.

Gorlick, D. L., P. D. Atkins, and G. S. Losey, Jr. 1978. Cleaning stations as waterholes, garbage dumps and sites for the evolution of reciprocal altruism. *Am. Nat.* 112:341–353.

Gotto, R. V. 1969. *Marine Animals, Partnerships and Other Associations.* New York: Elsevier.

Gronell, A. 1980. Space utilization by the cocoa damselfish, *Eupomacentrus variabilis* (Pisces Pomacentridae). *Bull. Mar. Sci.* 30:237–251.

Gruber, S. H. 1977. The visual system of sharks: adaptations and capability. *Amer. Zool.* 17:453–469.

——, and J. L. Cohen. 1981–82. Vision in sharks. *Oceanus* 24(4):17–29.

Gruber, S. H., and A. A. Myrberg, Jr. 1977. Approaches to the study of the behavior of sharks. *Amer. Zool.* 17:471–486.

Gundermann, N., and D. Popper. 1975. Some aspects of recolonization of coral rocks in Eilat (Gulf of Aqaba) by fish populations after poisoning. *Mar. Biol.* 33:109–117.

Hailman, J. P. 1977. *Optical Signals.* Bloomington: Indiana University Press.

——. 1982. Concealment by stripes during movement and bars at rest: field evidence from color changes in a goatfish and a coronetfish. *Copeia* 1982:-454–455.

Hamilton, W. D. 1971. Geometry for the selfish herd. *J. Theoret. Biol.* 31:295–311.

——, and R. M. Peterman. 1971. Countershading in the colourful reef fish *Chaetodon lunula:* concealment, communication, or both? *Animal Behavior* 19:-357–64.

Hanlon, R. T., and L. Kaufman. 1976. Associations of seven West Indian reef fishes with sea anemones. *Bull. Mar. Sci.* 26:225–232.

Hanlon, R. T., R. F. Hixon, and D. G. Smith. 1983. Behavioural associations of seven West Indian reef fishes with sea anemones at Bonaire, Netherlands Antilles. *Bull. Mar. Sci.* 33:928–934.

Hara, T. J. 1971. Chemoreception. In *Sensory Systems and Electric Organs; Fish Physiology,* W. S. Hoar and D. J. Randall, eds., vol. 5, 79–120. New York: Academic.

Harris, L. G. 1971. Nudibranch associations as symbiosis. In Cheng, op. cit., 77–90.

——. 1975. Defense mechanisms in nudibranchs. *Aquasphere* 9(2):2–9.

Hartline, A. C., P. H. Hartline, A. M. Szmant, and A. O. Flechsig. 1972. Escape response in a pomacentrid reef fish, *Chromis cyaneus.* In Collette and Earle, op. cit., 93–97.

Helfman, Gene, and Eric T. Schultz. 1984. Social transmission of behavioural traditions in a coral reef fish. *Animal Behaviour* 32:379–384.

Hendler, G. 1982. Slow flicks show star tricks: elapsed-time analysis of basketstar *(Astrophyton muricatum)* feeding behavior. *Bull. Mar. Sci.* 32:909–918.

——, and D. L. Meyer. 1982. Ophiuroids *Flagrante delicto* and notes on the spawning behavior of other echinoderms in their natural habitat. *Bull. Mar. Sci.* 32:600–607.

Henry, S. M. 1966. *Symbiosis,* vol 1. New York: Academic.

Herrnstein, R. J., and P. A. de Villiers. 1980. Fish as a natural category for people and pigeons. *The Psychology of Learning and Motivation* 14:59–95.

Hiatt, R. W., and D. W. Strasburg. 1960. Ecological relationships of the fish fauna on coral reefs of the Marshall Islands. *Ecol. Monogr.* 30:66–127.

Highsmith, R. C., A. C. Riggs, and C. M. D'Antonio. 1980. Survival of hurricane-generated coral fragments and a disturbance model of reef calcification/growth rates. *Oecologica* 46:322–329.

Hoar, W. S., and D. J. Randall, eds. 1971. *Fish Physiology*, vol. 5, *Sensory Systems and Electric Organs*. New York: Academic.

———, eds. 1978. op. cit., vol. 7, *Locomotion*.

E. S. Hobson. 1963. Feeding behavior in three species of sharks. *Pac. Sci.* 27:-171–194.

———. 1965. Diurnal-nocturnal activity of some inshore fishes in the Gulf of California. *Copeia* 1965:291–302.

———. 1968. Predatory behavior of some shore fishes in the Gulf of California. *U.S. Fish and Wildlife Service*, Research Report 73.

———. 1969a. Comments on certain recent generalizations regarding cleaning symbiosis in fishes. *Pac. Sci.* 23:35–39.

———. 1969b. Possible advantages to the blenny *Runula azalea* in aggregating with the wrasse *Thalassoma lucasanum* in the tropical eastern Pacific. *Copeia* 1969:-191–193.

———. 1972. Activity of Hawaiian reef fishes during the evening and morning transition between daylight and darkness. *Fishery Bull.* 70:715–740.

———. 1973. Diel feeding migrations in tropical reef fishes. *Helgol. Wiss. Meeresunters.* 24:361–370.

———. 1974. Feeding relationships of teleostean fishes on coral reefs in Kona, Hawaii. *Fishery Bull.*, U.S. Fish and Wildlife Services, 72(4):915–1031.

Hodgson, E. S. 1970. Sharkwatching. *Aquasphere* 16(1):10–17.

———, and R. F. Mathewson, eds. 1978. *Sensory Biology of Sharks, Skates and Rays*. Arlington, Va.: Office of Naval Research, Department of the Navy.

Hudson, R. C. L. 1977. Preliminary observations on the behaviour of the Gobiid fish *Signigobius biocellatus* Hoese and Allen, with particular reference to its burrowing behaviour. *Z. Tierpsychol.* 43:214–220.

Itzkowitz, M. 1974. A behavioural reconnaissance of some Jamaican reef fishes. *Zool. J. Linnean Society* 55:87–118.

———. 1977. Spatial organization of the Jamaican damselfish community. *J. Exp. Mar. Biol. Ecol.* 28:218–241.

———. 1978. Group organization of a territorial damselfish, *Eupomacentrus planifrons*. *Behaviour* 65:125–137.

Johannes, R. E. 1978. Reproductive strategies of coastal marine fishes in the tropics. *Env. Biol. Fish.* 3:65–84.

Johnson, R. H., and D. R. Nelson. 1978. Copulation and possible olfaction-mediated pair formation in two species of carcharhinid sharks. *Copeia* 1978:-539–542.

———. 1973. Agonistic display in the gray reef shark, *Carcharhinus menisorrah*, and its relationship to attacks on men. *Copeia* 1973:76–84.

Jones, O. A., and R. Endean, eds. 1973–1977. *Biology and Geology of Coral Reefs*, 4 vols. New York: Academic.

Jones, R. S. 1968. Ecological relationships in Hawaiian and Johnston Island Acanthuridae (surgeonfishes). *Micronesica* 4:309–361.

Kalmijn, A. J. 1978. Electric and magnetic sensory world of sharks, skates, and rays. In Hodgson and Mathewson, op. cit., 507–528.

———. 1982. Electric and magnetic field detection in elasmobranch fishes. *Science:* 218:916–918.

————, and D. Algom. 1981. Visual cues for predator face recognition by reef fishes. *Z. Tierpsychol.* 55:343–364.

Karplus, I., M. Goren, and D. Algom. 1982. A preliminary experimental analysis of predator face recognition by *Chromis caeruleus* (Pisces: Pomacentridae). *Z. Tierpsychol.* 58:53–65.

Karplus, I., R. Szlep, and M. Tsurnamal. 1972. Associative behavior of the fish *Cryptocentrus cryptocentrus* (Gobiidae) and the pistol shrimp *Alpheus djiboutensis* (Alpheidae) in artificial burrows. *Mar. Biol.* 15:95–104.

————. 1974. The burrows of alpheid shrimp associated with gobiid fish in the Northern Red Sea. *Mar. Biol.* 24:259–268.

Kaufman, L. 1976. Feeding behavior and functional coloration of the Atlantic trumpetfish, *Aulostomus maculatus. Copeia* 1976:377–378.

————. 1977. The threespot damselfish: effects on benthic biota of Caribbean coral reefs. *Proc. Third Intl. Coral Reef Symp. Miami,* 559–564.

————. 1981. There was biological disturbance on Pleistoscene coral reefs. *Paleobiology* 7:527–532.

Keenleyside, M. H. A. 1955. Some aspects of the schooling behaviour of fish. *Behaviour* 8:183–243.

————. 1971. *Diversity and Adaptation in Fish Behaviour.* New York: Springer-Verlag.

————. 1972. The behaviour of *Abudefduf zonatus* (Pisces: Pomacentridae) at Heron Island, Great Barrier Reef. *Animal Behaviour* 20:763–774.

————. 1978. Parental care in fishes and birds. In *Contrasts in Behavior,* E. S. Reese and F. Lighter, eds., 1–19. New York: Wiley.

Kelley, C. D., and T. F. Hourigan. 1983. The function of conspicuous coloration in chaetodontid fishes: a new hypothesis. *Animal Behavior* 31:615–618.

Keyes, R. S. 1982. Sharks: an unusual example of cleaning symbiosis. *Copeia* 1982:225–227.

Kinne, O., ed. 1982. *Marine Ecology,* vol. 5, *Ocean Management,* Part I. Chichester: Wiley.

Klimley, A. P. 1980. Observations of courtship and copulation in the nurse shark *Ginglymostoma cirratum. Copeia* 1980:878–882.

————. 1981–82. Grouping behavior of the scalloped hammerhead. *Oceanus* 24(4):65–71.

————, and D. R. Nelson. 1981. Schooling of the scalloped hammerhead shark, *Sphyrna lewini,* in the Gulf of California. *Fishery Bulletin* 79:356–360.

Knowlton, N., J. C. Lang, M. C., Rooney, and P. Clifford. 1981. Evidence for delayed mortality of hurricane-damaged Jamaican staghorn corals. *Nature* 294:-251–252.

Kummer, H. 1971. *Primate Societies.* Chicago: Aldine-Atherton.

Ladd, H. S. 1977. Bikini and Eniwetok Atolls, Marshall Islands. In Jones and Endean, op. cit., vol. 4, 1–19.

Lang, J. C. 1971. Interspecific aggression by scleractinian corals. I. The rediscovery of *Scolymia cubensis* (Milne Edwards and Haime). *Bull. Mar. Sci.* 21:952–959.

————. 1973. Interspecific aggression by scleractinian corals. 2. Why the race is not only to the swift. *Bull. Mar. Sci.* 23:260–279. *J. Exp. Mar. Biol. Ecol.* 47:77–84.

Lassig, B. R. 1977a. Communication and coexistence in a coral community. *Mar. Biol.* 42:85–92.

———. 1977b. Socioecological strategies adopted by obligate coral-dwelling fishes. *Proc. Third Intl. Coral Reef Symp. Miami,* 565–570.

Leis, J. M. 1983. Coral reef fish larvae (Labridae) in the East Pacific barrier. *Copeia* 1983:826–828.

———, and J. J. Miller. 1976. Offshore distributional patterns of Hawaiian fish larvae. *Mar. Biol.* 36:359–367.

LeSouef, A. S., and J. K. Allen. 1937. Breeding habits of a female octopus. *Aust. Zool.* 9:64–67.

Levine, D. M., and O. J. Blanchard, Jr. 1980. Acclimation of two shrimps of the genus *Periclimenes* to sea anemones. *Bull. Mar. Sci.* 30:460–465.

Levine, J. S. 1980. Vision underwater. *Oceanus* 23(3):19–26.

Levinton, J. S. 1982. *Marine Ecology.* Englewood Cliffs, N.J.: Prentice-Hall.

Lewis, J. B. 1977. Suspension feeding in Atlantic reef corals and the importance of suspended particulate matter as a food source. *Proc. Third Intl. Coral Reef Symp. Miami,* 405–408.

———, and W. S. Price. 1975. Feeding mechanisms and feeding strategies of Atlantic reef corals. *J. Zool. Lond.* 176:527–544.

Liem, K. F. 1968. Geographical and taxonomic variation in the pattern of natural sex reversal in the teleost fish order Synbranchiformes. *J. Zool. Lond.* 156:-225–238.

———. 1980a. Acquisition of energy by teleosts: adaptive mechanisms and evolutionary patterns. In M. A. Ali, op. cit., 299–334.

———. 1980b. Adaptive significance of intra- and interspecific differences in the feeding repertoires of cichlid fishes. *Amer. Zool.* 20:295–314.

Limbaugh, C. 1961. Cleaning symbiosis. *Scientific American* 205(2):42–49.

———, H. Pederson, and F. A. Chace, Jr. 1961. Shrimps that clean fishes. *Bull. Mar. Sci.* 11:236–257.

Lindsey, C. C. 1978. Form, function, and locomotory habits in fish. In Hoar and Randall, eds., op. cit., 1–100.

Lobel, P. S. 1978. Diel, lunar, and seasonal periodicity in the reproductive behavior of the pomacanthid fish, *Centropyge potteri,* and some other reef fishes in Hawaii. *Pac. Sci.* 32:193–207.

———, and R. E. Johannes. 1980. Nesting, eggs and larvae of triggerfishes. *Env. Biol. Fish.* 5:251–252.

Lorenz, K. Z. 1963. *On Aggression.* New York: Harcourt.

———. 1981. *The Foundations of Ethology.* New York, Wien: Springer-Verlag.

Losey, G. S., Jr. 1971. Communication between fishes in cleaning symbiosis. In Cheng, op. cit., 45–75.

Low, R. M. 1971. Interspecific territoriality in a pomacentrid reef fish, *Pomacentrus flavicauda* Whitley. *Ecology* 52:649–654.

Loya, Y. 1976. Recolonization of Red Sea corals affected by natural catastrophes and man-made perturbations. *Ecology* 57:278–289.

Luckhurst, B. E., and K. Luckhurst. 1977. Recruitment patterns of coral reef fishes on the fringing reef of Curaçao, Netherlands Antilles. *Canadian Jour. Zool.* 55:-681–689.

Lythgoe, J. N. 1968. Visual pigments and visual range underwater. *Vision Res.* 8:997–1012.

MacArthur, R. H., and E. O. Wilson. 1976. *The Theory of Island Biogeography.* Princeton University Press.

Mackie, G. O., ed. 1976. *Coelenterate Ecology and Behavior,* 237–245. New York: Plenum.

Macurda, D. B., Jr., and D. L. Meyer. 1983. Sea lilies and feather stars. *American Scientist* 71:354–365.

Magnuson, J. J. 1978. Locomotion by scombrid fishes: hydromechanics, morphology, and behavior. In Hoar and Randall, op. cit., vol. 7, 239–313.

Mahnken, C. 1972. Observations on cleaner shrimps of the genus *Periclimenes.* In Collette and Earle, op. cit., 71–83.

Major, P. F. 1978. Predator-prey interactions in two schooling fishes, *Caranx ignobilis* and *Stolephorus purpureus. Animal Behavior* 26:760–777.

Mariscal, R. N. 1970. The nature of the symbiosis between Indo-Pacific anemone fishes and sea anemones. *Mar. Biol.* 6:58–65.

————. 1971. Experimental studies on the protection of anemone fishes from sea anemones. In Cheng, op. cit., 283–315.

————. 1972. Behavior of symbiotic fishes and sea anemones. In *Behavior of Marine Animals,* H. E. Winn and B. L. Olla, eds., vol. 2. New York: Plenum.

Marshall, N. B. 1965. *The Life of Fishes.* London: Weidenfeld and Nicolson.

McCourt, R. M., and A. N. Kerstitch. 1980. Mating behavior and sexual dimorphism in dentition in the stingray *Urolophus concentricus* from the Gulf of California. *Copeia* 1980:900–901.

McFarland, W. N., J. C. Ogden, and J. N. Lythgoe. 1979. The influence of light on the twilight migrations of grunts. *Env. Biol. Fish.* 4:9–22.

Meyer, D. L. 1973. Feeding behavior and ecology of shallow-water unstalked crinoids (Echinodermata) in the Caribbean Sea. *Mar. Biol.* 22:105–129.

————, and N. G. Lane. 1976. The feeding behavior of some paleozoic crinoids and recent basketstars. *J. Paleont.* 50:472–480.

Meyer, D. L., and D. B. Macurda, Jr. 1980. Ecology and distribution of the shallow-water crinoids of Palau and Guam. *Micronesica* 16:59–99.

Miller, D. I., and R. S. Collier. 1980. Shark attacks in California and Oregon, 1926–1979. *Calif. Fish and Game* 67:76–104.

Milliman, J. D. 1973. Caribbean coral reefs. In Jones and Endean, op. cit., vol. 1, 1–50.

Molles, M. C., Jr., 1978. Fish species on model and natural reef patches: experimental insular biogeography. *Ecol. Monogr.* 48:289–306.

————. 1981. Mixed-species schools and the significance of vertical territories of damselfishes. *Copeia,* 1981:477–481.

Moss, S. A. 1977. Feeding mechanisms in sharks. *Amer. Zool.* 17:343–354.

————. 1981–82. Shark feeding mechanisms. *Oceanus* 24(4):23–29.

Moulton, J. M. 1958. The acoustical behavior of some fishes in the Bimini area. *Biol. Bull.* 114:357–374.

————. 1964. Underwater sound: biological aspects. *Oceanogr. Mar. Biol. Ann. Rev.* 2:425–454.

Moyer, J. T., and C. E. Sawyers. 1973. Territorial behavior of the anemonefish *Amphiprion xanthurus* with notes on the life history. *Jap. J. Ichthyology* 20:85–93.

Moyer, J. T., R. E. Thresher, and P. L. Colin. 1983. Courtship, spawning and inferred social organization of American angelfishes (*Genera Pomacanthus, Holacanthus* and *Centropyge;* Pomacanthidae). *Env. Biol. Fishes* 9:25–39.

Munro, J. L., V. C. Gaut, R. Thompson, and P. H. Reeson. 1973. The spawning seasons of Caribbean reef fishes. *J. Fish Biol.* 5:69–84.

Munz, F. W. 1971. Visual pigments. In Hoar and Randall, op. cit., 1–32.

———, and W. N. McFarland. 1977. Evolutionary adaptations of fishes to the photic environment. In *Handbook of Sensory Physiology,* vol. 7, no. 5, *The Visual System in Vertebrates.* F. Crescitelli, ed., 193–274. New York: Springer-Verlag.

Myrberg, A. A., Jr. 1971. Social dominance and territoriality in the bicolor damselfish, *Eupomacentrus partitus* (POEY) (PISCES: Pomacentridae). *Behaviour* 41:-14–229.

———. 1978. Underwater sound—its effect on the behavior of sharks. In Hodgson and Mathewson, op. cit., 391–417.

———. 1981. Sound communication and interception in fishes. In *Hearing and Sound Communication in Fishes,* W. N. Tavolga, A. N. Popper, and R. R. Fay, eds., 395–424. New York: Springer-Verlag.

———, D. D. Brahy, and A. R. Emery. 1967. Field observations on reproduction of the damselfish *Chromis multilineata* (Pomacentridae) with additional notes on general behavior. *Copeia* 1967:819–827.

Myrberg, A. A., Jr., C. R. Gordon, and A. P. Klimley. 1976. Attraction of free-ranging sharks to low frequency sounds, with comments on biological significance. In *Sound Reception in Fish,* A. Schuijf and A. D. Hawkins, eds., 205–227. Amsterdam: Elsevier.

Myrberg, A. A., Jr., and S. H. Gruber. 1974. The behavior of the bonnethead shark, *Sphyrna tiburo. Copeia* 1974:358–374.

Myrberg, A. A., Jr., and J. Y. Spires. 1972. Sound discrimination by the bicolor damselfish, *Eupomacentrus partitus. J. Exp. Biol.* 57:727–735.

Myrberg, A. A., Jr., and R. E. Thresher. 1974. Interspecific aggression and its relevance to the concept of territoriality in reef fishes. *Amer. Zool.* 14:81–96.

Neill, S. R. St.J., and J. M. Cullen. 1974. Experiments on whether schooling by their prey affects the hunting behaviour of cephalopods and fish predators. *J. Zool. London* 172:549–569.

Nelson, D. R. 1977. On the field study of shark behavior. *Amer. Zool.* 17:501–507.

———, and R. H. Johnson. 1980. Behavior of the reef sharks of Rangiroa, French Polynesia. *National Geographic Society Research Reports* 12:479–499.

———, R. H. Johnson, and L. G. Waldrop. 1969. Responses in Bahamian sharks and groupers to low-frequency, pulsed sounds. *Bull. So. Calif. Acad. Sci.* 68:-131–137.

Neudecker, S., and P. S. Lobel. 1982. Mating systems of Chaetodontid and Pomacanthid fishes at St. Croix. *Z. Tierpsychol.* 59:299–318.

Newell, Norman D. 1972. The evolution of reefs. *Scientific American* 226(6):54–65.

Northcutt, R. G. 1977. Elasmobranch central nervous system organization and its possible evolutionary significance. *Amer. Zool.* 17:411–429.

Nursall, J. R. 1974a. Character displacement and fish behavior, especially in coral reef communities. *Amer. Zool.* 14:1099–1118.

———. 1974b. Some territorial behavioral attributes of the surgeonfish *Acanthurus lineatus* at Heron Island, Queensland. *Copeia* 1974:950–959.

———. 1977. Territoriality in redlip blennies. *J. Zool. Lond.* 182:205–223.

———. 1979. Swimming and the origin of paired appendages. In *Readings in Ichthyology*, M. Love and G. M. Caillet, eds., 138–152. Santa Monica, Cal.: Goodyear.

———. 1981. The activity budget and use of territory by a tropical blenniid fish. *Zool. J. Linnean Society* 72:69–92.

Odum, H. T., and E. P. Odum. 1955. Trophic structure and productivity of a windward coral reef community on Eniwetok Atoll. *Ecol. Monogr.* 25:291–320.

Ogden, J. C., and N. S. Buckman. 1973. Movements, foraging groups, and diurnal migrations of the striped parrotfish *Scarus croicensis* Bloch (Scaridae). *Ecology* 54:589–596.

Ogden, J. C., and J. P. Ebersole. 1981. Scale and community structure of coral reef fishes: a long-term study of a large artificial reef. *Mar. Ecol. Prog. Ser.* 4:97–103.

Ogden, J. C., and P. R. Ehrlich. 1977. The behavior of heterotypic resting schools of juvenile grunts (Pomadasyidae). *Mar. Biol.* 42:273–280.

Ogden, J. C., and P. S. Lobel. 1978. The role of herbivorous fishes and urchins in coral reef communities. *Env. Biol. Fish.* 3:49–63.

Ormond, R. F. G. 1980. Aggressive mimicry and other interspecific feeding associations among Red Sea coral reef predators. *J. Zool. Lond.* 191:247–262.

Partridge, B. L. 1982. The structure and function of fish schools. *Scientific American* 246(6):114–123.

Patton, W. K. 1973. Animal associates of living reef corals. In Jones and Endean, op. cit., vol. 3, 1–36.

———. 1974. Community structure among the animals inhabiting the coral *Pocillopora damicornis* at Heron Island, Australia. In *Symbiosis in the Sea*, W. B. Vernberg, ed., 219–244. Columbia: University of South Carolina Press.

Pearson, R. G. 1981. Recovery and recolonization of coral reefs. *Mar. Ecol. Prog. Ser.* 4:105–122.

Perrone, M. Jr., and T. M. Zaret. 1979. Parental care patterns of fishes. *Am. Nat.* 113:351–361.

Pietsch, T. W., and D. B. Grobecker. 1980. Parental care as an alternative reproduction mode in an antennariid anglerfish. *Copeia* 1980:551–553.

Popper, D., and L. Fishelson. 1973. Ecology and behavior and *Anthias squamipinnis* (Peters, 1855) (Anthiidae, Telostei) in the coral habitat of Eilat (Red Sea). *J. Exp. Zool.* 184:409–424.

Porter, J. W. 1974. Community structure of coral reefs on opposite sides of the Isthmus of Panama. *Science* (N.Y.) 186:543–545.

———, J. D. Woodley, G. J. Smith, J. E. Neigel, J. F. Battey, and D. G. Dallmeyer. 1981. Population trends among Jamaican reef corals. *Nature* 294:249–250.

Potts, D. C. 1977. Suppression of coral populations by filamentous algae within damselfish territories. *J. Exp. Mar. Biol. Ecol.* 28:207–216.

Potts, G. W. 1970. The schooling ethology of *Lutianus monostigma* (Pisces) in the shallow reef environment of Aldabra. *J. Zool. Lond.* 161:223–235.

———. 1973. The ethology of *Labroides dimidiatus* (Cuv. & Val.) (Labridae, Pisces) on Aldabra. *Animal Behaviour* 21:250–291.

———. 1980. The predatory behaviour of *Caranx melampygus* (Pisces) in the channel environment of Aldabra Atoll (Indian Ocean). *J. Zool. Lond.* 192:323–350.

———. 1981. Behavioural interactions between the Carangidae (Pisces) and their prey on the fore-reef slope of Aldabra, with notes on other predators. *J. Zool. Lond.* 195:385–404.

Pressley, P. H. 1980. Lunar periodicity in the spawning of yellowtail damselfish, *Microspathodon chrysurus. Env. Biol. Fish.* 5:155–159.

———. 1981. Pair formation and joint territoriality in a simultaneous hermaphrodite: the coral reef fish *Serranus tigrinus. Z. Tierpsychol.* 56:33–46.

Randall, J. E. 1961a. A contribution to the biology of the convict surgeonfish of the Hawaiian islands, *Acanthurus triostegus sandvicensis. Pac. Sci.* 15:215–272.

———. 1961b. Observations on the spawning of surgeonfishes (Acanthuridae) in the Society Islands. *Copeia,* 1961:237–238.

———. 1967. Food habits of reef fishes of the West Indies. *Proc. of the International Conference on Tropical Oceanography, Studies in Tropical Oceanography* (Miami) 5:665–847.

———. 1977. Contribution to the biology of the white tip reef shark *(Triaenodon obesus). Pac. Sci.* 31:143–164.

Randall, J. E., and H. A. Randall. 1960. Examples of mimicry and protective resemblance in tropical marine fishes. *Bull. Mar. Sci. Caribb.* 10:444–480.

Randall, J. E., and H. A. Randall. 1963. The spawning and early development of the Atlantic parrot fish, *Sparisoma rubripinne,* with notes on other scarid and labrid fishes. *Zoologica* (N.Y.) 48:49–60.

Rasa, O. A. E. 1969. Territoriality and the establishment of dominance by means of visual cues in *Pomacentrus jenkinsi* (Pisces: Pomacentridae). *Z. Tierpsychol.* 26:-825–845.

Reese, E. S. 1964. Ethology and marine zoology. *Oceanogr. Mar. Biol. Ann. Rev.* 2:455–488.

———. 1973. Duration of residence by coral reef fishes on "home reefs." *Copeia* 1973:145–148.

———. 1975. A comparative field study of the social behavior and related ecology of reef fishes of the family Chaetodontidae. *Z. Tierpsychol.* 37:37–61.

———. 1977. Coevolution of corals and coral feeding fishes of the family Chaetodontidae. *Proc. Third Intl. Coral Reef Symp.* Miami, 268–274.

Reinboth, R. 1973. Dualistic reproductive behavior in the protogynous wrasse *Thalassoma bifasciatum* and some observations on its day-night changeover. *Helgol. Wiss. Meeresunters.* 24:174–191.

Richardson, C. A., P. Dustan, and J. C. Lang. 1979. Maintenance of living space by sweeper tentacles of *Montastrea cavernosa,* a Caribbean reef coral. *Mar. Biol.* 55:181–186.

Rinkevich, B., and Y. Loya. 1983. Intraspecific competitive networks in the Red Sea coral *Stylophora pistillata. Coral Reefs* 1:161–172.

Robertson, D. R. 1972. Social control of sex reversal in a coral-reef fish. *Science* 177:1007–1009.

———. 1973. Field observations on the reproductive behavior of a pomacentrid fish, *Acanthochromis polyacanthus. Z. Tierpsychol.* 32:319–324.

———, S. G. Hoffman, and J. M. Sheldon. 1981. Availability of space for the territorial Caribbean damselfish *Eupomacentrus planifrons. Ecology* 62:1162–1169.

Robertson, D. R., N. V. C. Polunin, and K. Leighton. 1979. The behavioral ecology of three Indian Ocean surgeonfishes *(Acanthurus lineatus, A. leucosternon* and *Zebrasoma scopus)*: their feeding strategies, and social and mating systems. *Env. Biol. Fish.* 4:125–170.

Robertson, D. R., and J. M. Sheldon. 1979. Competitive interactions and the availability of sleeping sites for a diurnal coral reef fish. *J. Exp. Mar. Biol. Ecol.* 40:285–298.

Robertson, D. R., H. P. A. Sweatman, E. A. Fletcher, and M. G. Cleland. 1976. Schooling as a mechanism for circumventing the territoriality of competitors. *Ecology* 57:1208–1220.

Roede, M. J. 1972. Color as related to size, sex, and behaviour in seven Caribbean labrid fish species (genera *Thalassoma, Halichoeres, Hemipteronotus*). *Studies on the fauna of Curaçao and other Caribbean Islands* 42:1–264.

Ross, R. M. 1978. Reproductive behavior of the anemonefish *Amphiprion melanopus* on Guam. *Copeia* 1978:103–107.

Ryan, P. R. 1977. A reader's guide to underwater sound. *Oceanus* 20(2):3–7.

————. 1981–82. Electroreception in blue sharks. *Oceanus* 24(4):42–44.

Sale, P. F. 1971. The reproductive behavior of the pomacentrid fish, *Chromis caeruleus*. *Z. Tierpsychol.* 29:156–164.

————. 1978a. Chance patterns of demographic change in populations of territorial fish in coral rubble patches at Heron Reef. *J. Exp. Mar. Biol. Ecol.* 34:-233–243.

————. 1978b. Coexistence of coral reef fishes–a lottery for living space. *Env. Biol. Fish.* 3:85–102.

————. 1979. Recruitment, loss and coexistence in a guild of territorial coral reef fishes. *Oecologia* 42:159–177.

————. 1980. The ecology of fishes on coral reefs. *Oceanogr. Mar. Biol. Ann. Rev.* 18:367–421.

————, and R. Dybdahl. 1975. Determinants of community structure for coral reef fishes in an experimental habitat. *Ecology* 56:1343–1355.

————, and R. Dybdahl. 1978. Determinants of community structure for coral reef fishes in isolated coral heads at lagoonal and reef slope sites. *Oecologia* (Berl.) 34:57–74.

Sammarco, P. W., J. C. Coll, S. LaBarre, and B. Willis. 1983. Competitive strategies of soft corals (Coelenterata: Octocorallia): allelopathic effects on selected scleractinian corals. *Coral Reefs* 1:173–178.

Santos, S. L., and J. L. Simon. 1974. Distribution and abundance of the polychaetous annelids in a south Florida estuary. *Bull. Mar. Sci.* 24:669–689.

Schmidt-Nielsen, K. 1972. Locomotion: energy cost of swimming, flying, and running. *Science* 177:222–227.

Schriever, G. 1977. In situ observations on the behaviour and biology of the tropical spider crab *Stenorhynchus seticornis* Herbst (Crustacea, Decapoda, Brachyura). In *Physiology and Behaviour of Marine Organisms, Proc. of the 12th European Symposium on Marine Biology,* D. S. McLusky and A. J. Berry, eds., 297–302. Oxford: Pergamon.

Schultz, L., P. W. Gilbert, and S. Springer. 1961. Shark attacks. *Science* 134(3472):-87–88.

Sciarrotta, T. C., and D. R. Nelson. 1977. Diel behavior of the blue shark, *Prionace glauca,* near Santa Catalina Island, California. *Fishery Bulletin* 75:519–528.

Sebens, K. P. 1976. The ecology of Caribbean sea anemones in Panama: utilization of space on a coral reef. In *Coelenterate Ecology and Behavior*, G. O. Mackie, ed., 67–77. New York: Plenum.

———. 1977. Autotrophic and heterotrophic nutrition of coral reef zoanthids. *Proc. Third Intl. Coral Reef Symp. Miami*, 397–404.

Seibt, U., and W. Wickler. 1979. The biological significance of the pair-bond in the shrimp *Hymenocera picta*. *Z. Tierpsychol.* 50:166–179.

Shapiro, D. Y. 1977. The structure and growth of social groups of the hermaphroditic fish *Anthias squamipinnis* (Peters). *Proc. Third Intl. Coral Reef Symp. Miami*, 571–577.

———. 1981. Sequence of coloration changes during sex reversal in the tropical marine fish *Anthias squamipinnis* (Peters). *Bull. Mar. Sci.* 31:383–398.

Shaw, E. 1962. The schooling of fishes. In *Life in the Sea, Readings from Scientific American*, 146–154. San Francisco: Freeman, 1981.

———. 1970. Schooling in fishes: critique and review. In *Development and Evolution of Behavior*, L. Aronson, E. Tobach, D. S. Lehrman, and J. S. Rosenblatt, eds., 452–480. San Francisco: Freeman.

Sheppard, C. R. C. 1982. Coral populations on reef slopes and their major controls. *Mar. Ecol. Prog. Ser.* 7:83–115.

Smith, C. L. 1965. The patterns of sexuality and the classification of serranid fishes. *Am. Mus. Novit.* 2207:1020.

———. 1967. Contribution to the theory of hermaphroditism. *J. Theoret. Biol.* 17:76–90.

———. 1972. A spawning aggregation of Nassau grouper *Epinephelus striatus* (Bloch) *Trans. Am. Fish. Soc.* 101:257–261.

———. 1975. The evolution of hermaphroditism in fishes. In *Intersexuality in the Animal Kingdom*, R. Reinboth, ed., 295–310. Heidelberg: Springer-Verlag.

———. 1977. Coral reef fish communities—order and chaos. *Proc. Third Intl. Coral Reef Symp. Miami*, xxi–xxii.

———. 1978. Coral reef fish communities: a compromise view. *Env. Biol. Fish.* 3:109–128.

———, and J. C. Tyler. 1972. Space resource sharing in a coral reef community. In Collette and Earle, op. cit., 125–170.

———, and J. C. Tyler. 1973. Direct observations of resource sharing in coral reef fish: *Helgol. Wiss. Meeresunters.* 24:264–275.

———, and J. C. Tyler. 1975. Succession and stability in fish communities of dome-shaped patch reefs in the West Indies. *Am. Mus. Novit.* 2572:1–18.

Smith, J. M. 1974. The theory of games and the evolution of animal conflicts. *J. Theoretical Biology* 47:209–221.

———. 1976. Evolution and the theory of games. *American Scientist* 64:41–45.

———, and G. R. Price. 1973. The logic of animal conflict. *Nature* 246:15–18.

Smith, W. L. 1977. Beneficial behavior of a symbiotic shrimp to its host anemone. *Bull. Mar. Sci.* 27:342–347.

Snodgrass, J. M., and P. W. Gilbert. 1967. A shark bite meter. In *Sharks, Skates and Rays*, P. W. Gilbert, R. F. Mathewson, and D. P. Rall, eds., 331–337. Baltimore: Johns Hopkins.

Spotte, S. 1973. *Marine Aquarium Keeping*. New York: Wiley.

Springer, S. 1960. Natural history of the sandbar shark *Eulamia milberti*. *U.S. Fish and Wildlife Service* 61:36–38.

————, and A. J. McErlean. 1962. A study of the behavior of some tagged south Florida coral reef fishes. *Am. Midl. Nat.* 67:386–397.

Stanton, G. 1977. Habitat partitioning among associated decapods with *Lebrunia danae* at Grand Bahama. *Proc. Third. Intl. Coral Reef Symp. Miami,* 169–175.

Starck, W. A. 1979. *The Blue Reef.* New York: Knopf.

————, and W. P. Davis. 1966. Night habits of fishes of Alligator Reef, Fla. *Ichthyologica* 38:313–356.

Steele, R. D., and N. I. Goreau. 1977. The breakdown of symbiotic zooxanthellae in the sea anemone *Phyllactis flosculifera. J. Zool.* Lond. 181:421–437.

Steers, J. A., and D. R. Stoddart. 1976. The origin of fringing reefs, barrier reefs, and atolls. In Jones and Endean, op. cit., vol. 3, 21–57.

Steinberg, J. C., W. C. Cummings, B. D. Brahy, and J. Y. (Spires) MacBain. 1965. Further bio-acoustic studies off the west coast of North Bimini, Bahamas. *Bull. Mar. Sci.* 15:942–63.

Stokes, A. W., ed. 1974. *Territory.* Stroudsburg, Pa.: Dowden, Hutchinson & Ross.

Swerdloff, S. N. 1970. Behavioral observations on Eniwetok damselfishes (Pomacentridae: *Chromis*) with special reference to the spawning of *Chromis caeruleus. Copeia* 1970:371–374.

Talbot, F. H., and B. C. Russell. 1978. Coral reef fish communities: unstable, high-diversity systems? *Ecol. Monogr.* 1978:425–440.

Tavolga, W. N. 1958. The significance of underwater sounds produced by males of the gobiid fish, *Bathygobius soporator. Physiol. Zool.* 31:259–271.

————. 1971. Sound production and detection. In Hoar and Randall, op. cit., vol. 5, 135–205.

————, ed. 1977. *Sound Production in Fishes.* Stroudsburg, Pa.: Dowden, Hutchinson & Ross.

————, A. N. Popper, and R. R. Fay, eds. 1981. *Hearing and Sound Communication in Fishes.* New York: Springer-Verlag.

Tester, A. L. 1963. The role of olfaction in shark predation. *Pac. Sci.* 17:145–170.

————, and S. Kato. 1966. Visual target discrimination in blacktip sharks *(Carcharhinus melanopterus)* and grey sharks *(C. menisorrah). Pac. Sci.* 20:461–471.

Teytaud, A. R. 1971. Food habits of the goby, *Ginsburgellus novemlineatus,* and the clingfish, *Arcos rubiginosus,* associated with echinoids in the Virgin Islands. *Carib. J. Sci.* 11:41–45.

Thompson, S. 1983. Homing in a territorial reef fish. *Copeia* 1983:832–834.

Thomson, D. A., L. T. Findley, and A. N. Kerstitch. 1979. *Reef Fishes of the Sea of Cortez.* New York: Wiley.

Thomson, K. S., and D. E. Simanek. 1977. Body form and locomotion in sharks. *Amer. Zool.* 17:343–354.

Thresher, R. E. 1976a. Field analysis of the territoriality of the threespot damselfish, *Eupomacentrus planifrons* (Pomacentridae). *Copeia* 1976:266–276.

————. 1976b. Field experiments on species recognition by the threespot damselfish, *Eupomacentrus planifrons* (Pisces: Pomacentridae). *Animal Behaviour* 24:-562–569.

————. 1977a. Ecological determinants of social organization of reef fishes. *Proc. Third. Intl. Coral Reef Symp. Miami,* 551–557.

————. 1977b. Eye ornamentation of Caribbean reef fishes. *Z. Tierpsychol.* 43:-152–158.

———. 1978. Polymorphism, mimicry, and the evolution of the hamlets (Hypoplectrus, serranidae). *Bull. Mar. Sci.* 28:345–353.

———. 1979. Social behavior and ecology of two sympatric wrasses (Labridae: *Halichoeres* spp.) off the coast of Florida. *Mar. Biol.* 53:161–172.

———. 1980a. Clustering: non-agonistic group contact in territorial reef fishes, with special reference to the Sea of Cortez damselfish, *Eupomacentrus rectifraenum*. *Bull. Mar. Sci.* 30:252–260.

———. 1980b. *Reef Fish.* St. Petersburg, Fla.: Palmetto.

———. 1982. Courtship and spawning in the emperor angelfish *Pomacanthus imperator*, with comments on reproduction by other pomacanthid fishes. *Mar. Biol.* 70:149–156.

Tinbergen, N. 1951. *The Study of Instinct.* Oxford: Clarendon Press.

Todd, J. H. 1971. The chemical language of fishes. *Scientific American,* May, 224(5):99–108.

Tricas, T. C. 1979. Relationships of the blue shark, *Prionace glauca,* and its prey species near Santa Catalina Island, California. *Fishery Bulletin* 77:175–182.

Tsurnamal, M., and J. Marder. 1966. Observations on the basket star *Astroboa nuda* on coral reefs at Eilat (Gulf of Aqaba). *Israel J. Zool.* 15:9–17.

Tyler, J. C., and J. E. Böhlke. 1972. Records of sponge-dwelling fishes, primarily of the Caribbean. *Bull. Mar. Sci.* 22:601–642.

Valentine, J. W., and E. M. Moores. 1974. Plate tectonics and the history of life in the oceans. In *Scientific American: Life in the Sea.* San Francisco: Freeman, 1982.

Van Heukelem, W. F. 1973. Growth and lifespan of *Octopus cyanea* (Mollusca: Cephalopoda). *J. Zool.* 169:299–315.

Vermeij, G. J. 1978. *Biography and Adaptation.* Cambridge: Harvard University Press. 1972.

———. Endemism and environment: some shore molluscs of the tropical Atlantic. *Am. Nat.* 106:89–101.

Vernberg, W. B., ed. 1974. *Symbiosis in the Sea.* Columbia: University of South Carolina Press.

Vine, P. J. 1974. Effects of algal grazing and aggressive behaviour of the fishes *Pomacentrus lividus* and *Acanthurus sohal* on coral-reef ecology. *Mar. Biol.* 24:131–136.

Vivien, M. L. 1975. Place of apogonid fish in the food webs of a Malagasy coral reef. *Micronesica* 11:185–198.

Walls, G. L. 1942. *The Vertebrate Eye and Its Adaptive Radiation.* Bloomfield Hills, Michigan: Cranbrook Institute Science Bulletin No. 19.

Warner, R. R. 1975. The adaptive significance of sequential hermaphrodites. *Am. Nat.* 109:61–82.

———. 1982. Mating systems, sex change and sexual demography in the rainbow wrasse, *Thalassoma lucasanum. Copeia* 1982:653–661.

Warner, R. R., and S. G. Hoffman. 1980. Population density and the economics of territorial defense in a coral reef fish. *Ecology* 61:772–780.

Warner, R. R., and D. R. Robertson. 1978. Sexual patterns in the labroid fishes of the Western Caribbean. The wrasses (Labridae). *Smithson. Contr. Zool.* 254:1–27.

Warner, R. R., D. R. Robertson, and E. G. Leigh, Jr. 1975. Sex change and sexual selection: the reproductive biology of a labrid fish is used to illuminate a theory of sex change. *Science* 190:633–638.

Weinberg, S. 1976. Submarine daylight and ecology. *Mar. Biol.* 37:291–304.

Wells, M. J. 1968. *Lower Animals.* London: World University Library.

———. 1978. *Octopus.* London: Chapman & Hall.

———, and J. Wells. 1972. Sexual displays and mating of *Octopus vulgaris* Cuvier and *Octopus cyanea* Gray and attempts to alter performance by manipulating the glandular condition of the animals. *Animal Behaviour* 20:293–308.

Wickler, W. 1968. *Mimicry in Plants and Animals,* R. D. Martin, trans. New York: McGraw-Hill.

———. 1967. Specialization of organs having a signal function in some marine fish. *Stud. Trop. Oceanogr. Miami* 5:539–548.

Wicksten, M. K. 1980. Decorator Crabs. In *Scientific American: Life in the Sea.* San Francisco: Freeman, 1982.

Williams, A. H. 1978. Ecology of threespot damselfish: social organization, age structure, and population stability. *J. Exp. Mar. Biol. Ecol.* 34:197–213.

———. 1979. Interference behavior and ecology of threespot damselfish *(Eupomacentrus planifrons) Oecologia* 38:223–230.

Williams, D. McB. 1980. Dynamics of the pomacentrid community on small patch reefs in One Tree Lagoon (Great Barrier Reef). *Bull. Mar. Sci.* 30:159–170.

———. 1982. Patterns in the distribution of fish communities across the central Great Barrier Reef. *Coral Reefs* 1:35–43.

———. 1983. Daily, monthly, and yearly variability in recruitment of a guild of coral reef fishes. *Mar. Ecol. Prog. Ser.* 10:231–237.

———, and A. I. Hatcher. 1983. Structure of fish communities on outer slopes of inshore mid-shelf and outer shelf reefs of the Great Barrier Reef. *Mar. Ecol. Prog. Ser.* 10:239–250.

Williams, M. M., and E. Shaw. 1971. Modifiability of schooling behavior in fishes: the role of early experience. *Am. Mus. Novit.* 2448:3–19.

Winn, H. E. 1955. Formation of a mucous envelope at night by parrot fishes. *Zoologica* (N.Y.) 40:145–147.

———, M. Salmon, and N. Roberts. 1964. Sun-compass orientation by parrot fishes. *Z. Tierpsychol.* 21:798–812.

Winn, H. E., and J. E. Bardach. 1959. Differential food selection by moray eels and a possible role of the mucous envelope of parrot fishes in reduction of predation. *Ecology* 40:296–298.

Winn, H. E., J. A. Marshall, and B. A. Hazlett. 1964. Behavior, diel activities, and stimuli that elicit sound production and reaction to sounds in the longspine squirrelfish. *Copeia* 1964:413–425.

Yarnall, J. L. 1969. Aspects of the behavior of *Octopus cyanea* Gray. *Animal Behaviour* 17:747–754.

Yonge, C. M. 1975. Giant clams. *Scientific American* 232(4):96–105.

Youngbluth, M. J. 1968. Aspects of the ecology and ethology of the cleaning fish, *Labroides phthirophagus* Randall. *Z. Tierpsychol.* 25:915–932.

Young, J. Z. 1962. Courtship and mating by a coral reef octopus *(O. horridus).* *Proc. Zool. Soc. Lond.* 138:157–62.

Index